Roosevelt and de Gaulle

⚜

By the Same Author

Dictionnaire Commercial (Librairie de Droit), Paris, 1936.
Les Actes de Montreux Annotés (Pedone) Paris, 1937.
Le Contrôle des Changes (Librairie de Droit), Paris, 1938.
French Laws (Steven and Sons), London, 1939.
War in the Desert (Henry Holt), New York, 1942.
The Fighting French (Henry Holt), New York, 1943.
L'Epopée de la France Combattante (Maison Française), New York, 1944.
Dictionnaire de Droit Américain-Français (Brentanos), New York, 1946.
De Gaulle et Roosevelt (Plon), Paris, 1984.

Roosevelt and de Gaulle

❋

Allies in Conflict
A Personal Memoir

RAOUL AGLION

THE FREE PRESS
A Division of Macmillan, Inc.
NEW YORK

Collier Macmillan Publishers
LONDON

The Free Press
A Division of Macmillan, Inc.
866 Third Avenue, New York, N.Y. 10022

Collier Macmillan Canada, Inc.

Printed in the United States of America

printing number
1   2   3   4   5   6   7   8   9   10

Library of Congress Cataloging-in-Publication Data

Aglion, Raoul.
  Roosevelt and de Gaulle: allies in conflict.

  Bibliography: p.
  1. Roosevelt, Franklin D. (Franklin Delano), 1882–
1945.   2. Gaulle, Charles de, 1890–1970.   3. World War,
1939–1945—Diplomatic history.   4. Aglion, Raoul.
5. World War, 1939–1945—Personal narratives, French.
6. Diplomats—France—Biography.   7. Diplomats—United
States—Biography.   8. France—Foreign relations—United
States.   9. United States—Foreign relations—France.
I. Title.
D752.A36   1988   940.53'22'730944   87–27187
ISBN 0–02–901540–5

Contents

Note from the Author

On June 18, 1940, de Gaulle made his historic appeal in London and created Free France and the Free French Forces (FFL). On September 24, 1940, he established the *Comité National Français* (C.N.F.) in London.

In 1942, the French underground resistance in France proper (the *Maquis*) joined de Gaulle. Together the FFL and the FFI (*Forces Française de l'Interieur*) formed the Fighting French.

Following a negotiated agreement, General de Gaulle joined forces with General Giraud. They created the *Comité Français de Libération Nationale* (C.F.L.N.) on June 3, 1943. Both generals were co-presidents. On July 31, General Giraud resigned and de Gaulle became the sole president.

The C.F.L.N. was a de facto government. It was recognized as the Gouvernement Provisoire de la République Française by the United States on October 23, 1944.

Preface

Anyone who might have imagined war to be the purposeful pursuit of national interest by a country, its representatives, and its people will perhaps be disappointed to learn that the conduct of war is more often the story of disorganization, ambition, petty squabbles, and small-minded recriminations.

For that is precisely what I witnessed through much of World War II when I was one of General Charles de Gaulle's first representatives to the United States. My position enabled me to be both a behind-the-scenes observer and a participant in the political and military events that shaped the relations between Roosevelt and de Gaulle. I was also informed about some revealing discussions between the two leaders and their assistants, and was often aware of the machinations that affected the relations between Free France and the United States in general, and of the growing discord between President Roosevelt and General de Gaulle in particular.

That there was discord between these two statesmen is quite well known; what is less known is the extent to which the large French community in the United States, its eminent exiles, the Vichy Embassy and its sympathizers, as well as some members of Free France's own delegation to the United States influenced the President's hostile attitude towards de Gaulle.

De Gaulle's reaction to America's policies further contributed to the hostility that characterized his relations with the President, and the latter, by his attitude towards de Gaulle, compounded the difficulties.

It is astonishing that the relations between Roosevelt and de Gaulle began as badly as they did. It is still more surprising, however, that the relations between the leader of the free world and the leader of a national movement of resistance against totalitarianism worsened instead of improved, even as the war progressed toward an Allied victory.

Finally, the American press, by its independent, vociferous moral commitment to the Free French movement, often played a significant role in the relationship between the two.

In these pages I have done my best to present the events that I witnessed during this period as they appeared to me at that time, and as I understand them now with the benefit of hindsight and a broader perspective. I have also tried to give the reader a sense of the day-to-day activities of de Gaulle's delegation to the United States, which, seen together with larger events, might well contribute to a more accurate understanding of Franco-American relations during the war. I have relied primarily on my personal notes taken at that time, and have used footnotes only to provide further corroboration when a particular event or situation was likely to strain the reader's belief.

May 1987

Acknowledgments

This book is more than a translation of *De Gaulle et Roosevelt*, published in Paris by Plon in 1984, and which, based on my personal notes, records, correspondence, files, and conversations with relevant political and military actors, received the history award of the Académie Française. In the past three years I have benefited from further correspondence and personal accounts. The present edition has been revised accordingly.

In addition, I have endeavored to offer the American reader more background for the events described, as well as more details of the events themselves. I have also ventured further to provide my own interpretation of and conclusions about the turbulent relations between the United States and France during the war.

Roosevelt and de Gaulle was completed with the invaluable assistance of my daughter Marie-France Aglion Foster, who was at the time with the French Embassy in Washington, and my son Michel Aglion.

I would like to express very special appreciation to Mrs. Betty Braun; Dr. Carol D. Lanham, professor at UCLA; Mlle Madeleine Cousin, of the French Press and Information Division; Mr. Hervé de la Ménardière, archivist; and Dr. Janice White of UCLA.

Among the many others to whom I am most grateful I would like to mention Mr. Erwin Glikes, president of The Free Press, Mr. Paul Teichman, senior archivist at the Franklin D. Roosevelt Library in Hyde Park, and Mr. Pierre LeFranc, Secretary General of the Institut Charles de Gaulle in Paris.

Roosevelt and de Gaulle

❊

CHAPTER I

❖

The War Is Not Lost

When World War II broke out on September 3, 1939, I, like most men my age, was not drafted, since the French government considered itself invulnerable behind the mighty Maginot Line, the massive chain of fortifications that lined the frontier with Germany. And the French people shared their Government's view, even though the Maginot Line stopped at the Belgian frontier, leaving it unguarded. In Paris the cafés and streets were filled with people who saw the signs of war but not the disaster to come. The few soldiers that were to be seen on the Champs-Elysées walked proudly in their new and well-tailored uniforms. And despite the nightly blackouts, Parisian motorists sped about the darkened streets, the headlights of their cars painted a dramatic blue.

We French were exuberant as ever. Proud of our impregnable border, and counting on the success of the British naval blockade of Germany, we were absolutely confident of an eventual victory against Hitler. Poland and the real war were far away. Like many others, I wanted to participate in some way in the victory, but in my capacity as attaché to the Ministry of Finance I felt removed from the war and saw little chance of engaging in it in any meaningful way.

As is often the case in chaotic times, it was by a combination of happenstance and decisions on my part that I was eventually able to involve myself in the war, but not as I might have expected.

In October that year I ran into Jean Pozzi, Minister Plenipotentiary in the Foreign Office, with whom I had worked at the Conference of Montreux two years earlier to negotiate the independence of Egypt.*

---

*The Conference for the Abolition of the Capitulations of Egypt was held at Montreux (Switzerland), April 12 through May 8, 1937.

He had just been appointed Minister to Cairo and suggested that I join him to help negotiate and draft questions relative to the blockade, the defense of the Suez Canal, and other problems of mutual interest between France and Egypt. I immediately accepted his offer. Thus I spent the winter of 1939 as attaché to the French Legation in Cairo.

In April 1940, as they had done in Poland, the Nazi Panzer Divisions rolled through Denmark, Norway, and the Netherlands. They advanced rapidly through Belgium, and then with equal speed rolled across the Franco-Belgian border where the French had built no fortifications in the mistaken belief that the Germans would respect Belgian neutrality. By May 1940 what had been named the *drôle de guerre,* the phony war, was over. The fighting was now in earnest.

Stunned by these almost unbelievable events, I immediately left my diplomatic post and sought out the nearest French military base, which was located in Lebanon. When I arrived in Beirut, I found a lovely peaceful city quietly basking in the sun. Everyone seemed to be leading a happy, leisurely life, quite oblivious of what was going on in Europe.

The French had a considerable concentration of troops and equipment in Lebanon, which at that time was under French administration. The forces numbered nearly 70,000 men. General Maxime Weygand had trained that army for one of the most absurdly grand military operations ever planned by the French High Command. Since it was considered impossible to cross the Siegfried Line to defeat the Germans, it was thought essential to attack them on their "soft underbelly" in the south of Germany. The French expeditionary force was expected to land in Salonica, cross Greece, Yugoslavia, Bulgaria, and Hungary in order to enter the unfortified southern part of Germany. The Germans were expected to be surprised and unprepared for their arrival. The quick collapse of the French army in France, however, prevented the launching of General Weygand's "ingenious" plan.[1]

The news we received from France grew worse every day. The German offensive had started on May 10. By June our armies were in disarray. On the sixteenth Reynaud resigned as Premier; on June 17 Marshal Pétain, who succeeded him, called for an armistice and capitulated. He surrendered the whole army, two million men, before even being notified by the Germans of the conditions they would impose. It was an unconditional surrender, with no power to negotiate. France now was dependent on the generosity of Hitler.

I was horrified, as were all of the officers and men. We could not believe that the war was suddenly over while we still had well-trained armies in Lebanon and elsewhere. It was the same story in North Africa. Most of us wanted to continue the war because we still had large armies that had seen virtually no action, and a modern fleet as well. At the same time we were overcome by shame, disgust, and humiliation. We had been reduced to nothing, and we had betrayed our British ally. What would our future be? What would become of our culture and our civilization under the Nazis? The armistice was without question dishonorable; we could not live with its terms.

Gen. Eugène Mittelhauser, Commander in Chief in Beirut of the French Expeditionary Forces and of the entire army in the Middle East, at first proclaimed that he would continue the war along with Britain. He advocated resistance, then hesitated, wavered, and was finally informed that General Noguès, Governor General of Algeria, had accepted the armistice. He was also under continuous pressure from General Weygand. On June 26, he finally gave in.

On June 19, while there was still some confusion and uncertainty as to what General Mittelhauser's final decision was going to be, I went to see him. He received me in his office. There I explained that I belonged to the French diplomatic staff in Cairo and felt I would now be more useful at my Cairo post than in the army, since the war was over. He did not accede. I was insistent, and finally he said: "Why are you in such a hurry to leave? Tell me the truth." I hesitated, but since I suddenly remembered that he was the brave man who had resigned his post of military attaché in Prague in protest over the Munich agreement, I replied: "If you don't have any major objection, I will join the British army." "It is madness," he exclaimed. "The British as well as the French have lost the war. How can you expect England on her own to beat the Germans when they can no longer do it with France's aid? Furthermore, Hitler has a new ally: Italy.* The war is lost; it is a fact. In Africa, the position of the British is desperate; they have fewer than 40,000 men with which to oppose a force of 400,000 Italians in Libya and 100,000 more in Ethiopia.† The Italians are also much better armed and equipped. The war is over! The British will surrender in three to six weeks." He thought for a while and then added, "I think you know the risks you will be taking: you will never be able to return to France, never see your family again; you will lose your nationality and your passport. If the Italians catch you, you will be shot."

*Italy had entered the war on June 10.
†In fact, the British had fewer than 27,000 men who were trained and equipped.

Realizing that despite his grim assessment I was firm in my resolve, he reluctantly authorized me to go. Before doing so, he instructed me to see M. Puaux, the French High Commissioner for the Levant in Beirut. I met with him in his beautiful white palace. He was extremely depressed, yet absolutely determined to follow the orders of Vichy. "The war is lost," he too told me. "The danger will be when the Italians invade Egypt, and this will happen within a few weeks. The Arab population will revolt, and the French residents will be in great danger. Plans should be made immediately to evacuate them to Syria and Lebanon, where they will be under the protection of the French army." He gave me a long letter and various documents to give to the French Minister in Cairo.

Within two days of this meeting I was able to secure my military permits (ordre de route) and a taxi willing to take me to the Lebanese border town of Nakoura. I was greeted on the other side, in Palestine, by members of the Australian Expeditionary Force, who offered to escort me to Haifa upon hearing I was going to join the British forces. I was lucky: a few days later, on June 25, the border between Lebanon and Palestine was sealed, since France and Great Britain were now on opposite sides of the war. All communications were severed.

At Haifa I boarded an uncomfortable and crowded train to the Suez Canal. I arrived that evening at El Kantara, a small Arab town, where I waited for the ferry to take me across. In an Arab café I met a French sergeant who, like me, was going to Cairo to join the British. He was turning the dials of a radio receiver and we faintly heard, in French, the words that in time changed my life and that of many other Frenchmen: "Has the last word been spoken? Is all hope gone? Is the defeat final? No, . . . France is not alone. . . . This war is not lost by the battle of France. . . . immense power of the United States . . . the British Empire . . . get in touch with me. . . ."[2]

We had no way of telling who had uttered these words, but they came to us as a distant ray of hope.

I then crossed the Canal and arrived in Cairo the following day, June 22. Jean Pozzi, the French Minister to whom I delivered the papers, was, like Puaux, extremely discouraged: "The war is over! The Nazis have won," he told me. "The defeat is complete. Hitler is so clever! We must accept defeat and abide by the terms of the surrender. A Nazi Europe may endure for hundreds of years. It will be painful for us, but our grandchildren will be able to live in the great Nazi empire of Europe."

Despite these hopeless assessments, I remained stubborn. I said I could not believe we had lost the war in one single campaign and that in thirty-eight days the Nazis had conquered France forever. We still had vast colonies that were loyal, and a powerful, intact fleet. We still had a chance. Everything was *not* lost. We also had pledged that we would never make a separate peace with the enemy while the British were still fighting. For the honor of France we had to continue the war. In our long history we had never betrayed our allies! The tragedy seemed to me incredible; we must have been betrayed.

A few days later I went to the British Embassy to meet with Sir Miles Lampson, their much-admired Ambassador. He told me that Colonel de Larminat, Chief of the French High Command staff in Beirut, had been arrested on June 28 for proclaiming the necessity of continuing the war. De Larminat had declared: "If we have to perish, we'll perish on our feet." Luckily, he escaped two days later to Palestine, though the borders had been closed. He then went to Cairo, where he arrived on July 2.[3]

I told the Ambassador that many of us wanted to continue the war. I told him that I wanted to join the British army. "It is impossible," he said. "We only have Britishers in our army. No aliens. We have no Foreign Legion." I did not accept his answer and went back to see him again and again. Finally he gave in and handed me a letter for Air Marshal Arthur Longmore, "who might take you."

I thanked him and, while he was showing me to the door, I turned around and looked at him and said: "You know my feelings, you know where I stand. I will be with your people up to the end, but I wonder how you are going to win this war. How will you be able to stop the Italian offensive?"

He answered calmly: "We will fight. Should the Italians push us out of Egypt, we will fight in the Sudan; if we lose the Sudan, we will fight in Kenya, Uganda, all the way to South Africa. We will never give up the fight; we will never capitulate. You know that the British Empire is so vast that before they can reach the end of it we will beat them back and they will have to give up. You see, in a war it is not the strongest who wins, but the one who can resist the longest."

This statement confirmed my belief that the war was not yet over. The British would not surrender nor seek an armistice, nor even a compromise peace. Obviously there would be a very long war before victory was achieved. I also thought that some if not all French colonies would eventually join with the British, and that our fleet would not remain neutral for long.

I also realized that I had involved myself in a terrible adventure.

There would be battles all over the world; I would be cut off from my family in Paris and from my country. Despite the heavy price I would have to pay, I was convinced there was no alternative for the liberation of France. I believed that sooner or later all Frenchmen, when they saw that the British continued to fight, would finally join them—not because they loved the British, but because it was the only way to save their own country.

When I went to see the Air Marshal at his headquarters in Cairo, I was warmly greeted by the officers of the Royal Air Force. But since I was not a pilot and they had no time to train me—and too few planes, besides—they did not know what to do with me. For a time I headed a liaison office to help receive volunteers who came from Lebanon, Syria, and Cyprus. I also held many other odd jobs during that period; in those days, because of the collapse of French authority, I was very much on my own. By July 3, however, I met Colonel de Larminat in Cairo. He was full of energy and hope. I asked him: "Who spoke in French on the London BBC?" "General de Gaulle, of course," he answered. "He is an officer whose theories always run contrary to those of his superiors on the General Staff."

De Gaulle had for many years before the war insisted on a system of national defense adapted to modern techniques, to keep in step with industrial advances. While still a Colonel, he had published three books—*Dissension Among Our Enemies* (1924), *The Edge of the Sword* (1932), and *The Army of the Future* (1934)—as well as articles in specialized reviews. De Larminat informed me that all of de Gaulle's ideas were opposed by Marshal Philippe Pétain and Gen. Maxime Weygand, who firmly believed that this war was going to be fought in exactly the same manner as the last one, in 1914–18.

Charles de Gaulle was a controversial man but one with unexceptional and rather modest beginnings. He was born in 1890 in Lille, a large industrial town in the northeast of France. He was one of four sons of a professor of literature and philosophy in the High School of the Immaculate Conception in Paris. At a young age he already displayed an interest in military matters. At 20 he entered the Military School at Saint Cyr, but his studies were not thought to be particularly brilliant. One of his instructors, according to popular lore, summed up his achievements in the following way: "De Gaulle is average in everything, except in height." He was, it is true, exceptionally tall, standing six feet four inches. As a soldier in World War I he was captured many times by the Germans but managed to escape each time. He was also recaptured each time. During his last escape, he had stolen the uniform of a German officer. Needless to say, it was too small for him: the coat barely reached his forearms, and the pants hardly reached his calves. He was easily spotted and recaptured.

After the war, de Gaulle decided to study the reorganization of French national defense. He was impressed by Britain's use of tanks for the first time in 1917, and was quick to foresee that tanks grouped together would have the impact of a moving fortress. He knew that their speed and fire power could disrupt enemy lines, and that their predecessor, the traditional system of passive defenses, had now become obsolete. The French General Staff vigorously opposed his ideas. Marshal Pétain and General Weygand believed that the Maginot Line was the best possible defense. The enemy would exhaust troops and energy trying to overcome it. Finally, they would have to give up.

De Gaulle also had another revolutionary idea. In modern times of mechanized warfare, a small army of professional and specialized soldiers was essential, to operate the complicated new machinery. The levée en masse, the mobilization and conscription of all of the nation's eligible men, was of little use. On this issue he met with opposition in political circles, from both the left and the right. France's long history had proved that professional armies and mercenaries were used by tyrants to oppress their own people. One of the great achievements of the French Revolution in 1789 had been the abolition of the professional army and the conscription of the whole nation into the national defense.

The General Staff, already opposed to de Gaulle's ideas of mechanized warfare, was equally opposed to his ideas about establishing a professional corps of specialized soldiers. Despite this opposition, and contrary to all the traditions of military discipline, de Gaulle lobbied stubbornly among the politicians, before as well as following the outbreak of World War II. He met with journalists, and appealed to the Prime Minister and to the Minister of Defense. His efforts were in vain.

The French General Staff—Marshal Pétain, General Weygand, as well as many others—were unwilling to reconsider their views. They believed in a static defense strategy. They even lacked hindsight. They had not learned a lesson from German warfare that, in 1939, had flattened Poland in less than six weeks. French defenses also crumbled in less than six weeks.

Paul Reynaud, the last Premier of the Third Republic, realized too late that de Gaulle had been right. He promoted de Gaulle from Colonel to Brigadier General and made him Under Secretary of War on June 5, 1940. De Gaulle did not believe the war to be lost. He thought instead that "many things could still be done." On this he was overruled by Marshal Pétain, General Weygand, and all the defeatists in the government.

When Pétain announced France's surrender to Germany on the seventeenth, de Gaulle rejected the armistice and flew to London to continue the war. On June 18 and 19 he made his historic call to arms, the one I had so faintly heard in El Kantara. He was going to have to build an entirely new French force on foreign soil, reestablish the nation out of disaster. In Vichy, Pétain's defeated government considered him an exile and a rebel, and sentenced him to death in absentia.

This was the man who had become our leader. When the Free French Forces were finally organized in Egypt, I left Colonel de Larminat (who went to Djibouti to persuade the garrison there to join our side) and placed myself under the orders of General Catroux, the former Governor General of Indochina, who had recently resigned from his post and had now joined himself to de Gaulle. In November 1940, he handed me an order from de Gaulle's headquarters in London to travel to the United States on a mission to recruit French volunteers from the important French community there, to form a special French brigade we would name "La Fayette," and also to buy arms. This was to be done with the help of de Gaulle's delegate in New York.

CHAPTER II

— ❧ —

Lending a Garden Hose

We seek to keep war from our firesides.[1]
—Franklin D. Roosevelt

On February 5, 1941, I arrived in New York from the Near East, traveling on a British travel permit. U.S. Immigration officers had the reputation of being meticulous, and the one I encountered was no exception. He looked with amazement at my unusual travel documents and asked why I, a Frenchman, was travelling under British diplomatic protection. I told him that I had been deprived of my French passport by the Vichy authorities. I then produced my mission "orders" signed by General Catroux along with a letter from the British embassy in Cairo confirming them. "So you're one of those Free French who are continuing to fight the war under General de Gaulle's leadership. If I were French, I'd do the same thing. Go right on through." It was a reassuring welcome, if somewhat misleading.

After clearing Customs, I bought the latest issues of the *New York Times* and the *Herald Tribune* and learned to my great astonishment that, for the most part, the United States did not want to become involved in the conflict that was raging in Europe. The majority of Americans apparently believed in isolationism. Charles Lindbergh, hero of the Atlantic, waged an unremitting pacifistic and defeatist campaign: "This war is lost. It is not within our power at this time to win it for England even if we were to put all our resources into the conflict." Later he would add: "Only the British, the Jews, and Roosevelt's Administration want the war."[1]

From the day of my arrival in New York, I noted that President

Roosevelt himself, great defender of democracies though he was, seemed dangerously isolationist, and in agreement with his country's pacifist public opinion. Everyone wanted to believe that the United States, without having to fight, could contribute to the defeat of the Axis powers merely by increasing the shipment of military equipment to Great Britain and its Dominions.

France's surrender had come as a great shock to the United States and had tremendously upset President Roosevelt. Premier Reynaud, facing almost certain defeat, had sent a personal appeal to Roosevelt begging for the immediate dispatch of troops and equipment. Churchill had supported his plea and cabled to Roosevelt on June 14:

> Reynaud felt strongly that it would be beyond his power to encourage his people to fight on without hope of ultimate victory, and that that hope could only be kindled by American intervention up to the extreme limit open to you. As he put it, they wanted to see the light at the end of the tunnel.[2]

Twelve hours later, Roosevelt clearly stated the American response in a cable he sent to Churchill:

> You realize as I hope Prime Minister Reynaud realizes that we are doing our utmost in the United States to furnish all of the material and supplies which can possibly be released to the Allied Governments. At the same time I believe you will likewise realize that while our efforts will be exerted towards making available an ever increasing amount of material and supplies a certain amount of time must pass before our efforts in this sense can be successful to the extent desired. As I asked Ambassador [Joseph] Kennedy last night to inform you my message of yesterday's date addressed to the French Prime Minister was in no sense intended to commit and did not commit the Government to Military participation in support of Allied governments. As Ambassador Kennedy also informed you when I sent the message I had very much in mind the question of the French fleet and its disposition for future use.... I have asked the Congress as a first step to appropriate fifty million dollars for the immediate furnishing of food and clothing to civilian refugees in France, and the Senate yesterday unanimously approved this recommendation.

Churchill, in the interim, had come to realize the degree to which Premier Reynaud felt vulnerable to the political defeatism of his cabinet. In a secret message he sent Roosevelt the following day, June 15, he explained again that France's decision to continue the war from overseas, should it lose to the Nazis at home, would depend on the American decision to intervene in the war at an early date. Knowing the limited powers of the President in committing his troops to war, he stressed that if Roosevelt's reply did "not contain the assurance asked for" then "the French would very quickly ask for an armistice," and, he added, "I much doubt whether it will be possible in that event for us to keep the French fleet out of German hands."

Churchill also made clear to the President that when he spoke of the United States entering the war he was not thinking of an expeditionary force—Congress would surely have disallowed that—but rather "what I have in mind is the tremendous moral effect that such an American decision would produce not merely in France but also in all the democratic countries of the world and in the opposite sense on the German and Italian people."[3]

Roosevelt was apparently unmoved by Churchill's messages. When he replied to Premier Reynaud's original request for assistance, he stated the American position clearly: The American people admired the heroic resistance of the French in the face of German aggression and promised to do all that was necessary to hasten the shipment of arms and ammunition, and added: "these statements carry with them no implication of military commitment, only Congress can make such commitments."[4] On June 17, after receipt of this telegram, the French government decided to surrender.

The defeat in less than six weeks of an army considered Europe's best, the neutralization of a modern fleet that had not even seen battle, the humiliating acceptance of the conditions of Hitler's armistice, and the betrayal of the alliance with Great Britain convinced Roosevelt that France—whose successive governments had been unstable for years—was finally and completely falling apart. For one brief moment, Roosevelt hoped that the fleet and the empire would continue to fight alongside the British, but here again he was disappointed. What remained was a vassal state of the Nazi empire, governed by an aged marshal who was surrounded by traitors. It then became President Roosevelt's opinion that France had ceased to exist, and he felt he could not change that fact.

Roosevelt had understood nothing of the drama and the intrigues that had taken place during the Third Republic. And he maintained a condescending attitude with regard to France after its defeat: during moments of pessimism, he came to believe the worst about France. He was convinced that it would never regain its status as a leading nation

and that it was therefore pointless to invest military might and diplomatic aid in trying to defend it.

Churchill's reaction was different. France represented to him a con-
crete entity with whom or against whom England had waged wars.
France had played an important role along with England in the construction of modern Europe and, like England, had created empires
throughout the world. Churchill was very knowledgeable about history and possessed a keen sense of the importance of maintaining an
equilibrium in European political affairs. He felt close to the French.
And although he had witnessed the instability and weakness of successive French governments, he understood that France was an essential force in time of war and would be an even more important partner
in any ensuing peace.

Churchill's reaction to the French armistice was to wait and see if
any French statesmen such as President Albert Lebrun, House Speaker
Édouard Herriot, Paul Reynaud, or some other officials would join the
resistance movement and set up a government in exile. The Dutch, the
Norwegians, and the Belgians had already done so. Churchill was
soon to be disillusioned; no French statesman or any high official came
forward.

Since the only one to come forward was de Gaulle, Churchill
extended his support to him and recognized him not as a French government in exile, but as the leader of all Frenchmen willing to continue the war alongside Britain. Churchill gave asylum to the Free
French Movement; he also equipped and armed its small army and
navy of volunteers.

The arrival of de Gaulle on the scene in London was probably not
noticed by Roosevelt. Later the President would consider him merely
a potential nuisance, capable of upsetting the good relations he
wanted to maintain with Marshal Pétain. It was a policy of expediency, prompted by fear that the Vichy government would intensify
its collaboration with the Nazis.

The situation of the United States was unique: It was neutral at the
time. Roosevelt, aware of the unpreparedness of his country and the
weakness of Great Britain, feared that Marshal Pétain would yield further under pressure from the Nazis, and eventually give them strategic
bases in the French colonies. He also feared that Pétain might be
inclined to order the mighty French fleet to join the Nazis. This danger was to him so real that it dominated most of the correspondence
between him and Churchill during this time.

Indeed, the situation appeared so desperate that Roosevelt, fearing the invasion of England by the Nazis, asked Churchill in that eventuality to send the British fleet to American or Canadian ports. Churchill replied:

> Although the present government and I personally would never fail to send the fleet across the Atlantic, if resistance was beaten down here, a point may be reached in the struggle where the present ministers no longer have control. . . . [5]

Roosevelt believed he had little alternative besides placating Vichy, to maintain the best possible relations with the old Marshal. He adopted a policy of "expediency" that was often criticized in the United States. He was of course even more harshly criticized by General de Gaulle, who cabled to Churchill: "It does not seem right to me, that in war the prize should be awarded to the apostles of dishonor."[6]

Despite Roosevelt's policy of expediency towards Marshal Pétain, he nevertheless procrastinated and initiated—albeit hesitantly—some measures to prevent Hitler from winning a global victory during these months. In May 1940 he asked Congress to rapidly transfer 35 destroyers to Great Britain. This was intended as a gesture of support by the United States, but the British considered it essential to protect the convoys to their ports. Congress rejected this proposal on June 28, ten days after the fall of France, an event which might have sparked the concern of a less isolationist body. The rationale was that the President was not entitled to transfer warships to a belligerent nation until the Chief of Naval Operations certified that these were not *essential* to the defense of the U.S.[7] After having obtained that decision Roosevelt procrastinated for nearly four months, until on August 13 he finally obtained the transfer of the 35 destroyers in exchange for bases on the British islands in the Atlantic and in the Caribbean.

Roosevelt continued to have misgivings about defending the allies by committing U.S. troops. He no doubt wanted the British to defeat Hitler, but the thought of engaging U.S. troops was still inconceivable to him. On October 30, nearly four months after the fall of France, in the Democratic Party's platform address, Roosevelt declared: "While I'm talking to you mothers and fathers, I give you one more assurance. I have said before, but I shall say again and again and again: Your boys are not going to be sent into any foreign wars . . . "[8] But by mid-December his parallel track of obtaining military support for the British was gaining strength. He made his now famous "lend lease" proposal that would enable the United States to transfer arms and ammunition to beleaguered England without obtaining immediate payment. Roosevelt compared this plan to the lending of a garden hose to a neighbor whose house was on fire. He wanted the United States to become the "arsenal of democracy." Congress, still unmoved by and unaware of the dangers of the war raging in Europe, deliberated for more than a month before adopting this bill, although its orientation was merely one of military supply and not of troop commitment.

Roosevelt further declared on December 29 that the government did not intend to dispatch any expeditionary force beyond its borders. "You can therefore nail any talk about sending armies to Europe a deliberate untruth."[9]

This, then, was the situation in the United States up to the moment of my arrival to secure arms and support for the Free French. There we were, a hopeful group of French resisters, wholly unknown in America, seeking political and material support at a time when supplies were being dispatched to the beleaguered British, but only with remarkable reluctance, by the country they regarded as their staunchest ally.

CHAPTER III

❋

Mission Impossible

My arrival in New York was, for a Frenchman who had lost his country, an absolute wonder. I marveled at this colossal city with its three towering buildings—the Empire State, Rockefeller Center, and the Chrysler buildings—standing triumphantly against the clear blue sky. No such buildings yet existed in Europe. The streets were alive. Well-dressed men and women (I had never seen so many mink coats) were busily moving about its clean and exceptionally wide streets. The stores were brimming with goods; their windows displayed bright fabrics, endless wares, and seductive mannequins. Few Americans could understand the dramatic effect such an active and exuberant city had on those fleeing from a war that was too rapidly changing the face of Europe.

At night, from my window in the old Murray Hill Hotel, I could see streams of cars speeding down Park Avenue. The city was completely illuminated at night, unlike Paris, Beirut, or Cairo. Under the blackouts these cities seemed somber and threatened compared to carefree New York.

New Yorkers themselves, too, seemed carefree. Europe and the war were far away. They reminded me of the men and women I had seen in Paris during the "phony war" in 1939. They also reminded me of the young people in Beirut and in Cairo, who even moments before the war seemed oblivious to it all.

The morning after my arrival in New York I went downtown to visit the British Consulate, where I received a warm welcome from the Consul General, Sir Geoffrey Haggard, who very authoritatively and competently handled a job that had grown disproportionately large due to the war and its repercussions. He managed, in the same capable way, all the problems dealing with security matters, mobilization, and blockades.

I handed over to him messages from Michael Wright, counsellor to the British Embassy in Cairo, that informed him of the situation in the Near East, where a tiny but heroic British army was facing a much-better-equipped enemy ten times its size. I told him of the unwavering faith of his fellow countrymen and of the Free French in that part of the world. The Italian offensive had been halted and General Wavell's men had repulsed the enemy beyond Sidi-Barani and Bardia in the Libyan desert.

He questioned me about the French in Lebanon and in Egypt, particularly those working in the administration of the Suez Canal. I told him that in June 1940, Jean Pozzi, French minister plenipotentiary in Cairo, had sent a message to General Mittelhauser telling him that if he wanted to resist, the French legation in Egypt was offering to act as a liaison with General Noguès, Governor General of Algeria. Mittelhauser replied that he had considered resisting at the outset, but that he considered the French army's function in Syria to be "purely decorative." He claimed that they had no military strength* and had neither tanks nor planes. Any resistance on their part he thought "would only draw the Germans to the Middle East."

I told Sir Geoffrey that the French citizens living in Egypt, especially those in the Suez Canal zone, had rallied behind General de Gaulle. However, the French diplomatic and consular personnel remained fiercely loyal to Vichy and not one of them had resigned in order to support Free France.

I informed him that on July 4 the French fleet from the Middle East had been anchored in the port of Alexandria, when the shore guns and the guns of the British ships were suddenly turned upon it. The British navy, afraid that the French navy would join the Germans, proceeded to send an ultimatum ordering the French to dismantle their fleet until the end of the war, or be sunk. Admiral Godfroy complied, realizing his ships, located deep in the harbor, had no means of escape. A negotiation took place between the two navies, and the French Admiral, to prove his sincerity, had to relinquish his ships' fuel and gun parts. In exchange, the French officers and sailors on board were permitted during the internment to go to Alexandria, and would be paid.

The details of this agreement were reported to me in Cairo by d'Es-

---

*This was of course untrue. The French had twice as many troops in Lebanon as the British had in Egypt. See de Larminat, *Chroniques*, Chapter III.

tienne d'Orves, a French lieutenant who was one of the few to leave the neutralized naval squadron to join the Free French Forces. Thus the important French fleet had been neutralized and would not participate in the war as Germany's ally, but neither would it fight against Germany and contribute to the liberation of its own country.

After reporting other military and political events in the Near East, I then asked Sir Geoffrey the name of the person I was to contact in New York and to whom I should hand over my mission orders and other important documents I was carrying. "It's difficult to say," he told me to my great astonishment, "because there is a good deal of confusion here. Mr. Garreau-Dombasle, Commercial Counselor to the French Embassy in Washington, resigned as soon as the armistice was announced. He now represents Free France and his offices are located in Rockefeller Center. Then there is Mr. Jacques de Sieyès, personal representative of General de Gaulle; his office is also on Fifth Avenue. Finally there is another official organization recognized by General de Gaulle that calls itself 'France Forever.' Its president, Mr. Eugene Houdry, whose name often appears in the papers, is a well-known engineer. If I were you, I would visit all three of them."

"Then I shall certainly do so," I replied, "but to whom should I turn over my 'orders'?" Sir Geoffrey told me, "You must decide for yourself, but I hope the choice will be fairly obvious. Please remember, if you have professional or personal problems with the American authorities concerning your visa, don't hesitate to call on me for help."

That afternoon, after what seemed to me a long subway ride, I arrived at Rockefeller Center, where the Free France delegate, M. Garreau-Dombasle, had his office. He gave me a very warm welcome, congratulated me on having joined the Resistance, and explained that he had been the sole member of the entire embassy to resign. Even his own staff had not followed him. Garreau-Dombasle told me of his final conversation with the Count of Saint Quentin, the ambassador in Washington, who refused to disobey Marshal Pétain and "could not assume a rebel stance and rally a handful of French in London." "Saint Quentin's attitude," he said, "can be compared to that of Corbin, the French ambassador to the Court of Saint James, who had resigned but said to General de Gaulle: 'I am an old civil servant; I resigned but dissidence is too much for me.' It is obvious," Garreau-Dombasle explained to me, "that if General Noguès had rallied behind de Gaulle, and behind General Mittelhauser in Syria, and if the other governors of the colonies had joined forces with him, the majority of diplomatic personnel would probably have followed suit."

As to the situation in the United States, Garreau-Dombasle did not pretend it was an easy one: first, because of the failure to win over diplomatic and consular personnel and their respective missions. "And then," he pointed out, "the Americans do not understand what is taking place in Europe. Finally, the new French ambassador, Gaston Henry-Haye, a Vichy supporter, is waging an anti-British, pro-neutralist campaign that is encouraging a policy of isolationism. It's really bewildering.

"I have joined forces with a small group of French patriots and Americans who have been branded 'warmongers' and 'leftists,' who are violently anti-Hitler because they are fully aware of what is happening. We are in an incredible mess. It is very difficult to accomplish anything of a serious nature. I have not a single aide, not one assistant. A committee of French and American patriots that goes by the name of 'France Forever' has just been established. I am in communication with de Gaulle's staff in London and have been designated as the delegate for Free France in the United States. What are my powers? I have no idea. I am more or less in charge of a diplomatic mission that has no staff, no funds, and no instructions to carry out. I must be constantly inventive and innovative. I hear people all around me claiming to be representatives of the Resistance movement outside of France. Houdry, who presides over France Forever, claims as much; de Sieyès as well. A war veteran who was a former schoolmate of de Gaulle, de Sieyès is now general manager of the Patou Perfumery. He was appointed personal representative of General de Gaulle and also claims to represent the Free French in New York. So who is representing what? What chaos! I am trying to sort it out in my mind. The British ambassador and the State Department know me and do not want to deal with anyone else. Nevertheless, Free France has no official status; we are not recognized in any way by the authorities. However, I am glad to hear the good news about our fighting men and the British victories in the Near East. That will bolster our cause here where so many people are pessimistic."

I then presented him with my order of mission and a letter from General Catroux. He looked them over and said: "You don't seem to know that there is a Neutrality Act here that forbids recruiting for foreign armies and does not allow the purchase of arms except in very special circumstances and under very strict rules." He concluded, "Your mission is impossible. Since I need personnel, I will cable de Gaulle that you should be assigned to my post here where I am badly in need of an assistant."

I was stunned, but since the beginning of the war I had heard so many things and lived through so many strange events that I did not argue. I wanted, however, a confirmation of his statement by de Gaulle's other representatives. Before leaving I asked him who was de Sieyès, the other representative of de Gaulle? "He's not qualified to deal with administrative or diplomatic matters," Garreau-Dombasle replied. "Go and see him certainly, and Houdry as well, but you will come to see that the center of activity is here."

I thanked him warmly and the following day paid a visit to Jacques de Sieyès, who received me very amicably at the Patou business office. "It's a difficult task," he warned me. "There are practically no supporters and very few volunteers. This is a result of the intense pressure exerted by Vichy's embassy on our compatriots to prevent them, by all possible means, from joining our cause. On the other hand, I receive a great deal of encouragement from Americans, many of whom are influential media personalities: Dorothy Thompson, William Agar, Edgar Mowrer, Louis Bromfield, Johannes Steel, Frida Kirchway, Richard De Rochement, Walter Lippmann, and many others. I am in direct correspondence with General de Gaulle, who has complete confidence in me, as I am a personal friend—I was with him at military school at Saint Cyr. He knows how I feel and confides in me and in me alone."

I then explained the nature of my mission. He confirmed that the Neutrality Act did not allow the recruiting of volunteers for de Gaulle, but that even without such a law the French in America were in no mood to join the Free French Forces. "There are sailors however who quit their merchant ships, and some Frenchmen from Central America who would volunteer, but they are few. Regarding the purchase of arms, it could be done through the British Purchasing Mission, with permission from the Department of State. I doubt that you could get it." I replied that I would inform our headquarters in London accordingly.

"And Garreau-Dombasle?" I asked him. "Oh, him," he replied, "he's just a civil servant, he only deals with the business world, whereas I know everyone here and in Washington. I alone am authorized to write directly to General de Gaulle, who has appointed me as his representative here."

Next I went to meet Eugène Houdry and found him to be a charismatic man—smiling, dynamic, and optimistic. He was a French engineer who, unable to get his "oil cracking" formula patented in France, had come several years earlier to the United States, where he had become remarkably successful in Philadelphia. With infectious enthusiasm he was gathering together French and American sympathizers of the French cause in an association that came to be known as "France Forever" *(France Quand Même)*. Houdry informed me that the Americans in the association considerably outnumbered the French. And this was because the Vichy embassy had strongly discouraged their movement. "But," he said, "the French will see the light just the same. My movement will snowball and in a few months' time, you will see. . . . Besides, the Association becomes stronger every day with the arrival of French notables in exile. We would love to have you in our movement. We are sadly lacking in competent personnel." I congratulated him on what he had accomplished, and thanked him for his time.

Having met General de Gaulle's three New York delegates, I was now in the strange position of having to choose my superior. De Sieyès was a charming businessman, Houdry a charismatic entrepreneur, but Garreau-Dombasle, the only diplomat among them, seemed to me the most competent to head a foreign mission. I handed him my credentials, a letter from General Catroux, and his file of guidelines regarding the recruitment of volunteers. Garreau-Dombasle immediately cabled de Gaulle suggesting that I be his assistant on a temporary basis.

A few days later, upon learning that a personal friend, Viscount Jacques d'Av, whom I had last met in Jerusalem in 1938, was Vichy's Consul General in New York, I went to see him to determine for myself the nature of his political views. I found him to be as charming a man as ever, but determined to follow Vichy to the bitter end. To me he said: "I read the interview that you granted the *Times* when you first arrived, and I am sorry that you feel this way.* Everyone here, as well as in France, considers de Gaulle to be a rebel, a soldier of fortune. He is being bankrolled by the British, who sank our boats at Mers-el-Kebir. His attempt to occupy Dakar† was repulsed by troops loyal to Pétain and he and the British had to retreat after heavy losses. No one is supporting him, either in France or in the Empire. In fact, the war is over now that Hitler has been victorious. Thanks to Marshal Pétain, France will enjoy a privileged position in Hitler's Europe. England continues to fight but is preparing to negotiate a peace with

---

*In this short interview I stated that the British were fighting bravely in Egypt and that French volunteers were joining them.
†See Chapter VII.

Germany, against our interests. You have to understand, my friend, that the Third Reich's victory is going to create a new empire that will dominate the world for centuries to come. The French community in New York has understood this and has remained loyal to Pétain. I advise you to break away from de Gaulle, and if you do so, I have enough connections to secure you a post in an American university. However, if you side with the rebels, you will not benefit from any further French diplomatic protection and you will eventually be deported by the American authorities."

My protests were brushed aside. None of my explanations would satisfy him. The war was lost and Pétain was our savior. How fast he had learned his new catechism! We had nothing in common anymore and our old friendship was gone. I realized that in my future activities in New York I would face a powerful and unbending enemy.

My duty was to serve Free France, join Garreau-Dombasle and the handful of followers of de Gaulle, and await instructions from our London headquarters.

CHAPTER IV

Patou's Perfumery

A week later, in mid-February, a telegram arrived from London, accepting Garreau-Dombasle's request that I be his assistant. The amount of work we had to do was staggering. We received visits from a truly amazing array of people: some very serious types, others who were not so serious, still others who were out-and-out crackpots. Everyone came to give advice or to ask that we send his congratulations, opinions, or messages to General de Gaulle. Some wanted him to proclaim all the Asian colonies independent and others wanted him to send parachutists to kidnap Marshal Pétain. Still others suggested contaminating the rivers, setting up ambushes or traps to halt the advance of German tanks, tarring the roads to stop the tanks, or printing counterfeit Deutsche marks to throw the German economy into confusion. Finally, there were those who suggested seizing the gold that was being stored in Martinique. In the realm of the more serious, letters were arriving from Frenchmen in Central America or the Caribbean islands offering their services. Much to Garreau-Dombasle's indignation, a group of convicts from Guyana even offered to enlist as volunteers in the Free French forces.

Most of the French colonial governors remained loyal to Vichy. In some of the territories the governors, after a great deal of pressure from Pétain, accepted the capitulation and the rule of the pro-Nazi Vichy government. However, in the Pacific and in central Africa there was a great deal of unrest and popular opposition to Vichy. In Africa, de Gaulle failed to win over Dakar, but in Chad, Governor General Felix Eboué (a black man from the Antilles) joined the Free French officially on August 26, 1940. In the Congo and West Africa there were real "coups" where Colonel de Larminat with the help of the local guard succeeded in ousting the Vichy governor. In the Pacific, the islands of New Hebrides (a Franco-British administration), Tahiti, and, after a popular uprising of the settlers, New Caledonia joined de Gaulle. Finally, by the end of 1941 de Gaulle had control of a far-flung empire stretching from central Africa to the faraway islands of Tahiti and New Caledonia. In all of these colonies, French settlers and natives joined Free France and sent young men to serve in the Free French forces.

One day we had a visit from a Lieutenant de Saint-André, who had come from London on a special mission. I soon learned that he had contacted a New York lawyer who had offered to negotiate with members of Congress in Washington, to have a certain proportion of the French gold that had been deposited in the United States by the French government in 1940 released and handed over to de Gaulle. Since this gold was the property of the French nation, "it was natural that it be turned over to de Gaulle who represented France and who would make use of it to outfit an army of liberation." This clever lawyer succeeded in having Saint-André, General de Gaulle's representative, sign a letter giving the lawyer a commission on whatever gold would be granted to either the General or to his government. Garreau-Dombasle was horrified when he learned of the transaction; however, no gold was transferred to the *Comité National Français* (the Free French authorities in London). It was not until after the war that another authority, the Provisional Government of the French Republic, gained access to the French gold.

We were also snowed under by requests from governors of the African and Pacific territories who had rallied behind General de Gaulle and whose economies, formerly dependent on the markets of continental France, were being forced to seek out new markets elsewhere. A case in point involved the minerals titanium and rutile, both of which were produced in the Cameroons. The territories had to find American buyers as well as obtain administrative authorizations from the Federal Government, which often got bogged down in paperwork and complicated regulations.

From a political as well as an economic standpoint, it was important to improve the administrative regime of Free France's territories in such a way that they would be treated like those Dutch possessions enjoying "open" license with the United States. It is true, however, that the Dutch colonies were being run by a government-in-exile that was recognized, a status that neither General de Gaulle nor the National French Committee in London enjoyed.

The Federal Government insisted on receiving samples of the products and then having them analyzed. Bank accounts had to be opened for French Equatorial Africa, Gabon, New Caledonia, and Tahiti. Then there was the problem of frozen assets in accounts held by the Bank of Syria and in Lebanon, as well as those in the Bank of West Africa. These accounts had to be operated in conformance with certain licenses granted by the American Treasury, which, generally speaking, was not quick to grant them. The Free French as well as the British were at war, the administration in some French territories had collapsed, and it was not easy to obtain formal legal documents from the temporary officers who had replaced the Vichy agents who had fled.

And then there were the Free French committees in Mexico, the Phillippines, Haiti, Venezuela, as well as the more-or-less underground committees in Martinique and Guyana, who thought that the Free France delegation in New York was powerful, organized, and capable of answering all their questions.

The British consulate often called on me to resolve the matter of French sailors who had abandoned their ships in the Caribbean and who wished to support de Gaulle rather than Vichy. These men were to be transported to London via Canada, but the American authorities were keeping them in quarantine in the port of New York.

The question of visas came up right away. Not only did the French sailors who joined the Free French Navy need them, but so did Frenchmen who were not already in military service but were volunteering to join the Free French force, as well as journalists, businessmen, and agents of the U.S. government who wanted to go to Brazzaville or Gabon or even to Tahiti. Obviously, they couldn't request visas from the Vichy consulate, nor in the middle of a full-scale war could they be allowed to enter the Free French territories without a visa. De Sieyès had been granting visas without keeping any record of them. I decided to set up a system for issuing visas and asked London what fees to charge for such documents.

I received stacks of letters from sympathizing Americans from San Francisco to Miami along with requests for meetings and visits. Reporters were constantly asking for information or visas so that they could visit the recently liberated territories.

Suddenly, without warning, on July 15, 1941, Garreau-Dombasle tendered his resignation to de Gaulle. I never learned the reason but suspected that he could not put up with the constant clashes with de Sieyès. He bid me adieu in a very dignified manner, and retired for a short time to Pasadena, California. (Later, de Gaulle entrusted him with various missions, including an Ambassadorship to Mexico.) I was left with no option but to move out of his office. This time I set up my offices with de Sieyès in the Patou perfumery office that was also located on Fifth Avenue, six blocks from the "France Forever" headquarters. It was a lovely, elegant place that smelled of French perfumes, but did not in my opinion have quite the dignity of a French diplomatic mission. It did not take long for the stacks of mail and the many visitors to catch up with me.

De Sieyès was beginning to have serious misgivings about his authority as de Gaulle's personal representative. Many Frenchmen were arriving from London, announcing that they had been empowered by the General to represent him. In addition, the France Forever committee also considered itself to be the legitimate representative in America of the Free French National Committee in London. Jacques de Sieyès wrote to Lord Halifax, British ambassador to Washington, in order to have his status confirmed. He also wrote to various State Department officials for the same reason. In order to convince me of his authority, de Sieyès gave me copies of the three letters that he had received on letterhead from de Gaulle's headquarters, signed by the General himself.

The first letter, sent from "Stephen's House" and dated July 11, 1940, specified:

> I am asking you to be my representative in all matters but I would especially like you to handle what information we release to the American press and the tone we would like it to have. I would also like you to handle all transactions that might arise concerning the purchase of different materials, particularly planes . . . , to accept much-needed donations and also, perhaps, to solicit contributions for our cause.

Obviously, at that time, de Gaulle did not seem to know that his orders were contradictory to the Neutrality Act.

The second letter was sent on letterhead bearing the address "Carlton Gardens" (the General's new headquarters) and was dated July 25. It stated:

> The first order of business is a political one. Mr. Winston Churchill of Downing Street, in the name of His Majesty's government, and I, in the name of the Free French forces, have signed an agreement outlining the organization, use, and enlistment conditions of the French volunteer forces. . . . The second order of business is of a military nature. Our Free France Air Force, bearing the French Air Force insignia, has col-

laborated with British forces several times. . . . You will see . . . a square blue flag decorated in the center with the red Cross of Lorraine, in contrast to the swastika.

Finally, the third letter, also on Carlton Gardens letterhead and dated August 12, read as follows:

> My dear friend: I have not yet received the letter of which your telegram of July 12 made mention. Also, in order to avoid wasting time, I would like to give you a general idea of how I view your mission on our behalf in the U.S. According to information I've received from various sources, it appears that many people who have visited me while passing through England declare upon their arrival in the U.S. either that they represent me or that they have been authorized to speak on my behalf. Such is not the case. Ever since the day you so kindly offered to assist me, I made the decision to appoint you as my sole representative in the U.S., and as soon as your letter arrives we will be able to come to an agreement by telegram concerning an official announcement of your appointment.
>
> I have heard it said elsewhere that the American press, at the time I first started soliciting support, published numerous sensational news items. I was described as being on the verge of setting up the sort of government which would include as members *the most disreputable politicians* of the regime. This news was completely untrue. During the first days following the signing of the armistice, London awaited the onslaught of French representatives who, in order to show their disdain for the policy of capitulation, would be setting up a National Committee. However, because the French government put a stop to all departures from France, the exodus the British were expecting never materialized and *I am not sure that we should regret* the fact that they [French politicians] were detained. [Italics added]
>
> As for me, the goal I have set for myself is very straightforward and has nothing to do with politics.
>
> I feel that all possibility of resistance is not dead simply because Marshal Pétain decided to give up the fight. With the fleet physically and morally intact, the French empire, alongside the British fleet, could con nue a battle that is by no means lost. . . . [1]

This last letter, copies of which de Sieyès sent to Garreau-Dombasle, Houdry, and Henri de Kérillis, was used, by the press and by others, quoting the preceding passage out of context to distort Free France's real aim. The phrase, "the most disreputable politicians," was quoted to convince the State Department and the French in America that General de Gaulle was anti-democratic, anti-republican, and paving the way for a dictatorship.

This same quote, coupled with de Gaulle's statement that he was "not sure we should regret" that many Frenchmen, dissatisfied with surrendering to the Germans, were unable to leave France and come to London, unleashed the anger of several French members of Parliament who had sought refuge in New York.

I was horrified. We really did not need that type of publicity.

It could be said that the origin of some of the misunderstanding between General de Gaulle and the American Administration dated from this famous letter, from which I was to hear repercussions and quotes for several years to come.

Among the administrative problems I had to handle, the sale and printing of postage stamps rapidly became a nightmare, ludicrous, but disturbing as well. The sale of stamps was a potentially important source of funds to supplement the advances given to us by the British government. At that time, we had no other source of funds. But our Financial Administration in London was finding it difficult to come up with a system for issuing and selling stamps that was similar to that implemented by the Crown Agent for the British colonies. It is difficult to imagine the persistence and aggressiveness of firms specializing in these matters. They offered considerable sums of money to obtain the exclusive contract to print stamps for the African or the free Pacific territories. They even telegraphed to General de Gaulle with more and more offers and propositions. An association in Canada offered to buy the franchise at face value for 100,000 French francs, payable in Canadian dollars. Philatelic associations were writing in asking for a monopoly in sales. Some Californian sent in a request for three stamps from Equatorial Africa! When on January 12, 1941, the Sunday edition of the *New York Times* announced that three stamps bearing a Free France surcharge had arrived in New York from the Cameroons, there followed a deluge of letters and telegrams, not to mention telephone calls and urgent visits to de Sieyès' office at Patou's.

Since London did not immediately deliver the stamps, the Delegation received the following threatening telegram from a Canadian collector:

> My lawyers advise me to hereby request one last time that you deliver the [stamp] collections offered by General de Gaulle for delivery by your agency. In case of default, we will undertake the necessary legal action.

I sometimes wondered whether these people believed General de Gaulle had nothing better to do than get involved in stamp-collecting and whether Free France was using the war simply as a pretext to issue a surcharge or to print new French stamps. The harassment from philatelists was doubly irritating to me because it prevented me from concentrating on more pressing matters, such as the plight of refugees and of their families, whom they were trying to get out of France.

We also had to maintain close contact with France Forever. Its members, primarily Americans but including some French patriots, were overly enthusiastic and had to be kept in line with the foreign policy of the National Committee in London. This was not always easy.

It was also important to maintain good relations with the press and radio commentators; this task took quite a lot of my time.

I told de Sieyès that he must cable General de Gaulle requesting personnel and funds so that we could provide adequate service. It was impossible for us to deal effectively with the multifarious problems that confronted us and, at the same time, recruit and train volunteer workers—all from the little sales office of Patou's perfumery. De Sieyès agreed. For my part, I wrote to Maurice Dejean and Camille Paris* and to all those that I knew on the French Committee in London, to warn them that the truly impossible situation in which we found ourselves threatened to impede our contribution to the war effort.

One sunny morning, December 11, 1941, I learned from the *New York Times* that Italy had just broken off diplomatic relations with the United States and that she was consequently closing her embassy in Washington as well as her consulates across the country.

The Italian consulate in New York occupied very plush offices in Rockefeller Center on Fifth Avenue. They were located on the sixth floor in the left wing of a very large complex. The consulate general of Vichy France was situated, appropriately enough, in the far right wing.

I immediately thought that it would be advantageous, for many reasons, for us to rent it for our delegation and spoke to de Sieyès about it. Although he hesitated, he didn't oppose it, saying: "Go and see the offices if you like. This area is very expensive, however, and the office that we are presently occupying in Patou's perfumery costs nothing." I went without further delay to the rental offices for Rockefeller Center and was courteously greeted. "I would like to rent a portion of the

---

*Maurice Dejean was a member of the *Comité National Français* in London. Camille Paris was in charge of diplomatic affairs.

premises of the former Italian consulate for the Free France delegation," I told the agent, "and would like to have an option on the other
portion." The rental agent had only a vague idea of who we were and
asked: "What connection do you have with the French consulate general?" "None," I replied. I then explained what our movement and
General de Gaulle stood for, telling him how the General had created
a movement that rejected the armistice accepted by Vichy, had organized forces to fight with the Allies, and that we therefore had nothing
to do with officials of Vichy, who, in fact, being under German control, were our enemies. The agent was dumbfounded, exclaiming, "I
had no idea all this was going on . . . I did not know such a thing was
possible! But what will happen after the war when the Italian consulate wants to move back in?"

"We will gladly give the space back because at that time the French
will be united and because we will be settled in the French consulate
which is presently being occupied by Vichy personnel," I replied,
becoming a prophet for the occasion.

This line of reasoning seemed to convince him. He gave me an
appointment for two days later. I cabled London to obtain permission
to rent the premises. Permission was immediately granted. However,
in the course of my second meeting at Rockefeller Center, the rental
agent stated that he was ready to rent the premises but that he wasn't
acquainted with the National Committee in London and that the Free
France delegation in New York was not a legal entity. He would only
be able to rent it to me under my name. "But I am only the representative for Free France," I protested. "I have no capital or collateral to
offer you." "That doesn't matter," I was told, "we are prepared to rent
these premises to you." Thus the sumptuous Fifth Avenue offices in
Rockefeller Center were rented on December 17, 1941, to an exile
with no references or fortune. The lease read, "Rented to Mr. Raoul
Aglion." It was only two years later, when the lease had to be
extended, that to it was added "and to his successors representing the
Free French." Looking back forty-five years later, I now wonder how
Rockefeller Center could have granted a lease to a complete stranger
without references. The Free France delegation did not yet officially
exist. I still wonder if someone intervened on our behalf—but who?

The first thing I did was to remove the name of the Italian consulate
from the entry door and have painted in its place: *Délégation de la
France Libre. Liberté, Égalité, Fraternité.* The next day, Johannes
Steel announced on the radio: "The Free French occupied Italian territory without a shot."

With almost no funds, we still had to recruit personnel and set up our offices, which was not an easy task. We had, of course, a very small staff, most of whom were inexperienced and knew nothing of the administrative rules governing French people abroad. Furthermore we had no archives of any sort on anyone or on anything. We had to run to the Public Library or to the Columbia University Library to read up on French legislation or Franco-American treaties, and if we could not find what we wanted, we had to rely on memory or imagination.

Late in December, after agreement with Washington, in my capacity as official delegate in charge of services in New York (in fact functioning as Consul General for Free France), I received French passport from London to be delivered to those of our compatriots who, having been stripped of their nationality, could not apply to the Vichy consulate. Soon our chancellery was very busy issuing visas, passports, passport extensions, affidavits certifying nationality, and identity cards, as well as "vital statistic" declarations that had to take the place of irretrievable documents left behind in France.

For my consulate office, my sole charge, I obtained the help of Xavier Charles and of Andrée Orienter, as secretary. The military department, including Colonel Brunschwig, Léon Brasseur, and Sacha de Manziarly, was set up on our premises, as well as a purchasing department with Levi and Chalon (two French businessmen who were refugees in New York). I started out without archives, regulations, or French law books. We had to improvise everything from ground zero, while constantly interrupted by refugees who came asking for assistance. I called on the British consulate general for help as seldom as possible in order to avoid becoming too dependent on their advice. However, they were very cooperative and helpful in telling me which American officials I should contact at City Hall, the Justice and Immigration Department, the holding offices for immigrants on Ellis Island, the OSS and the FBI, the Department of Censorship, etc.

In general, the attitude of American officials was sympathetic but extremely reserved; the public, too, was neutral, and didn't want to be considered as taking sides in the war. Imagine my surprise, then, when I visited City Hall to meet the dynamic Fiorello La Guardia, mayor of New York, for the first time in early May. "Long live France," was his greeting, "and long live de Gaulle! I think that the State Department should grant you the fullest legal and diplomatic recognition. All those who fight the Nazis are our real friends." He promised all the help his office could provide and assured me that he would facilitate any public demonstrations we wished to have. "You will be invited to all the meetings to which I invite accredited consuls general in New York. You could say the city of New York 'recognizes' you." And he concluded, "You are men without a country, but you represent a brave nation."

I had the pleasure of meeting La Guardia on several occasions and was always impressed by his boundless energy and his understanding of world politics (perhaps because he shared my ideas). "You cannot appease Hitler, and any attempt to appease Marshal Pétain is doomed to failure," he remarked one day, and he added that the Department of State was committing many errors. He criticized with humor the isolationist senators Borah and Taft. He was shocked by the refusal of the Administration to accept a greater number of refugees from ravaged Europe. "Do you know that the French quota is far from being filled, and that further French refugees should be admitted immediately and without hindrance?" He was indignant.

He asked me to keep him informed of the actions of the Free French Forces in Africa and the progress of the movement.

He never showed any sympathy to the Vichy partisans or did them any favors.

No doubt New York was a city that welcomed those who fought for freedom. New York was going to be the center of my activities, but the State Department, responsible for establishing American policy, was in Washington. It seemed to most Free French I met that de Gaulle should have an overall policy for the United States and send someone to the capital as soon as possible.

We had won a few victories for the Free French cause in New York, but Washington was another matter entirely.

CHAPTER V

❋

The Difficult Mission of Pleven

At that time, those who followed my banner were few.

—Charles de Gaulle

When Charles de Gaulle established his headquarters in London, he was of the opinion—as were many men of high military and political esteem—that all was lost for Europe only until America could be induced to intervene in the war. On June 18, 1940, he stated: "Nothing is lost because this war is a world war. In the free universe, numerous forces have not yet been brought into action. Someday, these forces will crush the enemy."[1]

The forces were the prodigious numbers of American military divisions supported by the greatest industrial strength in the world. De Gaulle could remember that American intervention in World War I had constituted the decisive factor in that conflict. By 1917, when the "Sammies" (after their Uncle) landed in Europe, chanting "Lafayette, we are here!" the French had lost more than a million men; the industries of England and France were on the verge of collapse. The arrival of the Americans had turned the tide of the war. This time, in 1940, de Gaulle was convinced it would be the same. America was the ultimate hope.

To de Gaulle, the intervention of the United States was infinitely more significant than appeared on the surface. Such intervention could lessen his dependence upon the British government, which advanced him funds and equipped his forces, and therefore make him more independent. Following his first appeal over the BBC, he received many cables of encouragement from numerous prominent Americans as well as from some of his friends, Frenchmen residing in the United States.

Actually, de Gaulle was suffering from completely understandable illusions. He could not comprehend that it would not be possible for him to raise a large volunteer corps from the ranks of the almost two hundred thousand Frenchmen residing in America permanently. This was at first the object of my mission. He visualized these volunteers organized into solid regiments—units fighting under the flag of Free France and the symbol of the Cross of Lorraine.

He had seen many refugees from France in London, whence they departed for New York, and they communicated to him their sole intention: the liberation of France. However, Jean Monnet (later the father of the Common Market), Henri Bonnet (later Ambassador to Washington), Henri de Kérillis, and André Maurois were but a few of those who refused to join his Committee and accept his leadership.

There were many problems to be resolved: the need for war equipment for his army and a resolution of the French navy's problems, the use of the French Merchant Marine in American ports, the use of French credits frozen in America, the French gold reserve, and questions related to the liberated French territories in Africa and the Pacific. De Gaulle was convinced that America would one day be forced into war against the Axis and, when peace finally ensued, the United States would emerge as the most important country in the Free World, assuming the master role in the post-war negotiations.

On May 19, 1941, General de Gaulle sent a telegram from Brazzaville to René Pleven in London:

> In view of the almost belligerent attitude of the United States toward the collaboration between Vichy and Germany which is becoming more apparent each day, and the special economic conditions of our colonies in Africa and the Pacific, the moment has arrived for us to establish relations with the United States. I intend to ask you personally to accomplish this mission. You will leave very soon. You will stay in the United States as many weeks as necessary to set up our program. You will:
>
> 1. establish our relations permanently and directly with the Department of State—these relations will have to be maintained afterwards through a fully qualified political representative of Free France;
> 2. organize economic and financial connections between Free French Africa and French Oceania and the U.S.;

3. organize, if possible, direct purchases of war equipment or equipment useful for war, according to the system similar to that used by the Belgians;
4. create or re-create our committees;
5. establish information and propaganda activities in the U.S.;
6. organize the cooperation and help of private sources in the U.S.

I ask you to prepare this mission right now. In the beginning, it must be treated discreetly, particularly with respect to the British, but it should be completed as soon as possible.[2]

Who was René Pleven? A Frenchman from Brittany, Pleven was born in 1901 in the small provincial town of Rennes. He received the degree of Doctor of Law and studied at the famed *Ecole des Sciences Politiques* in Paris. Preferring business to a government career, before the war he was General Director for Europe of an American firm, the Automatic Telephone Company of Chicago. His relations with American businessmen were excellent. Early in 1940, when he was with the French Supply Mission in London, he came to New York on an official visit to expedite the delivery of aircraft and military supplies.

Pleven joined de Gaulle almost immediately after the fall of France and was sent to Africa to gain the support of the colonies for the Free French movement. He was very successful in obtaining allegiance from Chad and proceeded with the economic reorganization of the Free Colonies.

Pleven was tall and handsome. He spoke fluent English, but with a marked French accent. A man of strong moral conviction and an idealist, he was nonetheless endowed with an acute sense of reality. He understood American politics and had been warned by many of his friends in the United States that his task would be difficult; indeed, it proved to be even more complicated than he had anticipated. The pro-Vichy position of the State Department was far stronger than he had expected. The Vichy Embassy was all-powerful in Washington. As for the attitude of the French in America, he would be keenly disappointed. He received virtually no support from them—most were hostile to his mission; some were indifferent; others were over-cautious. Only a few followed him. And they were very few indeed.

Upon his arrival, Pleven simultaneously carried out two negotiations: one with the United States Government for recognition of the Free French Movement, the other with the French in the United States to organize an official representation of that Movement and a National Committee to support it.

At first, as he told me, Pleven was of the opinion that the official delegation should be composed of five or six members, with a prestigious Frenchman at its head. For that post, he thought naturally of Alexis Léger, former French Ambassador and former Secretary-General of the French Foreign Office, a diplomat of great prestige and influence. By an extraordinary chance, Léger had left France a few days before the disastrous armistice and had come to the United States. He was held in high esteem by President Roosevelt, Cordell Hull, Sumner Wells, and members of Congress. He was critical of the errors of those French politicians who had been instrumental in the downfall of France and hostile to the Vichy French Government, but remained critical of General de Gaulle and the Free French movement as well.*

Had Pleven succeeded in convincing Léger to head the future mission, he would have scored a major victory. Not only would he have secured the services of the outstanding French diplomat, but would also thereby have been assured of some form of recognition by the State Department.

Léger, however, steadfastly refused. Although he was opposed to the Armistice, to Pétain, and to collaboration with the Nazis in any way, he could not accept that France could be represented by a General, however heroic, who had not received a mandate from the people. De Gaulle's call to arms and his rejection of the Armistice were the cry of the conscience of all Frenchmen. It was morally right; "however, it did not invest the General with any political power." Léger would have accepted a position with the Resistance as soon as a representative body could be formed abroad with, for instance, Lebrun, president of the French Republic, or Herriot, Speaker of the House, or Jeanneney, President of the Senate. Alexis Léger, the highest ranking diplomat of the French Foreign Office, could not join General de Gaulle and a committee of unknown patriots around him.

Pleven's insistence had no results. He then turned to another Frenchman of very great prestige: the Catholic philosopher Jacques Maritain, one of the greatest thinkers of our time, who had left France in January 1940 to serve as a professor at the Pontifical Institute of Medieval Studies in Toronto. He had originally intended to return to France at the end of June 1940, but the capitulation of the French armies and the German occupation of France prevented him from doing so. He later lectured at Princeton and Columbia universities.

---

*See Chapter XXI.

Because of his independence as a philosopher, Jacques Maritain had consistently refused to be a member of any political group. His moral position took precedence, of course, and he became—in those fateful days and years that followed the fall of France—the moral beacon for most of us in exile. While we had no government to look to, in those tragic times we did have the guiding light of the conscience of the great Maritain.

Pleven had considerable respect for him and asked whether he would be willing to represent the Free French Movement, or to be one of its delegates to the United States. Maritain refused. He would give advice when asked by Pleven, but could not accept any position with the future Delegation. He believed it necessary to respect the government of Pétain, although he judged it very severely. Our obedience to its orders, however, "could not go further than our conscience would allow."

He considered the opposition between political allegiance to de Gaulle and political allegiance to Vichy as an expression "void of sense as long as de Gaulle had not constituted a 'Government in Exile.'" He praised de Gaulle for having officers and soldiers to continue the war and to maintain every possible part of the French Empire on the side of Great Britain:

> ... the determination of General de Gaulle lifted a burden from many consciences. In a time of political collapse, he acted like a man. His action could be a considerable factor in future events. After all, however, it is not in a man, it is in the people of our country that we have our best hope.[3]

René Pleven, however, did ask Professor Maritain's opinion concerning the members of the Delegation he was about to form—without Jacques Maritain or Alexis Léger.

Jean Monnet, who was then in Washington as a member of the British Supply Council, told Pleven he was a greater help to the Allied cause in that position than he would be as a representative of de Gaulle in the United States. He also believed that a general had no political authority. He too would only join a government in exile recognized as such.

It was a baffling situation. Pleven realized he would be unable to find any outstanding personality of international reputation to take up the functions of delegate. He reported this problem to Lord Halifax, Ambassador of the United Kingdom in Washington, who very enthusiastically recommended a young industrialist who had escaped from

France through Lisbon on June 16, 1940—Étienne Boegner, whom he had met a few months earlier in London. He was the son of Rev. Marc Boegner, leader of the Protestant churches of France, a man renowned for his heroic opposition to the Nazis and his decision to remain with his flock and share their misery during the entire war.

Étienne Boegner, who was a friend of Léger, was then in Washington and was appreciated not only by the British Ambassador, but was warmly received by the various political and diplomatic circles there. He had the same moral principles of his father; he was a loyal patriot and, of course, a most desirable candidate. Pleven convinced him to assume the responsibilities of a delegate, despite their differing opinions concerning the future of the Free French Movement. Pleven, a great patriot, had a deep sense of devotion to the General and an almost mystic faith in his mission. Étienne Boegner was following a somewhat puritan ethic, with strong moral convictions and a deep belief in the democratic principles of his country. He wanted to be sure that after the liberation of France, the laws of the Third Republic would be applied.*

Boegner also desired an end to de Gaulle's unremittingly hostile attitude toward American policy. In view of such divergent points of view, it is surprising that Pleven nevertheless urged de Gaulle to appoint Boegner as his representative. He did so, I was told, because he believed that Boegner would gradually change his views and adopt the policies of London.

Seeking additional delegates René Pleven also met with Adrien Tixier in Washington. Tixier was one of the Directors of the Bureau of the International Labor Organization (ILO). During World War I, he had lost an arm and had sustained head injuries. His appearance was grim and forbidding. Yet he had the double advantage of being both a former war veteran and a labor leader, a friend of the different members of the French Unions and of socialist leaders now prisoners in France. In addition to his administrative abilities and training in an international organization, because of his leftist past, he had the great advantage of being the answer to all the critics in Washington who considered de Gaulle a "fascist" general.

Tixier did not respond immediately. He wanted an assurance that de Gaulle would enlarge the National Committee in London to

---

*A special law, the Loi Treveneuc of 1872, had foreseen a specific and detailed procedure to guarantee the legality of any government established after a national catastrophe. See Chapter XXI.

include labor leaders as soon as possible. He also wanted something to be done to plan the escape from France of Léon Jouhaux, the head of the Labor Unions, and other representatives of the Socialist Party. He believed it important to "democratize" the Free French Movement, which in many circles had the reputation of being under the influence of authoritarian members (the purported "fascists") of de Gaulle's staff. After receiving assurances from Pleven and after obtaining a leave of absence from the International Labor Organization, Tixier agreed to accept. He proved to be a rough man, rude, sarcastic, uncomfortable in the diplomatic and social circles of Washington. He was difficult to deal with, sometimes unpleasant, suspicious of everyone and everything. Many of these qualities must have appealed to de Gaulle, as well as the hope that this unpolished fellow would be loyal and unafraid of challenging the Americans. Tixier had terrible headaches as a result of his head injuries. He still suffered great pain from the high amputation of his left arm, and, as a chain smoker, was subject to episodes of violent coughing. He played a strange role, as we shall see, in the relations between de Gaulle and the State Department following the departure of Boegner a few months later.

To bolster the delegation, Pleven thought of Raoul de Roussy de Sales, whom he had met early in the year in New York, prior to the Armistice. Roussy de Sales was unquestionably a man of the world with great talent. He was a descendant of the illustrious family of St. Francois de Sales.* His father was French, his mother American. He had devoted many years to working with the International Red Cross. A talented author (he wrote *The New Order* and *The Making of Tomorrow*), he was also a journalist of great reputation. He died in New York in 1942 at the age of forty-six. When Pleven met him, he was already ill, and I remember many meetings in his Park Avenue apartment when he received us in his dressing gown. Later, as his health deteriorated further, he addressed our meetings from his bed. His body was weak but his brilliant mind seemed to sustain him through the daily physical indignities of those sad days.

Roussy de Sales was the correspondent of the French press agency *Havas,* and a brilliant lecturer, a man anyone would like to meet and talk to. At first, he turned down Pleven's offer; however, Pleven was a patient negotiator who would repeat his proposal many times until eventually some part of it would be accepted. Roussy argued that he was "not a Gaullist," that he did not like the people around de Gaulle

---

*Saint François de Sales, Catholic Bishop of Geneva, founded the Order of the Visitation (sixteenth century).

in London, that he totally disliked his foreign policy and his attitude towards the United States. Pleven persisted in his urging for months. In his diary, Roussy states that upon his return on July 28 from one of his trips to Washington, Pleven spent two days in New York:

> He wants to convince me to join the Delegation of de Gaulle, as a delegate or a political advisor.... It is without enthusiasm that I shall accept that duty. I have no faith, no heroism.[4]

On a subsequent visit, he saw Roussy again, who finally accepted on October 18 with great reluctance, many reservations, and the vague hope that he could change the policy of the Movement. "I am not a Gaullist," reiterated Roussy de Sales, "and probably will never become one."

Pleven's persistence and faith were admirable, but the authority or the actions of a "delegate" appointed under such conditions of disagreement and doubt were questionable. If they did not change soon, how could they speak for the General? Or, to put it differently, how could their statements in any way reflect the ideas of their leader? It is a fact that Roussy de Sales never concealed his opinions concerning de Gaulle's policies toward the Allies, of which he disapproved, nor of the membership in London of the governing body of the Free French Movement, the *Comité National Français,* which he considered not sufficiently democratic in its constitution.

René Pleven then decided to add to the future Free French delegation Jacques de Sieyès, the General Manager of Patou Perfumes, Inc., who was already de Gaulle's delegate. He also asked me if I would accept a position as delegate, explaining that there would be five altogether, each with a different function but combining our efforts for the common cause.

Not having found the "ideal" delegate, Pleven had decided to assemble five French patriots of varying backgrounds, tradition, training, and political conviction, who would join forces to help their country in a time of national disaster. In fact, he told me that Roussy de Sales would deal mostly with the press and information in New York; Boegner, with the State Department in Washington; Tixier, with members of Congress and the labor unions in Washington. De Sieyès would personally represent General de Gaulle at official functions as well as at meetings of Free French associations, and I would be coordinator of the four (Secretary-General) and also head of the Free French delegation in New York. Since I was the only one with some diplomatic experience, I was to help them and consult with them as closely as possible. On important matters, we were to seek instructions from the National Committee in London; on all other matters, we were to consult with each other before taking action.

The State Department, he informed me, had later accepted the names of the five delegates as accredited diplomats and was willing to give us certain—but not all—diplomatic facilities, especially concerning the cypher and pouch, but also exemption from the draft, access to certain restricted areas, exemption from the Alien Registration Act, etc. We were, however, not members of the accredited diplomatic corps of Washington. We did not represent a "legitimate" government. We did not benefit from diplomatic immunity and our offices did not benefit from extra-territoriality.

To bolster the Delegation, Pleven decided to organize a sort of Free French consulting committee, under the name of "The French National Committee to the U.S.A." To do so, he consulted with Jacques Maritain, as he had done for the appointments of the five delegates. It would be a sort of supporting committee (Comité de soutien), the prestige of whose members would impress the State Department and the American public. If his plan of a support committee had succeeded, the relations between the United States and Free France would surely have been smoother and devoid of much of their acrimony and hostility. Unfortunately, here too he met opposition from most Frenchmen in the United States who refused to be this closely associated with de Gaulle. Finally, Pleven settled for just the Delegation of five members. He also obtained a promise from General de Gaulle that the France Forever association would be its only recognized affiliate, dealing with information and grouping the Free French and the Friends of Free France in the United States.

Pleven cabled de Gaulle requesting his approval of the following five delegates: Boegner, Tixier, Roussy, Aglion and de Sieyès, and asking his preference for Chief Delegate. On September 23, 1941, de Gaulle's reply arrrived, accepting Pleven's suggestions of the five delegates and selecting Tixier as the senior delegate "because the French Labor Unions, Christian, Socialist, and CGT (Communist), had an excellent attitude in France."[5] Perhaps he did so because he found no one else; perhaps also because he was aware that it was rumored in Washington and in New York that he was a potential dictator surrounded by rightist officers. He must have calculated that a senior delegate who was to the left, a socialist or a trade unionist, would help counteract these rumors. Tixier fulfilled all those requirements and added to these qualities a passion for personal intrigue of which we—and de Gaulle—had as yet no knowledge.

CHAPTER VI

Men Without a Country

After Pleven's return to London, the Free French accredited delegates to the United States—Boegner, Tixier, Roussy de Sales, de Sieyès and I—began to meet as often as possible, sometimes once a week. The organization of a non-recognized diplomatic mission and its consular services was by no means easy. I will always remember our first meeting at Roussy de Sales' lovely apartment on Fifth Avenue. There we were, five delegates appointed by General de Gaulle, accredited as such by the Department of State. What did we represent in reality? Our leader had through René Pleven given us some very vague indication of his plans. We could interpret them as we thought useful or practical.

We knew very little about Charles de Gaulle other than his speeches on the BBC, and few of us had read the three small books he had published before the war. We differed in background and training. Roussy de Sales was an aristocrat, an excellent writer, a liberal, a skeptic (and mortally ill); Étienne Boegner was certainly more conservative and had rigid moral principles; Count de Sieyès was an aristocrat, a man of the world, and a businessman; Adrien Tixier was a socialist, a labor leader of the left, revolutionary in most of his ideas; and I was a jurist by training and had held minor diplomatic posts.

The confusion at our meetings was unbelievable. We all interpreted events in different ways: we had different political ideas, our views of the war had nothing in common, and we certainly did not agree as to the future structure of a liberated France.

We also had our personal problems. We were anxious about the whereabouts of our loved ones in France. We were without news of our families, but—for their safety—did not try to communicate with them.

The chief thing we had in common was that we believed we had to fight this war against Hitler to the end. We also had in common the fact that we were men without a country, representing an unknown "movement" led by a brigadier general who had been condemned to death by a French military court.

I learned later that there was just as much disorder and division among the French at our headquarters in London as we had in New York. Fortunately, we did not know this at the time!

To understand this confusion and this chaos one has to remember that the Free French Movement was a revolutionary reaction against the armistice and Pétain's policy of collaboration with the Germans. Revolutions usually start in great disorder. In times of national disaster, a nation naturally has need of, and indeed looks to, its legitimate constitutional leader. When the supreme authority of the state no longer exists, good and loyal people of good will become confused and do not know what path to follow. This was the unfortunate situation of the French people following the overthrow of the Republic and the destruction of its institutions in June 1940.

In Washington, Boegner and Tixier met with the State Department. Boegner openly expressed his misgivings and freely stated his disagreements with de Gaulle's policy. Tixier's attitude was somewhat elusive. To most of the Free French, he appeared as a tough hard-line representative. With the State Department he was quite different, as I have since discovered in reading its archives.

In the first weeks after his appointment, Boegner paid several visits to Lord Halifax, the British Ambassador, who gave him advice on diplomatic procedures in Washington. He was well received by the Assistant Secretary of State, Sumner Welles, and other members of the Department—Adolf Berle, Ray Atherton, and Sam Reber. There were various matters to be attended to, mainly those arising from the Lend Lease the Free French were now about to receive through the British. There were questions about economic negotiations concerning Free French Equatorial Africa, the purchase of medical and other supplies, the situation in New Caledonia and other Free French territories in the Pacific, the new radio station in Brazzaville (powerful enough to transmit to all the African territories, including those under the control of Vichy) and again, the definition of the official recognition to be given to General de Gaulle and the Free French Movement.

Boegner's frank approach to all problems was appreciated by everyone and he rapidly earned the trust of some members of the State Department with whom he was dealing. He never concealed his doubts about the authoritarian methods of the General or his hostility toward the U.S.

Tixier, who was also in Washington, did not at first disagree with Boegner. He too had his doubts and did not conceal them from anyone. He was critical of the people around General de Gaulle, critical of the fact that no leader of the labor party or of the French socialist party was with him in London.

Jacques de Sieyès, who had an unconditional admiration for the General, was completely at a loss to understand the positions of Tixier, whom he frequently accused of treason and told him once in front of me, "you are acting as though you were the enemy of General de Gaulle."

Roussy de Sales never concealed the fact that he was not a Gaullist, and though a "delegate," considered that his conscience did not permit him to support all the members of the London headquarters and what he considered the General's anti-democratic political ideas. He believed de Gaulle should remain a military leader and not intervene in political affairs. It is not unlikely that he played a role in the formulation of what would become the State Department's policy toward Free France.

These divisions among the delegates worried me, and I decided not to take sides. Consequently I avoided going to Washington as much as possible and concentrated my work in New York, where there was plenty to do.

In some instances, Tixier and Boegner went to the Department of State together and then, on their return, disagreed violently on what had been said by the official who had received them.

Due to his illness, Roussy de Sales could not readily leave his New York apartment. We therefore held some meetings there, expressing our concern about everything: the isolationist tendency of the United States, the pro-German attitude of the Embassy of Vichy, the shocking attitude of Marshal Pétain and Laval, our worries about our families and friends left in France, the regrettable attitude of most Frenchmen in the United States and the infighting in the Committee of France Forever in New York. More than anything we discussed the little we knew about what was going on in London at de Gaulle's headquarters. Roussy de Sales had very disturbing information about the poor organization of the Free French there and what he called de Gaulle's autocratic behavior. He felt that the National Committee was hardly confidence-inspiring.[1]

Finally, in March 1942, Tixier told us that he was so disturbed by what he heard about de Gaulle that he would go to London and have a talk with the General in order to find out what he was really like and what his policy was. He had friends such as Winant,* whom he knew from the International Labor Office. He would speak about the organization of our work and of our difficulties, the opposition of the Vichy officials and the distrust of the Department of State, and hoped we could obtain a declaration of the General's democratic principles.

It was difficult to find out what he did in London but upon his return he held a meeting with all of us at Roussy's home and told us that he had "grave doubts about the ability of de Gaulle to unite all Frenchmen." He was surrounded by men who had "no sense of realism." De Gaulle himself had "no idea that there was a people of France with whom he had no contact." Tixier thought it was indispensable that leaders such as Jouhaux, Léon Blum, or Herriot should be brought out of France to strengthen the National Committee in London and give it a democratic structure.

Finally, Tixier told us that the war was being fought on a different plan than the one de Gaulle could see. "Sumner Welles and Vice President Wallace have a realistic view of things while de Gaulle has a narrow idea of his mission. . . . When General de Gaulle left France to go to London, he was convinced that England was not going to be able to hold out for more than a few weeks and that it was necessary, for the honor of France, that a group of French soldiers, together with their officers, should die defending London." Tixier added, "as things turned out otherwise, it complicated the tasks of de Gaulle considerably, as he had to make other plans."† Roussy was quite interested. He had never been told that de Gaulle had been that pessimistic, and he deplored the fact "that de Gaulle had taken the position that he was a trustee to conserve the interests of France, while Pétain was also conserving the same interests. One does not defend a country by 'conserving' because the world is in constant evolution."[2]

Tixier had convinced de Gaulle to consider that the delegation should not remain in its present form, a group of delegates. Henceforth, the delegation would consist of one person—Tixier, with full power and authority, like an ambassador. The other delegates, Roussy,

---

*Soon after named U.S. Ambassador in London.
†Members of General de Gaulle's staff in London, Ambassador C. de Courcelles and Palewski, denied in a personal conversation with the author that de Gaulle ever made such a statement.

Boegner, de Sieyès and I were to become "counselors." Boegner disagreed, and Roussy stated that the clear result of Tixier's trip was a further division among members of the Delegation. Concluding that this must have been the real object of Tixier's trip, and noting his growing ambition, Roussy voiced concern over Tixier's qualifications to conduct successfully the very delicate negotiations with Washington. In any case we all dismissed his talk as meaningless haggling over titles since we were not even recognized as a legitimate government by Washington.

What did Tixier's London trip really change? It was he alone who now sent reports directly to the General and eventually received his instructions. Tixier could, and did, keep us completely in the dark not only about his correspondence with de Gaulle, but also about his activity in Washington. Of course, as there was no real French central authority, we corresponded with members of the *Comité National* in London who kept us informed.

One afternoon, after a long discussion about General de Gaulle and the advisors around him, Boegner finally got up and said: "I am going to go to London as soon as possible to find out what is going on over there. I want to have a frank talk with General de Gaulle to find out his ideas about political problems and his post-war plans for France. I also want to frankly discuss his attitude towards the United States. I want to know what his policy really is. Maybe I will be able to change his views. . . . " He had the blessings of us all. Before leaving Washington in May, he had further talks with Lord Halifax, and Sumner Welles at the Department of State, and also with Alexis Léger, with whom he had a long meeting. Léger encouraged him to go: "De Gaulle has a difficult character, so you have to be very patient." He added, "Don't forget that despite his irascible temperament, he can be an asset to us Frenchmen. We must make all possible efforts to come to an understanding." When Boegner promised to be patient, Léger concluded, "If de Gaulle can't get along with *you*, I am afraid no one will be able to work with him."

It was without enthusiasm but with a real sense of duty that Boegner left us in Washington for this trip to London to meet our leader. Before leaving, he told us how he would draft letters and telegrams to be sent to us in such a way that they would pass unnoticed by the Censor.

On June 2, Roussy called me to tell me that he had received a telegram from Boegner in London through the cypher of the British Consulate. It read as follows: "I am doing my best but things are difficult and I am pessimistic." Roussy commented that things must look pretty bad there if Boegner found it necessary to send such a bad telegram. Later, a letter dated June 3 reached Roussy:

> My first contact with the General was extremely violent. I have never been insulted like that in all my life. I failed to be impressed and defended my position. For one hour I was insulted, as were our (American allies). . . . It was like a storm. . . . de Gaulle is a phenomenon of patriotism.[5]

On his return after a long trip on a British bomber, Boegner came to see me at my office and told me he had officially resigned. He explained that when he arrived in London, he went to Carlton Gardens, the Free French Headquarters, where he was immediately introduced to the very angry General. He had been expecting him; he shouted at him, "What is going on in New York? Tixier has informed me that you are a traitor. Traitor!" he repeated in a violent explosion of rage. "I intend that everyone follow my policy toward the United States. . . . "

Then Boegner spoke of the necessity for friendlier relations with Washington and having a movement with a more democratic base.

"Are you a democrat?" Boegner asked the General.

"Yes, I am, and I will not repeat it again."

"Why are you seeking friendship with the USSR?"

"Because it is with the Russians that I will rebuild France and Europe. I have a policy and I insist that everyone follow it." Étienne Boegner replied again, "the United States is more important to us, more than any other country. They will, during and after the war, grant us military, financial, and economic aid. They will help us without any pre-condition. We need them."[6]

Boegner's contradiction of his views infuriated the General who now pounded on the table and shouted: "Get out, get out! Traitor!" The whole stormy meeting had lasted fifty minutes.

Boegner left the headquarters of the Free French, deeply distraught and disillusioned. On his return to Washington, he informed Lord Halifax, Alexis Léger, and other friends in the State Department of his meeting with de Gaulle.

Everyone was shocked. But the only conclusion I allowed myself to draw from his story, for now, was that, having started with five delegates, we were now only four.

At one of our subsequent meetings, Roussy de Sales, still sick in bed, declared that it really might be necessary for us to know more about

de Gaulle personally and suggested that I in turn go to London and
have a serious talk with him to determine his views on democracy in
general and democratic government in France after the war. I found
this request rather comical, and declined. By this time, in these circumstances, I felt we knew enough to stay or quit the Free French
Movement. According to the notes I made shortly after this heated
meeting, I concluded my excited and somewhat angry remarks as
follows:

> We are in chaos. A marshal of France has surrendered the whole army,
> two million men, and accepted a dishonorable armistice. The army, the
> navy, and the elite of the nation have accepted the surrender and the
> new pseudo government is ready to collaborate with the enemy. One
> man, only one, has said *no* to the defeat, *no* to the armistice, yes to war
> and sacrifice. I will follow that man.

We were not to be four delegates for long; Roussy de Sales died on
December 3, 1942. Soon de Sieyès, who always quarreled with Tixier,
was recalled by de Gaulle and sent to Syria. We were now only two—
Tixier and myself.

It was not easy to have political conversations with Adrien Tixier.
His style was an unvarying leftist harangue. He complained constantly of the chaos in London and endlessly, tiresomely, blamed generals, bankers, ambassadors, and traitors for the downfall of France.

In the absence of any instruction from our headquarters, I believed
I should have a talk with Alexis Léger. Perhaps this learned, worldly
wise, almost legendary figure could provide some insight into France's
problems and what was to be done now. Léger's real name was Alexis
Léger Saint Léger. He was born on May 31, 1887 at Guadeloupe
(French Antilles). He was a great poet who wrote in France under the
name of St.-John Perse, had a brilliant career as a diplomat, and held
for many years the rank of an ambassador. For the last eight years he
had been Secretary General of the French Foreign Office, a post similar to that of a Deputy Secretary of State. He had been the most highly
esteemed member of the staff of Aristide Briand, Prime Minister and
Foreign Minister of France. In May 1940 he was abruptly and without
explanation dismissed by Paul Reynaud, who was then Premier, and
replaced by Ambassador Charles Roux.

Léger was hurt and resentful. From then on he bore an unyielding
hostility and hatred for Paul Reynaud, and for all his appointees,
including General de Gaulle, who had been Reynaud's Undersecretary
of War.

On June 16, two days before France's surrender, Léger escaped on a boat to London where he stayed with Lord Vansittart. Invited by Churchill to Chequers, Léger conveyed the reasons for the French disaster. He blamed former Premier Paul Reynaud for all the errors made at that time. He did not want to meet and never met General de Gaulle.[4] Léger left England thereafter, arriving in Canada on July 14. From there, he proceeded to Washington. Léger was warmly received by his fellow poet and friend Archibald MacLeish, Librarian of Congress, and by a very good friend, Francis Biddle, U.S. Attorney General. Both of these men were very close to President Roosevelt. Léger was a proud man. He refused assistance from the American government, refused to write memoirs or articles for magazines and turned down posts offered by various universities. He finally accepted a modest post as literary advisor at the Library of Congress under his poet's alias of "St.-John Perse."

Léger had brought with him from France archives and documents of great importance from the French Foreign Office. In addition, he had also brought his own personal papers concerning the various political problems of the century and his notes on practically all the European leaders of the time. Léger was fervently anti-Nazi and viewed Marshal Pétain with scorn for having signed a dishonorable armistice and set up a puppet government controlled by the Nazis.

At my request he immediately granted me an interview. I had had a brief meeting with him in Paris two years before. He had received me then in his imposing office at the Quai d'Orsay (Foreign Office), where I was formally introduced by an usher in uniform. This time, to my surprise, he opened the door himself and welcomed me into a small, sparsely furnished room, whose windows looked out on a neglected cemetery. Léger seated himself behind a bare pine table and began to paint in the darkest shades the dreadful situation of the whole world. In rich detail he spoke of nations, territories, rulers and their ambitions and the unavoidable tragic fates of the millions strangled in the Nazi noose.

The hours passed; I was totally transfixed and hung on every word. When the room darkened he did not get up to switch on the light. I could see in the shadows his balding head and his dark eyes. He continued describing an image of a France that "had vanished into darkness" after the armistice. She was "no more"; no one, he insisted, had the right to speak in her name. Yet, in the dark room his words were like the disembodied voice of France lost in the night.

There was a long silence. "Of course," he said, "France will be res-urrected by the victory of the Allies, thanks to President Roosevelt." It was clear he had a profound admiration for the President. Although Léger believed de Gaulle had some merit as a military man, he thought the General had no right to get involved in political affairs and should not organize a committee as a "pseudo government."

We continued to talk in the dark. I would not accept his contention that France was gone and that only military, not political, means could revive her. "How could the colonies that had joined us survive without political and economic direction from outside?" I asked. He replied that "All territories could be administered locally." I was in no position to argue with him and to answer that I believed it impos-sible to wait for the liberation of France and free elections before administering the free territories. After having respectfully stated my position I thanked him for this long visit and departed.

I had been moved but not convinced by this man of great experi-ence. It seemed to me wrong to limit all our activities to the military. Someone in the free world should speak in France's name. It was by speeches and appeals on the radio that resistance had been fostered in France, and that territories overseas could be induced to join us and continue the battle.

Already New Caledonia and Tahiti in the Pacific, and colonies in Central Africa were joining us. I was convinced that one could be tempted to join a movement of liberation rather than a general limited to the command of a legion.

I was concerned, however, by all the divisions among Frenchmen in New York. Pleven's failure to rally outstanding exiles in America to our cause was hardly a good omen.

❈

CHAPTER VII

The Lonely Leader

France has lost a battle, but France has not lost the war.

—Charles de Gaulle

In London, the seat of General de Gaulle's headquarters, the French were more divided than ever. Despite the terrible German air raids, the bombings, the dangers of a possible invasion, and the hardships of war, the French in England could not unite under the only leader who had chosen to fight along with the British.

The number of non-Gaullists and enemies of de Gaulle in London was considerable. Most of the French residents as well as the new arrivals, the political exiles, opposed him. To make matters worse, the administration of the *Comité National Français,* the center of de Gaulle's power, was often itself divided. Even here, in his own committee, there was a plot to oust him.

The opposition started early, on June 17, 1940, when de Gaulle first arrived in London with Lieutenant C. de Courcelles. France was at that time in a state of complete chaos, the army was defeated, the government had resigned and Marshal Pétain was assuming full power, soon abolishing the Republic and establishing a Nazi-like puppet government in its stead.

On June 18 at 8 p.m. after receiving word of Marshal Pétain's surrender to Germany, de Gaulle spoke on the radio for the first time, severing his ties to the leaders who remained in France: "The leaders who, for many years, have been at the head of the French armies, have formed a government. This government, invoking the defeat of our armies, has entered in relations with the enemy, to bring a halt to the battle . . . but has the last word been said? No. . . . France is not alone! She is not alone! This war was not limited to the unhappy territory of our country. This war is not decided by the battle of France. . . . This war is a global war. . . . Overwhelmed today by a mechanized force . . . I, General de Gaulle, today in London invite all officers and soldiers on British soil . . . to join forces with me. . . . No matter what may happen, the flame of French resistance must not, and will not die. . . . Tomorrow, as I have done today, I will speak on the radio from London."

De Gaulle thus declared his rejection of the Armistice and announced that he was breaking with the traditional rules of the French army. He was calling on men to disobey their superior officers, to reject the Armistice and continue the war, to join their forces to his. He was, in effect, advocating insubordination, but at that time many French superior officers in the army and navy, as well as many governors of the colonies, were wavering. Their indecision explains why de Gaulle did not announce that he was leading a revolt against the Armistice; he was waiting for a superior officer to come to London. None did.

De Gaulle could not in those circumstances expect individual soldiers to continue to fight without a leader. Moreover, the Pétain government was placing itself under the control of the conquering Nazis, and France could therefore no longer be considered sovereign. During the night de Gaulle realized that he had to bring not only Frenchmen but France itself back into the war.

On June 19 de Gaulle made an important declaration. It was more than an appeal to arms. He declared: "In the confusion of French souls, facing the liquidation of a government that has fallen into servitude to the enemy, considering our institutions can no longer function, I, *General de Gaulle,* a soldier and a French chief, I am speaking in the name of *France.* . . . [Italics added.]"[1]

From that moment on, General de Gaulle considered that *France, the Republic, had not ceased to exist,* and that Pétain, who had abolished the Republic, had created a rebellious government against the permanent interests of France. In this view, it was Pétain who had no legitimacy.

De Gaulle now felt he represented not only a group of army volunteers but France itself. The assumption that an occupied nation's puppet government has no legitimacy and that the nation's sovereignty is transferred to its free citizens who continue to fight its oppressor was unknown in international law.

De Gaulle was more explicit on October 17, when in Brazzaville (Free French Congo) in Africa he created the *Conseil de Défense de l'Empire* and issued a proclamation declaring that "a government subject to the invader is in a state of servitude and lacks the basis of legitimacy...."* As no one outside the land that was dominated by the enemy had claimed that lost legitimacy, de Gaulle did so himself. Consequently the officers and soldiers who joined de Gaulle could claim they were loyal to France. Those who remained with Vichy were serving their country's enemy. Marshal Pétain was not chief of an independent country; no obedience was due to him; he was a rebel.†

This new form of legitimacy proclaimed by de Gaulle, over and above the Allies' objections, would create many difficulties, above all with Roosevelt, and to a lesser degree with Churchill.

Of course de Gaulle pledged that his political status was a temporary situation and that he would maintain his position only until the people of France could freely choose their government. On June 27 Churchill said to him, "You are alone! I will recognize you alone."² The next day a proclamation of the British Cabinet recognized de Gaulle as the "leader of all Free Frenchmen who would join his movement in defense of the Allied cause." A few days later de Gaulle formed a National Committee, recognized by His Majesty's government, responsible not only for military affairs, but also competent in civil matters such as transportation, purchasing, and finances, as well as information and propaganda.

In his numerous quarrels with de Gaulle, Churchill one day exclaimed: "You say you are France! You are not France! Where is France? I agree that General de Gaulle and all those who follow him are a respectable part of the French people. But we may find outside them another authority which may also have its value."

De Gaulle icily replied, "If in your eyes I am not the representative of France, by what right do you associate with me?" Churchill had no answer.

If instead of creating a National Committee and speaking in the name of France, de Gaulle had simply organized a "French Legion" to fight side by side with the British, he would have met much less

---

*This principle was later confirmed after the liberation of Paris, by an Ordinance of August 9, 1944 declaring all Vichy laws to be null and void because "the Republic has never ceased to exist."

†After the war Marshal Pétain and Pierre Laval, his premier, were sentenced to death by the High Court of France for treason and collaboration with the enemy. Pétain had his conviction commuted to life in prison in view of his advanced age. Pierre Laval was executed.

opposition, even from Vichy. The fact that he assumed a political role raised doubts concerning his integrity and his ambitions. Cordell Hull himself declared that it was de Gaulle's constant insistence on political recognition "that excited so much suspicion against him." If he, as an army general, had thrown himself wholeheartedly into the fight against the Axis in the military sense, if he had actually led French troops against the enemy *instead of spending his time in London* . . . he could have rallied more support. . . .[3] This view was shared by many Frenchmen in the United States as well as in England and to a certain extent in Vichy France, where officials and leaders felt their rule over the French being threatened and their legitimacy challenged.

Jean Monnet, the future father of the Common Market, in a letter to de Gaulle, admonished him: "You are wrong to want to set up an organization that might appear to be created under the protection of England. . . . I share your decision that France should not abandon the war. . . . But it is not from London that the resurrection can come. . . . "[4]

Among the very first and few who joined de Gaulle were members of the Information Office of the French Foreign Office such as André Weil-Curiel and Georges Boris. The members of the French press in exile were hostile to Vichy and sympathetic to de Gaulle but did not join him. André Labarthe and the renowned French historian Raymond Aron created a French magazine in London, *France Libre.* Maillaud and Comert created another magazine, *France,* with the support of the British Ministry of Information. They were independent and sometimes critical of de Gaulle, who had his own newspaper *La Marseillaise.*

The great majority of Frenchmen, although quarreling among themselves, opposed de Gaulle and led an incessant campaign against him. A leader of the French socialist group in London, the Jean Jaures club, drafted a scathing article against de Gaulle and asked Kingsley Martin—chief editor of the *New Statesman and Nation,* a leftist magazine—to publish it. Martin refused because of its defamatory character. David Astor, son of Lady Astor, manager of the *Observer,* considered that the French critics of de Gaulle were unjust, and he refused to publish their articles on the grounds that the enemies of de Gaulle were acting against the Allied war efforts.

The most bitter of de Gaulle's enemies was a high-ranking diplomat, Roger Cambon. He resigned from the French Embassy after the capitulation but did not join de Gaulle; instead he stayed in London and carried out an incessant campaign against the General. Unfortunately he was on very good terms with the members of the U.S.

Embassy and with British officials. De Gaulle was to him a future dictator. Cambon went so far as to claim that the General's headquarters
had jails where prisoners were tortured by the Gaullist secret police.
De Gaulle was, according to him, surrounded by fascists, spies, and
adventurers. These comments, not surprisingly, found their way to the
State Department in Washington.

There were also intrigues in the *Comité National* itself. Admiral
Muselier, the only admiral to have joined de Gaulle, outranked him;
he had three stars while de Gaulle, a brigadier general, had only two.
De Gaulle appointed him in charge of the small Free French navy. But
there were plots: Muselier wanted to replace de Gaulle. Labarthe
joined Muselier in stating that the *Comité National* was not functioning democratically and that decisions should not be made by de Gaulle
alone without a *Comité* vote on important issues. Finally after many
intrigues and fights de Gaulle dismissed Muselier and Labarthe.

During the entire course of the war, the BBC encouraged France to
resist. De Gaulle was able to broadcast to the captive people of France,
giving them courage and nurturing the movements of resistance to the
enemy. Maurice Shumann,* a man of great talent, a writer and a
remarkable speaker, had joined de Gaulle in June 1940. In his daily
broadcasts to France via the BBC, he broadcast news of the war on
the Allied side, reported the heroic feats of the Free French Forces,
and the increasing help given to Free France by the Allies. He was
also able to report what was going on in the France that resisted. His
messages were heard all over the ravaged country, despite the heavy
penalties imposed by Vichy on the listeners.

London was also the center from which the American, British and
French secret services communicated with members of the resistance
in the country occupied by the enemy. Unfortunately the rivalry
between them sometimes led to costly conflicts.

The situation of the French military was a disaster. By June 1940,
there were roughly 115,000 French troops in England—soldiers repa-
triated from Norway as well as those rescued from Dunkirk. Because
of the hesitation and the misunderstanding of some British and the
propaganda of the Vichy consuls, very few—indeed roughly only
7,000 men—joined the Free French forces.

This small force, however, soon proved itself heroic. It fought
bravely all over Africa. The fighting of the Free French Forces led by

---

*Later Minister for Foreign Affairs, Senator, and member of the prestigious Académie
Française.

men such as Leclerc, de Larminat, and Koenig saved France's honor by gallantly resisting the Nazis in battles such as Bir-Hakim, where with the entire British front in retreat, they stopped General Rommel and his Afrika Korps from invading Egypt. Rommel in his memoirs heaped praise on the gallant Free French defense.

The Resistance against the Nazis gradually grew stronger and stronger in France proper. Many individual Frenchmen joined London, some crossing the Channel on small fishing boats, others crossing the Pyrenées mountains into Spain. Sometimes young pilots arrived after stealing training planes. Every week volunteers escaped occupied France, despite the Gestapo and the Vichy police.

All the fishermen of the small island of Sein in Brittany, the whole male population, a total of 130 men, landed in Cornwall on June 15 in their fishing boats. Other fishermen came from the isle of Batz. A heroic fisherman, Jacques Gueguin, 64 years old, made five trips in his 25-foot long boat, bringing a total of 28 men to England before himself joining the Free French Navy. None of these volunteers came from well-to-do families; they were fishermen, peasants, workers—little people, not great intellectuals or civil servants of high rank but simple men who loved their country.

During the tragic days of June 1940, and the difficult establishment of a Free French movement, what was going on in the United States and what did President Roosevelt know about de Gaulle? Roosevelt was overwhelmed by the possible consequences of the great tragedy that he foresaw; his thoughts were on how to save America if England was invaded and her fleet destroyed. It is doubtful that his ambassador in London, Joseph Kennedy, a defeatist who predicted the lasting success of Hitler, had anything good to say about de Gaulle and his minuscule forces. Count René de Chambrun, whom the President saw socially and who was a son-in-law of the infamous Pierre Laval, probably did not know much of de Gaulle, was obviously not his friend, and could not be counted upon to present the cause of Free France impartially. The little the President knew was from Winston Churchill, with whom he had other, more important matters to discuss.

De Gaulle's ultimate policy was to bring France and her Empire into the war again, on the side of the Allies. He had no force permitting him to land on the continent or to fight the Nazi and Vichy armies. It was from Africa that the liberation would begin. With quick, bold moves a handful of de Gaulle's followers succeeded in taking Chad (August 26, 1940), Cameroon (August 28), Congo and Oubangui Chari (August 28), and later Gabon (November 20). The most important French outpost was Dakar, the capital city of Sénégal, a major strategic port on the Atlantic. In this, he consulted Churchill who enthusiastically agreed it should be captured and offered to bolster the small Free French Navy with his own battleships. The expedition sailed from Liverpool on August 31. De Gaulle was on the *Westerland* flying the Free French flag and reached Dakar on September 21. He sent emissaries with a white flag to negotiate— Free French Commander (later Admiral) Father d'Argenlieu and Captain Bécourt-Foch. Despite the flag of truce they were fired upon and both were wounded.[5]

Unfortunately the Royal Navy had failed to intercept Vichy naval and military reinforcements. There was then a violent exchange of fire between the shore batteries, Vichy's warships, and the Anglo–Free French force. The fierce opposition of the Vichy army and navy made the landing impossible and de Gaulle decided to withdraw. This fiasco was considered by the Americans as proof that the Vichy army and navy were loyal to the puppet government of Marshal Pétain, and that de Gaulle had no following. Because of this, de Gaulle felt he needed a new conquest. He therefore turned his ambitions to the French possessions on the American continent. Martinique was impossible to conquer, because a powerful Vichy fleet was there at anchor, but he believed that French Guyana (near Venezuela) could be taken, and also the tiny archipelago of Saint-Pierre-et-Miquelon.

We were informed of these efforts, and from New York we were rather fearful that anything should be done without the full cooperation of the Royal Navy and the tacit agreement of the United States. All our reports at that time discouraged him from taking action—at least for a while.

CHAPTER VIII

❧

The Day de Gaulle Invaded America (Saint-Pierre-et-Miquelon, Dec. 1941)

Our allies are also our adversaries.
—Charles de Gaulle

On the morning of February 11, 1941 in New York, shortly after my arrival, Garreau-Dombasle showed me a note he had received some days earlier from de Gaulle in London asking what he thought of a possible naval operation to liberate Saint-Pierre-et-Miquelon, two tiny French islands west of Newfoundland with a total population of 5,000 inhabitants, mostly fishermen. He had replied to de Gaulle with a lengthy memorandum pointing out the importance of the French fleet, which remained loyal to Vichy and could, from Martinique, under orders from Admiral Robert, launch a powerful counterattack on the tiny islands. Garreau-Dombasle also stressed the fact that Washington would be hostile to any such operation in the Western Hemisphere. This memorandum was followed by a coded telegram sent through the British Embassy's no. 32.

> February 1, 1941
> Following for General de Gaulle—London
> From Garreau-Dombasle no. 32 since the *Ville d'Ys** is in the West Indies, the liberation of Saint-Pierre-et-Miquelon would be very easy, since the population would surely welcome the arrival of a Free French warship. However, this operation would entail heavy financial obliga-

---

*French warship loyal to Vichy.

tions, since the administration receives from Vichy 8,000,000 Frs. sub-
vention plus about one million dollars in commercial credits.

Besides, Admiral Robert who is responsible would most likely try to
send the *Jeanne d'Arc** or the *Emile Bertin** to retake the islands and
this may lead to very far reaching complications. Should you decide on
any move on St.-Pierre, it would seem opportune to ascertain the cooperation of the British fleet and the tacit approval of Washington.

I am sending you a complete report with Sieyès.

The Roosevelt Administration had in fact, soon after the Franco-
German Armistice in June, met in Havana with representatives of the
Latin American nations to reassert mutual friendship and support and
to ensure hemispheric solidarity. On January 3, 1941, the American
nations had unanimously pledged to oppose, by force if necessary, any
attempted transfer of sovereignty within the hemisphere. The conference was vigorously chaired by Secretary of State Cordell Hull. Its
agreement was in fact a reassertion of the United State's long-standing
Monroe Doctrine (and its forty-year-old [Theodore] Roosevelt Corollary). After avowing their solidarity, the nations who were present,
in order to discourage seizure of islands or territories in the New
World by the Nazis or by governments under German control, all
declared their refusal to recognize any changes in administration. At
stake for France were French Guyana, Guadeloupe, Martinique, and
Saint-Pierre-et-Miquelon; for Holland, Dutch Guyana, Curaçao, and
its dependencies; for England, Jamaica and the Caribbean islands; and
for Denmark, the vast territory of Greenland.

General de Gaulle had been dismayed by the Havana declaration,
which clearly seemed to impose neutrality upon the remote French
territories. On October 27, 1940, he addressed a message to Secretary
of State Hull, through the American Consul General in Brazzaville,
Free French Africa. The General noted that the signatories to the
Havana treaty had taken it upon themselves to entrust the protection
of France's colonies in the Western hemisphere to the United States,
should certain European countries hand over, or allow Germany to
seize, their possession in the Americas. On behalf of those French citizens who rejected the Armistice with Germany, he told the American
government in no uncertain terms:

The Antilles and French Guyana, as well as the islands of Saint-Pierre-
et-Miquelon, are among France's oldest possessions. Occupation of

---

*French warships loyal to Vichy.

these colonies by armed forces of a friendly power such as the United States—if decided on unilaterally—would bring deep sorrow to all the French people. It would be all the more painful for occurring at France's hour of distress and humiliation.[1]

In his message, de Gaulle explained that he understood why the United States and the nations of the Western hemisphere had attempted to ensure that French colonies near to them would not be used by the Axis as potential bases and staging grounds. The General added, however, that Free France herself possessed naval, air, and land forces which, in cooperation with the American fleet, were capable of protecting these overseas territories. His newly created Council for the Defense of the Empire, in London, stood ready to negotiate an accord with the United States to put naval and air bases at their disposal, according to the same principles as those established with Great Britain. This declaration by the General was unquestionably received by the American State Department; it appears in its archives. But no reply was made.

In May 1941 de Gaulle again sent a note to de Sieyès, his representative in New York, asking his opinion regarding an expedition to Saint-Pierre-et-Miquelon.

Among the volunteers passing through my office were some seamen who had left Saint-Pierre to join the Free French Navy. They told me that the entire population, except for Governor Bournat and a few bureaucrats, was Gaullist. There had been a popular revolt on September 14, 1941, which was quickly suppressed by a Vichy warship then at anchor in Saint-Pierre. The seamen confirmed that Vichy troops were no longer stationed there and that the warship had since been transferred to Martinique for repairs. They also spoke of the powerful transmitter on the island that radioed messages and weather reports to fishermen—reports likely to be of great interest to enemy submarines. They claimed that Vichy agents were tapping Western Union's transatlantic cables which passed through Saint-Pierre and passed information on allied convoys to the enemy through fishing boats. They also said that the supervisor of the transmitter was anti-British and loyal to Vichy.

In early December, 1941, I was visited by Lieut. Alain Savary, who had arrived with additional information about the Free French position. In general, no one thought anything would be done about Saint-Pierre. The Japanese attack of December 7 on Pearl Harbor created the impression that, with the United States now involved in the war, the sovereignty of French territories off the American coast would be the subject of intense deliberation at the highest levels in Washington, and that any action would undoubtedly require Allied concurrence.

We did not know then that earlier that year the American government had secretly begun negotiating an accord with Vichy Admiral Robert, commander of the Vichy French fleet at Martinique, assuring him that, in exchange for neutralizing his powerful squadron at Martinique, the status quo of all of France's possessions in the New World would be maintained. On December 14, 1941, with America now at war and anxious to ensure the continuing neutrality of the French fleet and Empire, President Roosevelt sent a message to Marshal Pétain through Ambassador Admiral Leahy, assuring him of the status quo in the Antilles and North Africa, and hoping that the close relationship and friendship that existed between the two countries for so long would be maintained.

With regard to the war as a whole, however, American public opinion was now unequivocal. It would take an enormous and concerted effort to destroy Nazism and Japanese imperialism. The country had been humiliated by the loss of its Pacific fleet in Pearl Harbor and was divided only as to the priorities in the forthcoming war effort: would it be in Asia or Europe?

During one of our meetings at the home of Roussy de Sales on December 14, Tixier, who continued to complain about the "intrigues and the incoherence in London," told us he had just heard from a private source that Admiral Muselier, head of the Free French Navy,[2] had set sail from Scotland for Canada and the United States, the pretext being an inspection of the Free French submarine *Surcouf* in North America. In reality he was on his way to Washington to announce that General de Gaulle was putting Free France's Pacific bases in Tahiti and New Caledonia, as well as the bases in Africa, at the disposal of the American fleet. Additionally, Free French troops would be ready to cooperate with American units. It was to be negotiated at the highest level and was intended to make Free France the United States' true ally. In exchange, the United States would recognize the National Committee in London as a legitimate authority and Free France would have the status of an allied nation. Of utmost importance, the forthcoming negotiations would radically alter relations between the two countries. The rumor that Tixier brought us was to be confirmed by an article that appeared the same day in the *London Sunday Dispatch,* written by Genevieve Tabouis, a well-known French reporter. One must wonder how she learned of the flotilla's departure for Canada, carried out as it was with the greatest secrecy. Didn't the Free French know how to guard their secrets?

"Muselier is coming to Washington," claimed Tixier, "to disrupt the negotiations I'm involved in. It is I who must handle the role of negotiator!" He added that his suspicions had been confirmed. Indeed, he had just received a message from Colonel Pierrené, General de Gaulle's delegate to Canada, asking him to receive Admiral Muselier in Washington. Tixier told us indignantly that he had refused to do so because de Gaulle had not advised him directly of the mission—a mission that, in his view, was inopportune. But Colonel Pierrené had insisted, deeming it a matter of the greatest urgency. Tixier said he would do nothing without first receiving the Admiral's "papers," that is to say, his orders. "He must not come," he repeated. "I will not submit to scheming."

De Sieyès was not at the meeting. I filled him in on what had taken place. He told me that Colonel Pierrené had telephoned him to express amazement at Tixier's attitude, which had been, to say the least, less than courteous during their conversation. On December 20 I received—as did Tixier, Roussy and Boegner—the following telegram from our headquarters in London via the British Consulate:

No. 306—We have the honor of informing you that the Foreign Office has apprised us confidentially that Canada proposes to take control of the radio transmitter on St.-Pierre, either peacefully or by force.

It seems the project has been approved by the American Government, which would, however, oppose any action by the Free French aimed at acquiring the islands that neighbor America.

One of the goals essential to the French National Committee is to bring into the battle, for the cause of France's allies, all portions of the French Empire that can be freed from the authority of a government under enemy control.

The National Committee would lose its justification if it permitted any violation of the sovereign rights of France by the Allied governments anywhere in her Empire.

Please insist upon this point to the State Department.

In the same context, invoke the arguments in our telegram no. 3553 regarding the French Antilles.

Make it clear that any operation like the one being considered would be particularly inopportune at a time when Germany is manifestly pressuring Vichy to effect a united defense of the German-occupied North

of France in accordance with the Indochina precedent. This telegram
is strictly confidential.

Tixier assured us that he had communicated the contents of this
telegram to the State Department in Washington. But the Secretary of
State later denied any knowledge of it and claimed he had not been
told of the National Committee's position.

Had the communiqué been transmitted? The surprise of the Americans in the wake of ensuing events seems to indicate that the State
Department was indeed unaware of the text of this telegram. It is true
that on December 16 de Gaulle, furious over the article by Genevieve
Tabouis, had ordered Muselier by telephone to return to London.
Muselier thought it prudent, however, to delay his departure. When
he embarked from England to prepare the liberation of Saint-Pierre-
et-Miquelon, America was still neutral. It could have been presumed
at that time that the status of these islands was unimportant to her.

However, after the Japanese attack on Pearl Harbor, which
destroyed most of America's Pacific fleet, a large Vichy French navy
at the disposal of the Axis represented a very serious danger. Muselier
thought it necessary to inform the Americans of the purpose of his
mission, and to avoid doing anything that might complicate things for
them. He thought it best to prepare a trip to Washington, before anything else, in order to be briefed on the new situation. De Gaulle, however, instructed him to keep the operation secret and not to go to
Washington. Unable to go and confer there with either Tixier or the
State Department, he decided to meet with J. Pierrepont Moffat, the
U.S. Minister in Canada. A meeting took place on December 17, 1941.
A day later, on the eighteenth, Muselier received a peremptory telegram from de Gaulle ordering him to immediately occupy the islands
"without notifying the foreigners." Muselier hesitated but considered
it his duty to obey and not to create further discord. Matters were in
this state when, around seven o'clock on Christmas morning in New
York, I was awakened by a phone call from the State Department asking me for Tixier's whereabouts. I did not know. The voice at the
other end insisted: "Look for him. You tell him to come at once to
the State Department. If he does not contact us shortly, I will have to
ask you to come to Washington."

I was amazed. What was happening? The reason for the call became
clear, however, when I received my copy of the *New York Times*.
"The Free French have landed at Saint-Pierre and Miquelon,"

announced the *Times'* front page headline. It coincided with a report of the "disaster of Wake Island" in the Pacific, where the Marines, after losing a large part of their forces, had to retreat.

This is how de Gaulle's delegates came to know about Admiral Muselier's landing, and his small contingent, and of the plebiscite to be held among the island's several thousand inhabitants. But the real drama had yet to unfold.

Secretary of State Cordell Hull, like the rest of the State Department, was furious. Hull, who had rushed home from vacation that same Christmas Day, made a memorable speech that he was later to regret, condemning in no uncertain terms "three so-called Free French ships" for carrying out an arbitrary operation contrary to the accords of all concerned parties, and without having notified the State Department in advance. He added that he was asking the Canadian government what measures it planned to take to restore the status quo in the islands.[3]

To Cordell Hull, the islands themselves were of little importance, but their occupation by the Free French proved highly embarrassing. It could well endanger the then delicate U.S. relations with the Vichy government of Marshal Pétain. Indeed, it was only eleven days before the occupation that President Roosevelt had sent Pétain his message concerning maintenance of the status quo in France's possessions in the Antilles and in North Africa.

De Gaulle's expedition to Saint-Pierre could have provoked Vichy into sending its fleet to recapture the small islands; or worse, it could have been the pretext to send the whole fleet to join the German fleet against England. The Vichy government vehemently protested to Washington the occupation of the archipelago by the Free French. Cordell Hull's violent reaction against the Free French was considered a diplomatic success by Pétain, who then decided to take no futher action.

Roussy de Sales was rather ironical and extremely critical of the whole operation. He called it "probably a diplomatic mistake," and ventured the most pessimistic predictions about future relations between Free France and the United States. Boegner saw in the operation a clear expression of the contempt General de Gaulle felt for the Americans. Tixier called it a crazy adventure and insisted that none of us communicate a word about it to the press.

De Sieyès was worried and stated he would go see one of his friends at the State Department, adding that it was necessary to have further

clarification from the Free French delegation at Ottawa and to determine from Muselier the situation in the islands.

I myself was horrified. I feared a strong reaction on the part of the
State Department, whose trust we had now lost. How would we
regain its confidence? Our political position was so weak that any
adverse event could wipe us out completely. Why weren't we
informed so that we could prepare ourselves for the predictable consequences of such independent action? I suggested that we insist that
in the future London headquarters keep us informed of any major
decision.

A few days later I saw de Sieyès, who had made a short trip to
Washington. "Tixier is betraying the General," he said. "He told the
State Department that he disapproved of the entire operation. I sent
Colonel Pierrené a telegram and will leave tomorrow for Saint-Pierre
to talk to Muselier and apprise him of the situation." Muselier himself
later confirmed the charge by de Sieyès: "Colonel Pierrené, the Free
French delegate to Canada, told him that Mr. Tixier had suggested
demilitarization of the islands to Washington."[4]

Later Tixier was to go to the State Department with Boegner. During their meeting there, Tixier openly declared his disapproval of the
entire operation. On their way back, the two men argued angrily over
the wording of the report to be sent to London. Finally, Tixier sent a
version that, according to Boegner, did not correspond to what had
been said at the meeting.[5]

In the meantime, the American press had learned that the plebiscite
in Saint-Pierre-and-Miquelon, held in the immediate aftermath of the
seizure, had gone overwhelmingly (97 percent) in favor of Free France;
this in the presence of American journalists, among whom was Ira
Wolfert of the *New York Times*. Suddenly there was an outburst of
sentiment in favor of de Gaulle all over the United States. Until that
moment, the democracies had suffered defeat everywhere: the Americans at Pearl Harbor and Wake Island, the British in Libya, the Free
French and the British at Dakar. But now a handful of Free French
had liberated a territory controlled by Vichy and the Axis. It was the
democracies' first victory. Yet the State Department did not understand its emotional significance!

The *New York Herald Tribune* in its evening edition vehemently
criticized the State Department, which it referred to as "the so-called
State Department." Many Americans sent protests to the "so-called
Secretary of State." The American press was unanimous and relentless
in attacking Hull who, for his part, was furious.

The following is a sampling of the editorials and articles which appeared after the "invasion":

December 26, 1941:
The *New York Times* (from an editorial entitled "Saint-Pierre and Miquelon"):

... The bloodless investiture of these surprised islands by four little Free French warships under command of Admiral Muselier was accomplished with a display of style and manners in the best tradition of Alexander Dumas.

The *Christian Science Monitor* (from an editorial entitled "Beau Geste"):

For many Americans, seizure by Free French forces of the little islands of Saint Pierre and Miquelon off the Newfoundland coast bespoke an initiative and flair that had often been lacking in Allied strategy.... Some may wonder at the haste to rebuke this Cyrano-like gesture. The answer seems to be that war is practical business.

The *New York Herald Tribune* (from an editorial entitled "Tempest in a Teapot"):

Admiral Muselier seems to have embarrassed the cause to which he himself has been devoted.... It is obvious that a clearer policy regarding Vichy would help to avoid such complications as the Free French are likely to create.

The New York Post (from an editorial entitled "Must We Betray de Gaulle?"):

Americans, Canadians, Britons and all others who are struggling to defeat the Axis have experienced great joy this Christmas Day on learning that the Free French have occupied these two French islands.... The Department of State has tried cajolerie, corruption, self-delusion and stupidity in attempting to prop up Vichy against Hitler. Today it tries treason—for there is no other word to describe its sellout of the Free French at Saint Pierre and Miquelon and its attempt to restore Vichy to power there.

On December 28, the *New York Herald Tribune* (from an editorial entitled "A Moral Victory"):

The bluntness with which Washington has reprimanded the Gaullists had created a most unpleasant impression.... And naturally the moral victory rests with the cause of the Free French—which is also our own.

On December 29, from a syndicated article by Dorothy Thompson entitled "The State Department's Crime on Saint Pierre," appearing in more than one hundred papers:

> It is regrettable that General de Gaulle believed that he could conduct his operation without advising us. But that is no reason for calling our comrades-in-arms the 'so-called' Free French. It is a gratuitous insult. . . .

From a *New York Post* editorial:

> In a manner that becomes more and more flagrant, anonymous bureaucrats have been dominating American foreign policy. They outdo themselves today in brutally abandoning de Gaulle at Saint Pierre.

On December 31, from a *New York Herald Tribune* editorial:

> The Prime Minister (Churchill) has without a doubt thrown open a pernicious window at the State Department on the question of Saint Pierre and Miquelon and this 'so-called Free French.' For Mr. Churchill, this is no time to be calling the Free French 'so-called.'

On January 2, 1942, from an article by Walter Lippmann entitled "Concerning the State Department," syndicated in more than one hundred papers throughout the U.S.:

> The real lesson in the affair is that the State Department was not awake. . . . The State Department this Christmas season maintains its regular routine. . . . But this blunder, this little diplomatic Pearl Harbor should put us on guard. We are right to ask if the State Department is too bureaucratic in spirit to adjust rapidly enough to the new and immense responsibilities of war.

Finally, Anne O'Hare McCormick, supporting the Administration position, made her own appraisal of the events in the January 7 *New York Times:*

> Whether our policy toward France has been wise will be proved by events. It is a considered policy, however, patiently followed in the face of opposition, and fully understood by the Free French as well as the British. It may be argued that our entry into the war changes our relation to the 'United Nations' fighting Hitler, but our belligerency does not diminish the necessity of waging diplomatic battles as successfully as we can until we are ready for military battles. . . .
>
> The Saint Pierre affair cannot be considered apart from our policy toward France as a whole, and to criticize it as State Department policy is absurd to anyone who knows the facts. . . . The fact is that Washing-

ton has been fighting a delaying action in France as truly as General MacArthur has been playing for time in the Philippines. And every week gained in the campaign against French collaboration with Germany is as important as any action in the field.

Roosevelt, who had originally approved the unfortunate protest by his Secretary of State, was not long in seeing where public opinion stood. He then "shrugged his shoulders over the whole affair"[6] and declared the whole matter a tempest in a teapot, having had, it was rumored, a difficult talk with Cordell Hull who threatened to resign.

Henry-Haye, the Vichy Ambassador, protested vigorously and repeatedly, invoking America's commitments to his government and to Admiral Robert.[7]

MacKenzie King, the Canadian Prime Minister, tried on his part to placate the angry Hull, who had demanded that the Canadian government send warships to oust the Free French from Saint-Pierre. The Prime Minister reminded Hull that the Free French were "our allies," and that Canadians, especially those in French-speaking Quebec, would not tolerate military action against them.

In Washington, Britain's Ambassador Lord Halifax exerted all his influence to appease Hull. Churchill, who was Roosevelt's guest there, assured his host that any action against the operation in Saint-Pierre-et-Miquelon would weaken the Free French and, consequently, the resistance inside France itself. Roosevelt replied, predictably, that it was essential to maintain good relations with Vichy to prevent the surrender of the French fleet to the Nazis and to preserve North Africa's neutrality. In Ottawa on December 30, Churchill delivered a resounding speech, partly in French, in which he heaped scorn and irony upon "Pétain, Darlan, and the whole Vichy gang," lauding General de Gaulle and the brave Free French who had joined him.

"I have good reasons," he said, "to fear that the present attitude of the State Department in Washington toward the Free French and Vichy may be doing a great deal of harm to the Free French fighting spirit in France and elsewhere. . . . " Continuing his indictment of Vichy, he called them "men who lay prostrate at the foot of the conqueror." The Free French he praised eloquently as "Frenchmen who would not bend their knees and who under General de Gaulle have continued the fight on the side of the Allies. They have been condemned to death by the men of Vichy, but their names will be held, and are being held, in increasing respect by nine out of ten Frenchmen throughout the once happy, smiling land of France. . . . And everywhere in France, occupied and unoccupied, for their fate is identical, these honest folks, this great people, the French nation, are rising again. Hope is springing up again in the hearts of a warrior race.... We shall never lose confidence that France will play the role of free men again, and by hard paths will once again attain her place in the great company of freedom-bestowing and victorious nations.[8]

De Gaulle, who did not often praise Churchill, would on this occasion cable him that "What you said yesterday in the Canadian Parliament has touched the entire French nation." Churchill replied to de Gaulle, "I have received your telegram. You can be certain that I have pleaded your cause before our friends in the United States. You have broken an accord on the matter of Saint-Pierre and Miquelon and raised a storm that would have been serious had I not been on hand to speak to the President. There is no doubt that your action has made policy more difficult with the United States and prevented certain favorable happenings."[9]

Still angry over the affair, Cordell Hull had to explain himself publicly. He told the press that he had never intended to discredit or insult the Free French, that his use of the phrase "so-called" did not apply to them but to the warships. This new explanation provoked outbursts of laughter and a number of cartoons in the press lampooning the "so-called State Department" and the "so-called Secretary of State."

Tixier decided on his own to suggest a settlement to the impasse over Saint-Pierre, one that would let the Canadian and American governments take over defense of the islands, with civil administration entrusted to a governor elected by the population. The American archives reveal that, during a meeting with Under-Secretary of State Sumner Welles, Tixier had alluded to the situation in Saint-Pierre and Miquelon. "He stressed the fact that he had not made any public declaration concerning the question and that he had been criticized by his headquarters in London for not having vigorously upheld de Gaulle's policy."[10] He did not mention, however, that he had prevented Admiral Muselier from going to Washington to be informed of the State Department's position concerning the landing in Saint-Pierre and Miquelon. It is doubtful that Muselier would have proceeded had he known the opposition from the U.S.

Tixier "sometimes took initiatives," Muselier wrote later, "that were contrary to his instructions and to our general directives."[11] This behavior was as obvious in Washington as it was in Ottawa. It was reconfirmed to Muselier by one of the British Embassy counselors in Washington and also reported to him by Bret and Brenda, two of de Gaulle's agents in Halifax. In London, however, there was apparently no knowledge of Tixier's true demeanor. It was believed on the contrary that the irascible and outspoken Tixier was stoutly facing the Americans on the General's behalf.

Finally, Cordell Hull threatened to resign if Roosevelt did not use every possible means to reestablish the status quo on Saint-Pierre and Miquelon: namely, the departure of the Free French and a vague formula for the island's neutralization. Roosevelt could not allow his Secretary of State to continue this way without risking a political crisis. The President attempted to get Churchill to pressure de Gaulle, going so far as to threaten sending the powerful warship *Arkansas* to drive the Free French off the islands with cannon fire. At the same time though he also sent a note to Hull requesting that he "not bring up the question again." Admiral Muselier had already made it known that he would not leave Saint-Pierre. Privately, Roosevelt admitted: "We cannot afford to send an expedition to bomb him out."[12]

Meanwhile, de Gaulle—having weighed the matter and become convinced that the Americans had no alternative but to accept the situation as it stood—remained intransigent. His *Mémoires* tell us that he resisted every pressure. Anthony Eden came to see him to suggest that the islands be "neutralized" under face-saving conditions for the Free French, pointing out that failing such an agreement, the Americans would consider sending one of their cruisers with two destroyers to Saint-Pierre. "What will you do in that case?" he asked de Gaulle.

"The Allied ships," replied de Gaulle, "will stop at the limit of territorial waters and the American Admiral will come to lunch with Muselier, who will be delighted."

"But if the cruiser crosses the limit?"

"Our people will summon her to stop in the usual way."

"If she holds her course?"

"That would be unfortunate, for then our people would have to open fire."

When Eden threw up his arms in dismay, de Gaulle smiled. "I understand your alarm," he said to Eden, "but I have confidence in the democracies."[13]

Upon his return to London, Churchill too had what he called "a severe conversation" with de Gaulle concerning the settlement of the whole affair.

As for Cordell Hull, with the turmoil over the incident subsiding, he recommended to Roosevelt in a memo dated February 2 that the "wisest course would be to let the matter rest until the end of the war. . . . Our relations with the de Gaulle movement," he added, "have not been helped by the incident." There was no doubt in either Roosevelt's or Cordell Hull's mind that de Gaulle had been personally responsible for violating his commitment to Britain and for contravening the wishes of the United States and Canada. They considered him even more personally ambitious, and less reliable, than they had before.

Saint-Pierre was a tactical victory for Free France, but it cost her very dearly in the long run, weighing heavily in her subsequent relations with the United States. Roosevelt and Hull were not forgiving when, a short time later, the Declaration of the United Nations was drafted. Churchill suggested that Free France be admitted as a signatory. After some hesitation, Roosevelt seemed on the verge of relenting, but Hull was flatly opposed under the pretext that Free France was not a "nation" but a political "movement." His opposition carried the day. The Declaration was signed by the United Nations on January 1, 1942, without de Gaulle. Only in 1945 was France invited to sign.

Perhaps from the standpoint of principle, as well as tactics, de Gaulle had been victorious. He had also succeeded in rallying American public opinion around him. He had proved to America's leaders that the State Department's policy of "expediency" toward Vichy did not represent the desires of most Americans. He had scored one large point against the grand American strategy of appeasing Vichy and neutralizing France, her colonies, and her dependent territories.

However, distrust of the general in the wake of the Saint-Pierre incident was so great that in the future there would be no genuine cooperation between the Free French and the Americans. There is no question that, thus stung, the Americans planned the subsequent landing in North Africa and later in Normandy without consulting General de Gaulle who was from then on considered an unreliable ally. It also marked the beginning of a deep mistrust between President Roosevelt and General de Gaulle that would last for years to come; its effects would be noticeable for a long time after the war was over.

What is most perplexing about the entire affair is the role Tixier played. Had de Gaulle's newly appointed senior delegate transmitted telegram no. 306, in which de Gaulle had so clearly expressed his displeasure about the handling of French territories, and in which there was a veiled warning of his intentions? Probably not. There is also the question as to why Tixier would voice such opposition to Muselier's request to go to Washington. Had he gone, he would no doubt have learned of the American opposition to the plan, and may have abandoned it altogether. Finally there is something strange in the fact that Tixier voiced to the State Department his opposition to the landing, although he cabled quite the contrary to General de Gaulle in London.

❊

CHAPTER IX

The Strange Policy of Adrien Tixier

De Gaulle and his entourage are equally devoid of all sense of realism ... De Gaulle and his followers have no contact with the people ...

—Adrien Tixier

In Washington Adrien Tixier had to cope with the heated opinions surrounding the Saint Pierre and Miquelon affair. Cordell Hull and the American administration were furious; the American press, favorable. The French in America were, for the most part, resolutely antagonistic towards de Gaulle's attempt to gain power and influence. They were in large part succumbing to the influence of Vichy's consuls. It was no doubt a welcome development to United States government officials that the majority of the French in the United States agreed with their position.

As a result, we of the Free French delegation had a difficult task. We had somehow to regain some degree of credibility. Unlike what de Gaulle believed at the time, and even long after the war was over, as his memoirs prove, Tixier did not *represent* de Gaulle's position to the State Department. On the contrary, he let it be known that he disapproved of the entire operation. At some point he lost the understanding that his duty was to defend de Gaulle's position vigorously.

I will not attempt here a full definition of a "Diplomatic Mission," nor of the duties the head of such a mission must fulfill. But it is clear that embassies or other official agencies of foreign governments are appointed to represent their government's views, and not their personal views, and that they must make them clear, when necessary, to the host governments to whom they are accredited. Ambassadors are chosen among the elite of a nation's diplomatic service or its citizenry. An ambassador must possess great patience and understanding, and a capacity to mitigate intergovernmental difficulties when they arise. He or she must be likeable, capable of establishing cordial relations—even friendship—with a nation's chief of state, its minister of foreign affairs, or other public officials, and—in an open society—with the press. And he must win their confidence.

At times when relations between governments are tense, the ambassador's role is especially delicate and all the more so when the ambassador represents, not a sovereign state, but some lesser political entity, such as an occupied country or a government in exile.

French diplomatic representation in America during the early years of the war was, to say the least, peculiar. The Vichy government, although it represented a country two-thirds occupied by the enemy (and the other third governed by Marshal Pétain under the occupier's thumb) nonetheless enjoyed all the diplomatic privileges and had a full-fledged ambassador. Vichy was a country, of course, without sovereignty, and with only the vaguest legitimacy. Free France, on the other hand, controlled strategic territories in Africa and the Pacific, and commanded a small army and navy fighting alongside the British. General de Gaulle, its leader, had enviable prestige with his followers both outside and within continental France.

The British, for their part, had given General de Gaulle qualified recognition, acknowledging him as "leader" of the Free French volunteers, although they did not recognize him as a chief of state. When Pleven had come to the United States, he had obtained a very limited form of recognition from the Americans. No embassy could be established, but an official "delegation" of the Free French was recognized by the Department of State. Tixier became the senior delegate, with semi-diplomatic privileges, representing de Gaulle and his National Committee to the government in Washington.

In appointing Tixier, de Gaulle miscalculated. For that sensitive post, he should have appointed one of his highest-echelon staff— someone like General Catroux or René Pleven. Unfortunately, both preferred to stay in London "where the action was."* The post was offered to a number of esteemed Frenchmen in the United States: Alexis Léger, Jacques Maritain, and Jean Monnet. They all refused.

---

*Conversation of René Pleven with the author.

As a result, the extremely difficult task of representing a non-recognized non-government was handed by de Gaulle to Adrien Tixier, and four other delegates.

Tixier's task was made more difficult because he had no backing from the French in America; he also had many doubts of his own concerning General de Gaulle and the National Committee.* Tixier was truly concerned that no elected leader, no member of the Senate or the Chamber, or any Union leader, had been made a part of de Gaulle's National Committee in London. During his stay in London in March 1942, Tixier spoke openly to the General about the distrust of high officials in the U.S. State Department toward the Free French movement, a distrust attributable primarily to incessant propaganda from the Vichy Embassy, characterizing de Gaulle as an ambitious, authoritarian, anti-democratic adventurer. Members of the French Parliament in exile in the United States—de Kérillis, Pierre Cot, Jonas, Ferdinand Laurent, Stern—could neither comprehend nor accept their exclusion from de Gaulle's National Committee, and they made clear their dissatisfaction.

Tixier, who had deep unionist and socialist ties, explained to de Gaulle the necessity of dealing with problems other than those that were nationalistic or military; he wanted to see the movement take on a program of social and economic reforms as well. He apparently failed to convince the General to abandon his nationalistic line, and he became openly resentful on a number of occasions, complaining to British and American officials about de Gaulle's attitude. On March 26, 1942, before returning to Washington after a meeting with the general, Tixier on his own initiative went to the U.S. Embassy in London where he had a most unusual conversation with chargé d'affairs H. Freeman Matthews, complaining in the most bitter terms about de Gaulle, who had just appointed him.

Chargé d'affairs Matthews summarized the meeting in a telegram he sent the Secretary of State that same evening:

> I received a call from Tixier, chief of the Free French Delegation in Washington, who is shortly returning to the United States. I found him unhappy over the situation he has found here. He feels that neither the British Government nor our own "understands" the situation in France and that General de Gaulle and his entourage at Carlton Gardens are equally devoid of all "sense of realism."

---

*See Chapter V.

To this already unflattering assessment of de Gaulle, Tixier leveled a further attack on whatever credibility de Gaulle might have had, adding that,

> France must again become a battlefield before the end of the war. The seeds of resistance which exist in France should therefore be carefully nurtured. Those seeds of resistance are only to be found in the "people." De Gaulle and his followers, he says, have no contact with 'the people.'

Tixier then suggested to the American chargé his own personal vision of the means by which France was to be liberated. Again, in Matthews' words:

> Specifically, what he wants, apparently, is to have the British through clandestine means bring over a few trusted persons who will subsequently return to France and organize for 'the day.'

These trusted persons, not de Gaulle, would then form the future government of France after the liberation. And, ironically, Tixier told Matthews that

> He finds the Free French headquarters so occupied with 'their own petty squabbles' as to be unable to give that leadership 'devoid of self-seeking' which the movement requires.[1]

While touching on it only briefly, Tixier criticized the United States government, not for maintaining relations with Vichy, but for its alleged efforts to discourage generous and well-disposed groups in America from supplying the material aid that he would like to see.

Tixier's candor in this passage, coming as it did from the newly appointed senior delegate of de Gaulle's own choosing, was duly reported to Washington and widely circulated in the State Department as an important statement. That interview was later quoted repeatedly in a variety of reports and books.[2] I had heard rumors about such a statement during the war and afterwards. But I was skeptical. I could not believe the report could possibly be accurate. Such a thing would certainly not have contributed to a better understanding between de Gaulle and the State Department, which did not understand Tixier's brand of sincerity.

Returning to Washington on May 2, after another trip to London, Tixier attempted a very complicated negotiation, declaring that his visit to London had convinced him that the General was the only possible representative of the French Resistance but that he needed help from the United States. He stated that labor leaders in France were willing to accept de Gaulle as head of the Resistance provided the General would make a three-point statement of democratic principles. De Gaulle had agreed to do so, stipulating however that he must receive from the United States government an official "statement of encouragement to the Free French Movement under General de Gaulle." The Department, however, would provide such official encouragement only along military, not "political" lines, thus dooming Tixier's initiative.[3] The State Department's offer was rejected by Tixier although it more or less conformed to Britain's limited form of recognition, and could therefore have become a stepping stone to later negotiations between the State Department and the Free French.

Interestingly enough, in many instances, Tixier assumed a position completely contradictory to the instructions he had received from de Gaulle. On one occasion, at the end of a meeting with Sumner Welles, who was at that time the Under-Secretary of State, he openly alluded to Saint-Pierre and Miquelon, stressing that he had made no public statement concerning the incident, and that he had been severely criticized by Free French headquarters in London for not having more effectively propagandized the episode to de Gaulle's advantage.[4] In another meeting, when the General had requested that the State Department accredit a full Free French military mission, Tixier urged, on his own initiative, that "there not be a military mission," but instead "a couple of regular attachés" stationed in Washington.[5] The State Department did not follow his advice and accepted instead a *full* military mission.

Tixier maintained an independent position because he wanted the State Department to believe that he retained complete autonomy of thought and action. He must have believed such a posture would enhance his own prestige and authority. Rumor had it, however, that he had ulterior motives. Tixier was, of course, as blunt and outspoken with General de Gaulle as he was with other people. But his constant criticism of de Gaulle, whom he ostensibly represented, considerably weakened the diplomatic situation of the Free French delegation. Yet de Gaulle himself, unaware of his chief delegate's statements,[6] never considered Tixier other than a tough, loyal, and trustworthy representative.

Why did Tixier insist on publicizing to the American administration that he did not share de Gaulle's views? For a long time Tixier did not believe that de Gaulle had any great following in France and that a profound revolution after the war would liquidate the old political and social structures. That revolution, led by extreme-left underground fighters, would finally set up a government excluding de

Gaulle and other conservative Frenchmen. Incidentally this view was shared by some people outside France, both Americans and French alike. Keeping himself aloof from de Gaulle, Tixier must have calculated, would increase his chances of being included in that future administration. He changed his mind toward the end of 1943, however, after the General obtained the support of the *Comité National de la Résistance* and the French communists in Algiers.

Relations between the United States and Free France were never easy. Early in February 1942, with the Allied situation in the Pacific fast deteriorating, it became necessary for Americans to find a secure alternate route between the United States and Australia. Pointe-Noire, in Free French Equatorial Africa (West Africa), had an airport that could be improved and converted into a practical stopping-off point.

At the outset, negotiations for the base encountered no unusual problems. The French National Committee in London expressed its willingness to help, and asked in return that Washington grant its officials "recognition of its status," that the United States bear the cost of rehabilitating the base, that the base be returned to France after the war, and that eight Lockheed warplanes be provided under Lend Lease for immediate delivery. Before sending off an answer, however, the War Department dispatched engineers and equipment to construct the air base. Problems then arose. De Gaulle's National Committee in London instructed the High Commissioner in Equatorial Africa, General Sicé, to block the use of Pointe-Noire, owing to the failure of the United States to recognize the Free French National Committee and to its failure to deliver the eight airplanes.

Sicé cabled London that he would not obey the order, and that he would take up the matter during his next visit to London. He then informed the U.S. Consul in Leopoldville, Mr. Mallon, that, in spite of the National Committee's wish, he, as High Commissioner of Free French Africa, would "permit Pointe-Noire to be used as a base.... Runway installation and housing construction will proceed uninterrupted."

In Washington, of course, Tixier also became involved in the Pointe-Noire affair. On February 22, he saw Adolf Berle, assistant Secretary of State, and showed him a telegram he had received from de Gaulle. Tixier said "he had carried it around for three days before daring to present it." What a strange way for a diplomat to carry out his official instructions! The telegram stated that if the United States expected to request help from the Free French, it ought to recognize them as a full ally. De Gaulle did not, however, make this a condition for granting landing rights at the airbase. Permission to use it would be given "as soon as the Free French received a binding assurance from the United States of eight Lockheed transport planes." Tixier commented disparagingly about the message to Berle, who told him he appreciated Tixier's frankness and would be candid with him in return. In matters like this, he said, it was infantile to think one could "bargain" with the United States. The United States would sympathetically consider requests for assistance, quite irrespective of the use of any airbase. It expected, in turn, that the Free French would do the same with requests made of them. Tixier understood this "perfectly well," and was unhappy about the instructions he had received. He said he thought he could exercise a certain amount of discretion in the matter, and asked whether he could officially restate the message and soften its edges. Tixier went on to tell Berle that London (meaning General de Gaulle) was extremely difficult to deal with, and he expatiated on his problems in doing so. Berle dictated the memorandum of their conversation, and forwarded it to the Secretary of State.[9]

On April 4, de Gaulle relented and sent a telegram to Sicé, withdrawing his objections to the air-ferry base but expressing his disapproval of Sicé's show of independence in the matter. This episode was followed by feuding between Sicé and Governor General Eboué. De Gaulle finally recalled Sicé; and when I saw him later in New York he expressed bitterness toward those in London who, he claimed, instead of relinquishing the base to an ally, "were instead playing politics with the war effort."

Here, then, are but two of the bizarre activities of de Gaulle's chief representative in the United States during the war years. Although it is clear that Tixier's task may not have been easy, it seems equally clear that because of his disagreements with de Gaulle and his suspicion of him, he was less than loyal in representing the General who had appointed him. The most common rule of diplomacy would have required Tixier to have either served de Gaulle with the requisite loyalty, or, upon disagreeing with him, tendered his resignation.

Tixier, whose main activities were in Washington, did not come to New York often. He did not want to see the Vichy partisans or the "neutrals." He made no effort to win anyone over to our cause. He had little inclination to meet the Free French. They in turn did not like him and found him always insensitive and seldom interested in their problems. As for the refugees, Tixier regarded them as a nuisance and had no time for them. He left this problem to the rest of us, and we soon had our hands full.

CHAPTER X

— ⚜ —

The Divided French

While Tixier was spending his time waging political disorder in Washington, the French community in New York contributed to the difficulty of their representation by the chaos of their condition.

During the four years that I headed the French Delegation in New York, I spent a great deal of my time trying to help the constantly increasing number of refugees. They were desperate. They had left their loved ones in France, and they were without news. They felt guilty to be eating well, sleeping peacefully, and living in security while their relatives and friends were suffering in France. What would become of their homes, their country? Would they ever see them again? Each battle lost by the Allies during 1941 or 1942 felt like a knife in the heart, another postponement of their return home.

The exiles had many problems: that of surviving the humiliation of the surrender of France, the betrayal of their British ally, and the neutral position of the powerful French navy and the armies in the colonies, all of which were working in Germany's favor. There were other problems. They had to make some semblance of a new life in New York, find people to talk to and also find employment. Most refugees did not speak English; only some learned it. The ways of life in America were strange to them. The jobs most of them had held in France were very different from those they could fill in the United States. Most did not have the skills needed to work in America. Lawyers, of course, could find nothing; the French law they knew was completely different from the American. Doctors were faced with stiff medical examinations that very few succeeded in passing. Newspaper people and reporters found only temporary jobs at the time of their arrival, when the public was anxious to have news of the war and of the occupation of France. Business people had no capital to start something

new, and office employment in New York for new arrivals was very
limited. The French immigrants were the last wave of Hitler's victims
to arrive. The other foreign refugees—Austrians, German Jews,
Czechs, Poles, and even Italians—had arrived before them and taken
the few jobs available to foreigners.

The French immigration, moreover, was largely composed of intellectuals, professors, writers, journalists, and members of parliament of
the most different shades of opinion, from the extreme left, like Pierre
Cot, to the Catholic right, like Henri de Kérillis, who had offended
the Nazis and would have been arrested. There were also some French
people who discovered that they were partly of Jewish ancestry and
thus condemned to be deported to the dreaded concentration camps.

The refugees' main problem was to get members of their families
out of France. The Free French delegation and representatives in
Washington or in London did their very best to obtain American
entry visas, with little success. The Congress of the United States had
enacted strict quotas and the State Department enacted regulations
and strict requirements to enforce the law. The direction of the visa
department was under the control of Brekenbridge Long, a powerful
and rigid man whose name was pronounced with fear by those who
sought to save their loved ones in France.

In June 1941, at a social gathering, I was introduced to Mrs. Eleanor
Roosevelt as the head of the Free French delegation just established in
New York. I met her with some embarrassment, knowing that we
were probably seen as outcasts at the White House. Mrs. Roosevelt
reassured me, and with her charming smile said she was happy to meet
someone who represented "the brave men" who were fighting with
their British allies. She told me how distressed she was at the news of
the terrible disaster that had engulfed France: the refugees, the whole
population on the roads, the women and children. She would later say:
"The plight of the poor refugees of France is appalling, but the chance
of doing anything seems so slim. I have been working all week with
no result as yet. . . . "[1]

I thanked her for the generosity of her country which had admitted
some French refugees, but I added that many of them were requesting
visas for their relatives or friends whose lives were in danger; I knew
how strict the immigration law could be, but I wondered if within the
framework of the law regulations could be made more flexible, in
view of the present disastrous situation.

I told her that although the Advisory Committee on Refugees had
requested visas for 546 people whose lives were in danger, the proce-

dure adopted by the State Department was so slow and so complicated that after more than one month only forty had been granted. I drew her attention to the urgency of the situation and implored her to suggest simplification of the procedure. She was the only one who could obtain from the President the precious temporary emergency visas we needed so desperately.

I pointed out how difficult it was for people hunted by the Nazis to obtain all the documents and certified legal papers that had to be submitted with a visa application. Certificates of birth, of domicile, and of good conduct were impossible to obtain. The procedure took so much time, that often when the American Consul received the permit, he could no longer find the refugee, who by that time might either have been captured by the Nazis or have gone into hiding. The case of the Alsatians was particularly tragic. Alsace had been annexed by Germany. All correspondence to obtain documents from that province was impossible, since it had to go through the Nazi authorities. Mrs. Roosevelt promised to help, but the President himself could not change the law.

The First Lady, who always had been concerned for the plight of children, had supported a plan to evacuate a great number of children from England and France to a safe haven in the United States during the war. That plan had to be abandoned after the rapid advance of the German armies in Holland, Belgium, and France.

We spoke then of the possibilities of sending powdered milk and vitamins to French children in the non-occupied part of France. She agreed, of course, that all precautions should be taken so that nothing would fall into the hands of the Germans. Since America was neutral at the time, I asked whether she could, with the help of the International Red Cross, send ships to carry the goods. She agreed to inform the British and make requests for a partial lifting of the blockade and for the obtainment of navicerts. In fact a few months later the U.S. freighter *Cold Harbor,* then the *Exmouth,* hauled cargo in the south of France with $1,250,000 worth of food.

Unfortunately the total occupation of France by the Nazis on November 12, 1942, suspended further relief. The American consulates were closed and no more visas could be granted. There were no more shipments of relief for children, nor any hope to save the victims of Hitler.

Even now it is painful to recall the pitiful plight of the refugees. Their financial and economic disaster was outweighed by their anguish for relatives and friends who had been left behind in France, to whom they could not write, and from whom, in turn, they received no word. When would that nightmare end? In 1941 and 1942 there was little hope that it could be soon; each Allied defeat, whether at Singapore, in the Pacific, or in the deserts of Libya, only added to their anguish. I remember early in 1941, when America was still neutral, a young French woman who had obtained her own visa for the United States and was expecting her mother to follow. Waiting for her mother's visa, day after day, she begged us to help obtain it, but there was delay upon delay. Finally, she felt she could no longer wait and despite our warnings returned to France. She was promptly picked up by the Vichy police and vanished.

Despite their pitiful state, the refugees were grateful for American hospitality and for the help and understanding they found among their hosts. They were welcomed everywhere, invited into homes, and treated with warm consideration.

The old French colony consisted of the French who had emigrated before the war. They had settled in the United States, and held secure jobs; they had also acquired American citizenship while retaining their French nationality for sentimental reasons. They congratulated themselves for having had the foresight to leave Europe in time, and were contemptuous of the naïveté of the new arrivals. They were proud to be far from the war that was destroying their old country. They were proud too to be beyond the realm of French politics and French confusion. They had left their old country where opportunities had been few, salaries low, and obstacles to promotion many. Most of them claimed that they had predicted that there would again be war. And most believed that they should trust Marshal Pétain, Weygand, Darlan, and all the other heroes of World War I, who they felt knew better than any of us the reasons for the defeat. Since these soldiers "won" in 1914–18, it was they who could best judge the situation. Acceptance of the Armistice was a duty toward these war heroes. Pétain had stopped the war, he had stopped the senseless killings, he would bring peace; France would perhaps be smaller, but peace was of course mankind's greatest gift. With peace, even with a *pax Germanica,* they believed that all things would be restored, that life would return to normal, that two million prisoners would return home, and war would cease. "To wage war, you have to be two; if one refuses to fight, well, there can be no war," they confided to one another.

A small minority of French, particularly the new arrivals among the exiles, were interventionists, and pointed out that it was the unpreparedness of their country that had made it easy prey to the bellicose

Nazis. They hoped that Americans would draw a lesson from the defeat of the peace-loving nations of Europe. The new wave of refugees brought terrifying news of the German occupation and of the growing underground resistance to Nazi domination. They admired de Gaulle and the resistance movement of Free France, cautiously while America was neutral, and openly afterwards.

After Pearl Harbor, when all Americans were united, French confusion in America took on a different aspect. The majority continued to admire Marshal Pétain, some believing that he would trick the Germans and finally turn against them and join the Allies. For them the capital of France was now Vichy. Others regarded General Giraud as the new head of the new French army, and now considered their capital Algiers. Finally, a small number followed de Gaulle, approved his stand, and joined the Free French forces. *Their* capital was now in London.

The American administration was anxious to know where the French in the United States stood, and closely followed the attitude of the residents and exiles in order to get an idea of what the French in Occupied France might think and do. Many of them went to Washington from time to time to try to influence the State Department to adopt their political views, but most of the time to warn against the dictatorial tendencies of General de Gaulle.

Jacques Maritain, the philosopher, told me many times he was not Gaullist, although he joined Free France after the liberation of Algeria in 1943. Of course, in Washington Léger was a formidable enemy of de Gaulle. André Maurois, the famous author of *The Silences of Colonel Bramble, A History of the United States,* was openly pro-Vichy (despite his Jewish ancestry). Antoine de Saint-Exupéry, the talented writer, poet, and pilot, arrived with his wife Consuelo on January 1, 1941. He too refused to join de Gaulle. In answer to de Gaulle's famous appeal "France has lost a battle but France has not lost the war," he cried, "Tell the truth, General; France has lost the war, but her Allies will win it!" He declared that France would not win because there were twice as many German soldiers as Frenchmen and that German war equipment was five times superior. He accused American neutralism and isolationism of being responsible for the success of Hitler all over Europe. While in New York, he had published *Flight to Arras* and *Letter to a Hostage* in 1942; and of course *The Little Prince* in 1943, a charming and philosophical story written in the guise of a children's book. He and I were on very good terms, and often he, his wife, and I would have dinner at my apartment. Our discussions were always about the war, about America's isolationism, and about Pétain and de Gaulle.

"We must credit Pétain for having saved France from destruction by the Nazis," he would say. I would reply that neither the Norwegians, the Dutch, nor the Belgians had signed an armistice, nor had they placed their police under the orders of the Gestapo; they had not collaborated with the enemy as some French had done, nor had they been destroyed as a result. "Thanks to Pétain," I would add, "French factories are working for the Nazi war effort," as was the Renault factory. This would not move him and he would switch to a different tack. "De Gaulle's small army is not independent! It is paid for by the British! And besides, de Gaulle is ambitious." To which my reply was always the same, "How can you expect him to be otherwise? Ambition is the source of leadership." Pleven and many sympathizers of de Gaulle did their best to convince him but with no success. His constant criticism of the Free French caused some Americans as well as some Frenchmen not to support our cause. It was not until after the liberation of Algeria by the American Army that he volunteered under General Giraud, not de Gaulle.

In February 1941, I was visited by Mr. and Mrs. Maurice Maeterlink, a charming, elderly Belgian couple. He was the author of the famous play, *The Blue Bird,* translated throughout the world. "I fled the German invasion once in 1914. Now for the second time the Germans have invaded my country, and I had to leave my home," he told me. He also recounted the difficulties of fleeing from the Nazis and of crossing France, Spain, and Portugal. His wife, close to tears, said that she was able to carry her two beloved blue nightingales in their silver cage from their home to America despite many difficulties. The customs officer at Hoboken, New Jersey, refused to let them enter the country with the bluebirds. "What could we do? We bid them goodbye as we did to the good old days, and gave them to the captain of the Norwegian ship that had brought us to the New World."

Among the newly arrived there were also a few former members of the French Parliament now in exile in New York. There was Edouard Jonas, Henri Laurent, Jacques Stern, Pierre Cot, Henri de Kérillis, and Camille Chautemps. It was a strange group, ranging from Pierre Cot, a left-wing socialist and former Minister of Aviation, to de Kérillis, of the most conservative right. None of them understood why de Gaulle had initially refused their cooperation, why they were kept outside the "Movement" at its inception. Pierre Cot was anti-colonialist and insisted that de Gaulle should make a declaration announcing the end of the colonial regime. Stern, former Minister of the Colonies, wanted to keep them and improve their economic status. Jonas was a member of Parliament for Nice, hoping that the Germans would not destroy his constituency. However, Camille Chautemps and de Kérillis, who hated each other, were the only ones to have some influence in Washington.

Henri de Kérillis, *député* of Paris,* arrived in New York in May 1941, having stayed a few days in London where he met General de Gaulle and for whom he had boundless admiration. He expressed this in a book: "Charles de Gaulle has become the leader for whom one prays in thousands and thousands of poor churches in France. He has become the leader whose blessed name is taught to small children on the knees of their crying mothers. He has become the leader of unfortunate hostages who salute his name, before being shot for crimes they have not committed. He has become the leader, on the battlefields of Libya and elsewhere, of the sons of France who fight fiercely under his orders. He is the leader of a multitude of slaves and martyrs. He is the leader of the large faction of the French people who fight for her independence. . . ." [2]

"You are a good French citizen, who has seen, and who sees clearly," replied General de Gaulle. In those days de Kérillis often declared that he was a "Gaullist" before de Gaulle. He was one of those rare patriots who denounced the colossal rearmament of the German Reich. He had been the only non-communist member of Parliament to vote against the Munich agreement..He was the head of a very conservative party and founder of a patriotic newspaper, the *Epoque,* in which he exposed Hitler's treachery daily and warned against any policy of appeasement. There is no doubt that if he had remained in France, he would have been murdered by the members of the French Nazi party and members of the fifth column. He was obsessed by them, and saw fifth columnists everywhere in London and also in New York.

De Kérillis arrived in New York with funds from members of his party (the *Républicains Nationaux*), amounting to $100,000, a very large sum in those days. He was free to use this sum according to his own judgment. Soon after his arrival he wrote to de Gaulle offering to share it with him. The General thanked him profusely and suggested that a part of the capital could be donated anonymously to help build a powerful radio station in Brazzaville (Free French Africa), from

---

*A *député* in France is the equivalent of a congressman in the United States.

where it could broadcast all over Africa. The cost was estimated at
$200,000. De Kérillis replied to de Gaulle that in his opinion the funds
would be better used to help the escape from France of a number of
statesmen whose lives were in danger, such as Édouard Herriot, Paul
Reynaud, Mandel, Édouard Daladier, Léon Blum, etc. . . . De Gaulle
refused, and relations between the two men rapidly grew sour. De
Kérillis began to consider de Gaulle ambitious for wanting to use the
funds for his own propaganda and not hesitating to sacrifice statesmen
who might compete with him in London.

De Kérillis, who had his own channels of communication with people in France, came to see me often, on some occasions providing
interesting information, although it was not always accurate. He was
convinced that General Weygand would not follow Marshal Pétain's
collaboration with the Germans. He was convinced, and I believed he
convinced many officials in Washington, that Weygand would soon
head a resistance movement in North Africa, and that the rest of
Africa and the Free French would subsequently join the Allies.

De Kérillis had access to Sumner Welles and many important officials in Washington. He did his best to convince them that it was
important to smuggle out of France many statesmen who could form
a government in exile in London or in Washington and replace de
Gaulle, whom he now called an "apprentice dictator." He no doubt
contributed to influencing Sumner Welles and the State Department
to woo General Weygand and later General Giraud, whom he characterized as a "magnificent soldier who does not interfere in politics
and has no political ambition."

De Kérillis was always in a great state of exaltation. He had always
been right, he thought, and continued to consider himself a prophet.
He supported General Giraud, whom he considered as the future lib-
erator of France, the greatest patriot of all time. He wrote many articles in the French paper *Pour la Victoire* in his favor.

The admiration de Kérillis had expressed for General de Gaulle in
Français, Voici la Verité[3] was replaced by a far different sentiment.
That book had been published in 1942; a scant three years later with
de Gaulle victorious and installed as President of France, de Kérillis
published in Montreal a vengeful book, *De Gaulle Dictateur,* in which
he not only exposed the weaknesses of the exiles, their ambitions,
their divisions, and their treacheries, but also criticized de Gaulle in
an inflammatory style: "The man who is writing this book is an exiled
writer, chased from his country; he is weak, isolated, solitary,
destroyed by his excruciating pain; he has for himself this conscience

and the belief that he is fighting for the truth. . . . The man that he attacks has benefited from the troubles of war to place himself at the top of honors, celebrity, of the height of power. He governs France as her master. . . . "[4]

His hatred for de Gaulle became such that he did not want to return to France while de Gaulle was its president; he feared the vengeance of his political enemies. He died in New York in 1958, alone and forgotten by everyone.

A French writer of great talent, Jules Romains, also arrived in New York in May 1941. Very soon he found that most of the French who were anti-German were not for de Gaulle. He then attempted to form a patriotic organization of his own, *Le Comité National des Français d'Amérique,* which would unite and represent all the non-Vichy French citizens in America (similar organizations existed in Egypt and Argentina). He considered France Forever, the Franco-American association whose American members outnumbered the French nine-to-one, as a propaganda agency of de Gaulle that was not interested in representing French public opinion or acting on its behalf. His committee would not oppose General de Gaulle, nor interfere with his military operations: it would in civilian affairs act along "parallel" lines. Jules Romain had several meetings with groups of exiles. They all quarreled and were never able to organize themselves as a committee.

Another committee was created, *Les Amis de la République Française,* which had meetings with intellectuals: professors, writers, and newspaper reporters. Its aim was to support the Republic. In the United States the majority of its members were not Gaullists or were actively anti-Gaullists; a survey revealed that 11 percent were Gaullists and 4 percent said they did not care. No wonder then that the perception of the State Department and of the French in America was that de Gaulle had little standing and should be disregarded.

The consulates of Vichy were of course very active. They led fierce campaigns against the British and, of course, against the Free French. They also sent reports to Vichy on the activity of the French colony. The results were not long in coming: by Vichy decree, 29 French citizens in the United States were deprived of their French nationality. The most eminent were Eve Curie, and Henri Bernstein, the playwright.

Eve Curie, the daughter of Pierre and Marie Curie, twice Nobel Prize winners for their discovery of radium, was condemned by Vichy for having prevented the sending of relief ships to France. The accusation was untrue. She was also falsely accused of supporting the British blockade of France and thereby contributing to the starvation of women and children. Vichy was angered because she was one of the first to support the Free French Movement and to wage a campaign of resistance to the Germans. She traveled all over the world and lectured in favor of the Resistance. She often said she belonged to two martyr countries, France (by her father) and Poland (by her mother). In Africa she met the British and the Free French forces who, under General Wavell, were blocking the advance of the Italians and Germans. She also visited the armies in Asia and the Pacific. On her return she wrote a best seller, *Journey Among Warriors*,[5] that one could see in all the New York bookstores. In 1942 she joined General de Gaulle's Women's Auxiliary.

Henri Bernstein, who was a renowned playwright and author, wrote a series of articles for the *New York Times* revealing the treacheries of Pétain, Laval, Darlan, and other collaborators with the Nazis in France. These articles, written with his usual humor and talent, aroused the anger of the Vichy Consul General in New York who reported them to his superiors in Vichy. They took steps to denationalize him.

Bernstein was not surprised. "This decision appears logical," he told me. "Since 1934 I have not ceased to attack Hitler in my plays and in my books. I returned my decorations to Mussolini, when he joined Hitler, together with a letter that was published in all the newspapers of Europe. Since that time my royalties due to me for my plays have been confiscated by the fascist regime. I am thus accustomed to confiscations, and the seizure of my books in France by Pétain does not worry me! Morally, the action of Vichy against me has no significance; materially, it is different, but I am accustomed to sacrifices. Since my arrival in New York I have been informed by Vichy that they would be kind to me if I did not write anything on Vichy but I am a free man in a free country, and no one will prevent me from writing what I think."

The American press praised the courage of the group of denationalized citizens, and expressed the hope that the federal government would promptly grant them United States citizenship.

One morning I was visited by Louis Rougier, professor at the University of Besançon (France), who was pro-Vichy. He believed he could impart great diplomatic secrets to me concerning the serious negotiations being held in Madrid, between the ambassadors of Great Britain and Vichy France, concerning the colonies and the fleet. He said he had been appointed by Pétain in October 1940 to carry on important negotiations with the British. He went to London and held secret talks with Churchill in order to obtain an agreement with Marshal Pétain. According to him, the Germans would not be permitted to use the French Colonies, and all parties would respect the status quo of the colonial territories if the Free French would remain as they were. Vichy France would take no action to reconquer the countries conquered by de Gaulle. Great Britain for its part would prevent de Gaulle from conquering colonies still under Vichy domination and would also partially lift the blockade that prevented France from importing goods that were needed for the winter. He also told me that according to that agreement Churchill would no longer attack Marshal Pétain in his broadcasts. He stated he had met Churchill personally and had come to an understanding and that negotiations would follow.*

Rougier then remarked that since I had a reputation for uniting the exiles I should neutralize their vocal political opinions. "Everything must be done," he said, "to prevent agitation among the French people and promote the union of all." He concluded that it was "essential to stop attacking Marshal Pétain." We are in a free country, I replied, where everyone is free to say what he thinks. And I pointed out that here one can openly attack even President Roosevelt.

Although I gave him little encouragement, he came to see me again and again, once to request that I see Camille Chautemps. I told him I was willing to see any Frenchman, but not former Premier Chautemps, who was among those responsible for the dishonorable Armistice and for scuttling the last cabinet of the Republic. If Chautemps had a message for General de Gaulle I said I would transmit it, or if he preferred he could send it thorugh Tixier in Washington.

On another occasion, Rougier informed me that the Consul of Vichy wanted to see me and talk to me about important matters concerning the French colony in New York. I had seen him eighteen months earlier when I had just arrived in New York and saw no reason why such a meeting could not take place, but not of course in my Delegation or at his Consulate; instead, we met discreetly in a hotel. He was an interesting man who, although a member of the Vichy

---

*What Rougier did not say I learned only after the war: The day after his meeting with Churchill, Marshal Pétain made an agreement with Hitler at Montoire (France) promising the complete collaboration of France, far beyond the terms of the Armistice. After this, of course, Churchill declined to see Mr. Rougier anymore.

clan, had been an acquaintance of mine before the war. We met alone and discussed problems concerning the French colony for which we were both responsible. He stated sternly: "I have learned that you deliver passports, you issue visas, you sign documents, as an official of France. You have no right to do that. I am the one who represents the sole legal authority of France, in Vichy now. By performing official acts you are committing a felony; you are guilty of falsifications!" The Vichy official then criticized the few French newspapers that were sympathetic to the cause of Free France.

Finally, he brought up the real reason for the meeting: "Can you not calm your partisans who write articles and open letters to the press again Marshal Pétain? He is the hero of Verdun. He is loved in France and should be respected abroad." I replied that I did not want to discuss the case of Pétain, and that he would have to justify his actions to the French people after the war. Regarding the articles in the press, I could not, and did not want to, control my Free French compatriots. "You have an old colony on which you have various means of applying pressure," I pointed out. "You can give subsidies or decorations. You can even threaten. My case is different. I have a colony of "stars," Henri Bernstein, Eve Curie, Jean Perrin,* Jacques Maritain, Henri Torrès, Jacques Hadamard, all celebrities—they are free in a free country." I insisted once again he abandon Vichy. He answered, "I admire the Marshal. I am loyal to his policy and to his government. If ever the American government decides to sever diplomatic relations with Vichy—and I don't believe it will—I will return there and place myself at the orders of Marshal Pétain.

"How can you do that? Pétain enforces a policy of collaboration with Hitler," I replied. "Pierre Laval, his Premier, is a tool of the Nazis."

He interrupted me. "You forget that the war is lost. France is committed to live in the Reich's Europe, where she will play a role equal to her genius. Anyway, Marshal Pétain is the legitimate ruler of the French State."

I was amazed that a highly educated man and a distinguished civil servant could say such things and decide to join the politicians in Vichy who were making France a vassal of the Nazis. When he started to tell me that all would be forgotten if I joined Vichy, I replied that

---

*Nobel Prize winner in Science and Atomic Research.

if he would renounce Vichy, everything he was doing now would also be forgotten by us. It was the end of our conversation. I met him only once later, after Pétain had severed diplomatic relations with the United States and closed Vichy's embassy and consulates. As he had promised, he then returned to Vichy.

CHAPTER XI

A French Press in America

The French exiles who read American newspapers were astonished to see that the American press almost always sided with Free France. This posture often transcended the isolationist tendency of certain newspapers. In New York, the *New York Times* was on very good terms with my delegation. On several occasions its editor-in-chief, Edwin James, wrote articles in our favor. Even more favorable to us was the *New York Herald Tribune,* an evening daily of Republican leanings, whose hostility to Roosevelt and his entire policy automatically caused it to line up on our side. Mrs. Ogden Reid, its owner, defended our cause with particular zeal. Other papers, such as *P.M.,* an afternoon daily, for example, supported us with enthusiasm, convinced as they were that General de Gaulle—who had abandoned Marshal Pétain and General Weygand—was a man of the left who would reestablish a socialist republic after liberation. Frida Kirchway of the weekly *Nation* shared the same opinions, as did the editors of the *New Republic.*

American news editors could not accept the State Department's policy of expediency, which contradicted their principles of moral conduct. The American press, therefore, ignored no opportunity to publish articles on the military successes of the Free French Forces in Africa (FFL) or the naval victories of the Free French Naval Forces (FNFL). It was beyond their comprehension that the American government—at war with the Germans and Italians—would nevertheless maintain an embassy in Vichy and allow the Vichy government to be represented in Washington.

Since de Gaulle, his "nasty temperament" notwithstanding, was fighting the common enemy, the press could not understand why his movement was not recognized as an allied government.

I was quite disappointed, on the other hand, by the small French-language press in America. Infinitely less important and much less influential than the American papers, it was divided in its opinion on many things, yet generally united in its unfavorable attitude towards General de Gaulle and the Free French. In 1940, its readership was made up of the French population in the United States, which at that time stood at between 150,000 and 200,000 people, plus approximately 20,000 refugees. There were, of course, American readers, in particular the descendants of people of French ancestry who had migrated from Canada and now lived in the New England states. Their memory of the fight against the British that had forced them to abandon their homes in Quebec to settle elsewhere had made them fiercely anti-British. This population was also Catholic and, having never accepted the secularization of France, was convinced that the 1940 defeat was punishment from on high. In short, the Third Republic was to them the devil incarnate, with Pétain pointing the way to redemption. The Free French were much criticized in this regional press by a readership that hoped to see the old *Maréchal* "save" France.

It should not be surprising that the local French press, instead of promoting some community of purpose, would reflect instead the political and material chaos of its divergent groups of readers.

Some newspapers were published by recent French emigrés. In San Francisco, Paul Verdier, of Gaullist leanings and the president of a large department store in the city, published *Le Courrier du Pacifique* (Pacific Mail). *L'Amérique* was published in New York by a Polish printer who had no understanding of France or of its policies. *Le Messager* (The Messenger), a university-style paper managed by Jules Dubois, appeared three times a month. The frequently published *Voici la France de ce Mois* (Here is this Month's France) was subsidized by the Vichy Embassy, and continually attacked Free France. *Voici*, another large newspaper, also assumed a collaborationist posture very early on, and stood behind the pro-German policies of Vichy.

Finally, *La Voix de France* (The Voice of France) belonged to a printer named Demilly, who gradually became pro-Gaullist. Demilly came to see me to ask for a $2,000-a-month subsidy, over and above the income from 500 subscriptions; $2,000 was at that time a fortune which, in any case, we did not have. He then called upon a prominent French trial lawyer, Henri Torrès, for help. Torrès was happy to acquire the paper. For several months, Torrès and M. Vogel, once chief editor of the French *Vogue*, published pro-Gaullist articles incessantly. These were followed by violent disputes within the paper as well as by intrigues to replace Torrès by Émile Buré, who had once been chief editor of *L'Ordre,* a patriotic, anti-Hitler daily in Paris. Finally, the intrigues and financial difficulties brought the publication of the paper to a halt.

In 1943, a group of refugee businessmen—Eugène Gentil, Myrtil Schwartz, Jules Jeandros, along with Henri Torrès—founded a purely Gaullist paper, *France-Amérique,* of very high literary and journalistic quality.

With the exception of *France-Amérique,* these French newspapers were written by amateurs for the most part, and had a circulation of perhaps 500 for the less successful; some, in exceptional circumstances, reached a circulation of 10,000 copies. None of these small newspapers exerted any influence on the American press, which ignored them entirely.

In view of all the talented French writers and journalists in New York, I too thought it might be possible to establish a real French newspaper—one which would enjoy a certain prestige, regularly report news from France, and be in a position to influence the French in the United States, both those who had been long established and those who had recently arrived. I even thought that articles by renowned writers might be reprinted in the Greater New York press. To this end, on October 7, 1941, I wrote a report to the National Committee in London in which I suggested either purchasing an existing French newspaper and restructuring it completely, or helping a group of exiled journalists to establish a new paper. According to Albert Grand, the representative of the Havas agency, the creation of a new paper would cost $4,000. The National Committee answered that it did not have the funds to help, but encouraged me to pursue my project nonetheless.

Among the famous journalists who were French refugees were Geneviève Tabouis (whose article on Admiral Muselier's mission had so angered de Gaulle), André Géraud (Pertinax), Henri de Kérillis, Émile Buré, and Michel Pobers.* Mrs. Tabouis, who had been on Hitler's blacklist for having fought him for years in the press, narrowly escaped the Gestapo. Upon her arrival in London in June 1940, she was greeted by Churchill, who strongly encouraged her to go to the

---

*Geneviève Tabouis was famous for her articles in *L'Oeuvre,* Émile Buré was chief editor of *L'Ordre,* Lucien Vogel was the founder and director of *Vu,* Pertinax wrote in *L'Echo de Paris,* and de Kérillis had founded *L'Époque*—all influential anti-Hitler papers published in Paris before the war.

United States, where her uncle Cambon had been Ambassador and where she had many friends, in order to convince Roosevelt and the Americans in general that it was imperative to send arms to Britain forthwith, and to prepare to enter the war the following year.

Mrs. Tabouis arrived in New York on July 26, 1940. She was warmly greeted by Mrs. Eleanor Roosevelt at Hyde Park, where she had been invited to attend a press conference by the President. He shook her hand and said with emotion, "Dear Madame Tabouis . . . France . . . France, I care so deeply about it!" He went on to speak sadly about the tragic news he had just received of the fall of France. Mrs. Tabouis was physically very weak and was constantly ill. She often despaired, deprived as she was of news from her husband and her daughter, who had remained in France, but she was endowed with extraordinary courage and energy. She succeeded in bringing together talented journalists, such as Philippe Barrès, Henri de Kérillis, Michel Pobers, and Professor Fred Hoffer of Columbia University. I helped her to meet Frenchmen who would be willing to give substantial financial help to found and support a French newspaper of prestige.

One morning, she came to see me, glowing: "I have found a generous benefactor; Horace Finaly (former president of the *Banque de Paris et des Pays-Bas,* who was a refugee in New York) has put the necessary funds at my disposal to allow me to start a Free French newspaper! He only stipulated one condition: I must be the director and the editor-in-chief. I thanked him, but told him that I was only a journalist and had never managed a paper, and that he should choose someone else. But he was inflexible, so I chose Pobers, who has editing experience. As for de Kérillis, he was offended and, after a thousand difficulties, made me sign a huge contract permitting him to publish anything he wanted unconditionally." Mrs. Tabouis accepted this clause, and was later to regret her decision.

The Japanese attack on Pearl Harbor occurred just as the negotiations with the writers had come to a standstill, but in its wake there was no longer any hesitation; America was at war, and an anti-Vichy French newspaper now became a necessity. The first issue of this newspaper, which adopted *Pour la Victoire* (For Victory) as its name, appeared on January 10, 1942, with a moving message from Mrs. Roosevelt. About twenty French writers of all political tendencies, from the extreme right to the extreme left (excluding, of course, the Vichyites), sent their message of support. General de Gaulle himself sent a congratulatory telegram to de Kérillis.

Pour la Victoire quickly acquired an impressive reputation, and its articles were reprinted in the large American newspapers. The paper attempted to bring the French together and to promote Franco-American friendship. While maintaining a somewhat favorable posture toward the Free French, it requested no subsidy from London, and strove to remain completely independent from de Gaulle, which was not always easy. Adrien Tixier, for instance, tried on several occasions—but in vain—to publish articles of his choosing. Later, there were problems with his successor Hoppenot, who also wished to impose his own politics on the paper.

In their editorials, the editors maintained an anti-Vichy stance but preserved their freedom of expression when it came to other French problems. Robert Valeur, one of the delegation's press attachés, became involved in a violent conflict which took on comic overtones. *Pour la Victoire* one day announced that in order to prove his patriotism, Valeur had volunteered to join the Free French forces. He then received with a great deal of embarrassment a series of congratulatory letters applauding his heroic initiative, when in fact he had no interest at all in leaving his New York office.

Published in London and edited by François Quilicy, *La Marseillaise* was a paper that strictly followed de Gaulle. *La Marseillaise* signed an agreement with *Pour la Victoire* in order to publish a full issue in each edition that appeared in the U.S. However, as *La Marseillaise* became progressively more hostile to President Roosevelt, on September 2, 1942, *Pour la Victoire* refused to continue publishing its articles. I tried in vain to arbitrate between them and to prevent their conflict from becoming public knowledge. Hoppenot, who at that time had succeeded Adrien Tixier in Washington, intervened in turn. "In liberated France," he told Tabouis, "there will be no room for the opposition. One is either for or against us: those who will have chosen to be against us will be banished from French soil forever."[1] To this Mrs. Tabouis responded that she had chosen exile in order to safeguard freedom of the press, and that she would no more submit to orders from Algiers than from Vichy.

Pour la Victoire was to see new problems. One morning de Kérillis rushed into the offices of the paper yelling: "My son has been handed over to the Germans by de Gaulle's services. He was captured while on a mission. He died horribly tortured. I will avenge his death!" He then presented an extraordinarily violent article against de Gaulle, accusing him of murder. Mrs. Tabouis refused to publish it. De Kérillis reminded her that under the terms of the agreement that bound them, she was obligated to publish it verbatim. The following Thursday, he brought in another article entitled "Pétain faisait mieux" ("Pétain did better"), in which he dragged de Gaulle through the mud. Geneviève Tabouis refused to publish this as well, whereupon de Kérillis took her to court, along with Philippe Barrès and Pobers, to enforce the provisions of his contract. After interminable and shocking discussions, de Kérillis' suit was dismissed.

Despite those setbacks, *Pour la Victoire* continued to be published, and on the day the provisional government was recognized, Geneviève Tabouis wrote a moving article calling on the French people to unite. She was one of the very first to board the Liberty Ship for France. The paper was then handed over to Pobers, a talented writer and journalist. *Pour la Victoire* later merged with *France-Amérique,* which is published to this day.

The question of French publications continued to be an issue. Indeed, between blockade and maritime war, the shipment of books from France to French-speaking areas such as Quebec and to French-speaking South America had been cut off. Meanwhile a number of important French writers were exiled in New York, where there existed a well-stocked French library run by Mr. Molho and Mr. Crespin in the Rockefeller Center. The two men decided to start a publishing house called *Éditions de la Maison Française.* Steadfastly refusing to be Gaullist, Vichyite, or even Giraudist, it published over a hundred works by Raymond Aron, Julien Benda, Gustave Cohen, Julien Green, Eve Curie, Pierre Cot, Henri de Kérillis, Jacques Maritain, André Maurois, Jules Romains, Geneviève Tabouis, Paul Vignaux, Saint-Exupéry, Pertinax, and others; and it even published a book in French by Edward Stettinius, who was later the American Secretary of State. It also published my book *l'Épopée de la France Combattante.*

These works, published in a common format on excellent paper, with covers reminiscent of the *Nouvelle Revue Française,* were extremely successful not only in the United States but also in Canada, Egypt, Brazil, and even in North Africa after the American landing. The successes of the *Maison Française* inspired competitors, and Brentano's, an American firm, opened a service for the publication of French books under the supervision of Robert Tenger, a Parisian lawyer.

Maison Française Didier also published works by Pierre Mendès-France as well as the moving *Message aux Pays Libres (Message to the Free Nations)* by Édouard Herriot, President of the Chamber of Deputies, who, fearing for his life, entrusted his manuscript to Admiral Leahy, who forwarded it via diplomatic channels to the United States.

When North Africa was liberated these three publishing houses, especially the *Maison Française,* successfully published a whole literature that, had they not been in existence, would never have seen the light of day in the French-speaking world.

CHAPTER XII

The Global Strategy of Colonel Cunningham

The defense of any territory controlled by the French Volunteer Forces is vital to the defense of the United States.
—Franklin D. Roosevelt

My duty was to keep close contact with the American and local French press, to support and win the French exiles and residents over to de Gaulle's cause. I also had the responsibility of negotiating with the American authorities. I quickly learned that the initial contacts between Free France and the United States were plagued with difficulties due to errors, confusion, and misunderstandings. Not all of these were the fault of the Free French.

As a matter of fact, although René Pleven had executed his assignment with a great deal of savoir-faire and discretion, three events over which he had no control were to disrupt our position. General de Gaulle's direct offer of bases in Africa to the American government, about which our delegation first learned through the American press, did not strengthen our position in New York. Then, there was the unfortunate publicity accorded to an interview de Gaulle gave on the same subject to the *Chicago Daily News*. And finally, an American colonel was sent on an astonishing fact-finding mission to the Free French territories.

On July 6, 1941, General de Gaulle, who was in the Near East, sent a long memorandum to A. Kirk, U.S. Minister in Cairo, explaining that in the context of the war, military activity consisted of "engagements executed from airbases [and] drawing progressively closer to the sources of enemy strength." He then skillfully explained that the deployment of planes and ground transport was possible only if they possessed a good communications network. Foreseeing an end to U.S. neutrality, de Gaulle added: "If America is induced to take part in this war, . . . she will need bases progressively closer to the front in order to attack the enemy." He stated that England, whose base was too narrow, could only offer "limited strategic possibilities." Communications between England and the United States were precarious because of the enemy. He also thought that the ideas and the methods of the American people were different from those of the English and that mixing of the two should be avoided.

De Gaulle also added: "In reality, America must actually plan to use Africa as the place where she will install her bases of embarkation." Then came a long explanation of the geographic and strategic position of Africa. The General mentioned as possible bases Pointe-Noire, Brazzaville, Douala, Yaounde, Bangui, Fort-Archambault and Fort-Lamy, concluding that "Free France is ready to welcome, to the African territories that she administers on France's behalf, any installation that the United States of America would wish to place there in view of its eventual military intervention in the war. A commission to be either covertly or overtly sent by the U.S. government to study the matter on location would be welcomed on behalf of the authorities of Free France with the greatest possible compliance."

The offer had no doubt been immediately transmitted to the American government, which did not reply. De Gaulle then decided to make his offer public so as to force the U.S. government to take an official stand in the matter. It was obviously not the most diplomatic way to carry on negotiations. Thus several weeks later, on August 27, General de Gaulle granted an interview—about which his own delegation, incidentally, was not informed—to George Weller, correspondent for the *Chicago Daily News* in Brazzaville. This interview was vital to understanding the political thought and military aims of General de Gaulle over the course of the war. Speaking on his own soil without the inhibitions natural in Cairo or London, General de Gaulle predicted a Nazi invasion of Africa, in the same uncompromising terms in which he had foretold the German invasion of Syria two months before it occurred, and had predicted the blitzkrieg technique six years before Hitler launched it.

"Through a suitable intermediary," said de Gaulle, "I have offered the United States Douala in the Cameroons, Port Gentil in Gabon, and Pointe-Noire in French Equatorial Africa as naval bases. I always had faith that the United States would keep her word and I know that America does not covet territorial aggrandizement in Africa.* Especially, I am sure that France's African possessions would be in safe hands if strategic points were occupied by the American Navy. I observe that one of the cardinal points of the conference between President Roosevelt and Prime Minister Churchill was respect for the integrity of all nations. Moreover, I believe in the American conception of international honor," he continued.

The interviewer asked whether he believed the United States should break off relations with Vichy.

"I do," said the General. "Without delay. Immediately."

Was there any hope that Vichy might, despite all evidence to the contrary, still change its color and resist Hitler's orders if Britain and her allies started to gain victories? "Not only is there no evidence, but the men of Vichy could not now turn back even if they wanted to," said de Gaulle.

"They have taken three deliberate steps, one after another, and they cannot retrace them even if they should develop a desire to do so. The first step was that they lost the military campaign; the second step was that they concluded an armistice with Hitler; and finally they undertook to collaborate with Hitler's plans. Those steps were separately taken and each closed a new door to retreat. They cannot go back; they can only go further in the same direction."

De Gaulle further explained British action. "If America both breaks with Vichy and recognizes our Free French government, your people will have gone further against Vichy than Britain herself," he suggested to the interviewer. "Britain has taken the first of these steps, should she not also take the lead in the second? Why, in your opinion, does not London finally close the door upon Vichy by recognizing your government?" asked Weller.

General de Gaulle answered without hesitation:

England is afraid. England is afraid of the French fleet. What, in effect, England is carrying on is a wartime deal with Hitler in which Vichy serves as a go-between. Vichy serves Hitler by keeping the French people in subjection and selling the French empire piecemeal to Germany. But do not forget that Vichy also serves England by keeping the French fleet from Hitler's hands. Britain is exploiting Vichy in the same way

---

*Later, when the U.S. government dealt directly with local authorities, de Gaulle became very suspicious.

as Germany; the only difference is in purpose. What happens, in effect, is an exchange of advantages between hostile powers which keeps the Vichy government alive as long as both Britain and Germany are agreed that it should exist. If Vichy should lend or lose its fleet to the Nazis, Britain would quickly bring the suspense about recognition to an end. And if Vichy should cease serving Hitler and dismembering its empire for his benefit, Germany would herself dismantle Vichy. . . .

In a final question, the interviewer asked General de Gaulle whether Syria had given him any solution to the painful problem of giving orders to Frenchmen to fight against Frenchmen. "The task itself is in that way an unhappy one," he answered. "But when I assumed this work I realized I would have to fight Frenchmen. Today I expect to be obliged to fight Frenchmen from here all the way to the very gates of Paris. I am ready to do my duty."

Like all de Gaulle's speeches and declarations, this interview was no accident. Its obvious aim was to shock public opinion. It must have been done with the dual purpose of affirming his complete faith in the United States and—incredibly enough—of gaining its sympathy by bitterly attacking Great Britain. Perhaps he thereby intended to prove that he was completely independent despite British military and financial support. He always made a point of showing that despite the fact that his headquarters was in London he was the head of the sovereign nation of France. He was no puppet.

The day the interview appeared in the *Chicago Daily News,* I received calls from the *New York Times,* the *Herald Tribune,* and other newspapers, wanting to know whether the interview was genuine, and asking for my comments. Since at that time we'd been kept in the dark, I was most embarrassed, and could not answer.

Later de Gaulle denied having given such an interview, at least in those words. Ironically I learned from the American archives, many years later, that he had cabled from Lagos to try to stop the interview from being printed.[1] The paper went ahead and printed it, however, since Weller was a correspondent of integrity and had conducted many interviews with de Gaulle. Churchill took the interview seriously, and had a violent confrontation with the General upon his return to London. Needless to say, the interview also created an uproar in Chicago, the capital of isolationism. In New York and Washington, Vichy's agents used this pretext to shout: "England is the enemy; that's what we have always proclaimed!"

One can well imagine that Roosevelt, who was pro-British and had supported by all possible means Britain's fight against Hitler, was not thrilled with the Weller interview. An indignant State Department official denied that it had negotiated with de Gaulle. Cordell Hull openly expressed his discontent. Further, the State Department considered the interview to have destroyed all possibility of secretly negotiating the use of the preferred bases. Moreover, it seemed evident that de Gaulle had used this pretext as an opportunity to attack the British government, a U.S. ally, in a region of the country (Chicago) where support for the policy of isolationism was strongest. In addition, the State Department deemed that de Gaulle was unjustly criticizing the only country which had "recognized" him, given him asylum, financially supported his movement, and equipped his small army.

Nevertheless, the offer made by de Gaulle had been genuine. The geographic position of his bases was such that it soon became evident to military strategists that it would be useful to consider their eventual use. The Free French territories in Africa strategically occupied half the continent, allowing the British to travel in a westward direction to reach the Middle East. Would it still be possible to send a mission to very discreetly probe the situation?

Pleven's negotiations in Washington, although they had not yielded all he had hoped for, had had the advantage of making the atmosphere less strained and drew the public's attention to the possibility of cooperation between the Americans and the Free French. Therefore while remaining as cautious as possible, the State Department, at the request of the Navy and the Defense Department, decided to send a mission to investigate on site the possibilities offered by the immense territories rallying behind Free France in Africa.

The State Department acted very cautiously and in great secrecy. It accepted the suggestion of the Defense Department to appoint Lieutenant Colonel Harry Cunningham to head the small mission to Free French Africa that also included Lieutenant Commander John Mitchell of the Naval Reserves and Lawrence Wilson Taylor, a medium-ranking officer (class 8) in the Foreign Service. (The Department chose low-ranking officials in order to avoid arousing suspicion at Vichy's Embassy.)

Although intrigues often stymied French unity and certainly made the task of representation difficult, the French were not the only ones subject to mistakes wrought by the chaos of war. Thus, on a beautiful morning in September 1941, I received a visit from a very statuesque and charismatic man, a cowboy type who eerily resembled a John Wayne character: Colonel Cunningham in person. He said he had always admired *le grand Charlie* (Charles de Gaulle), and was going to join forces with him to win the war. The Free French were "famous boys, our real friends," and Free France, following Cunningham's visit to Africa, was going to be recognized as a legitimate and lawful ally while America was still neutral. He expressed himself fluently in French but with a very strong American accent. The man was so bizarre and his manner of speaking so strange that I telephoned the State Department to get confirmation of his mission. And yes, Cunningham was for real! I was warned however that his mission had to be "secret," not to offend the Vichy government.

Having made the rounds of the French organizations in New York, and announcing the importance of his covert mission, the Colonel set sail on the SS *West Lashaway* for Pointe-Noire.

The arrival of the first official American delegation in Free French Africa aroused indescribable enthusiasm. A crowd, from the moment the ship arrived, swarmed into the port to greet the secret mission. The road was packed with French settlers, and the natives brandished American and French flags. The local press wrote articles that were more than glowing. The New York press received word of this delirious enthusiasm in telegrams from its correspondents.

The U.S. Consul at Leopoldville (then the capital of the Belgian Congo) didn't hesitate to contact Cunningham early in October. Dr. Adolph Sicé, the High Commissioner of Free France, told me how he welcomed the tiny mission with open arms and, during a dinner held by the French Chamber of Commerce at Brazzaville, presented Cunningham with a gold Cross of Lorraine on which his name had been engraved. Official receptions and banquets followed one after the other. The Colonel praised General de Gaulle and those who had supported him, and promised generous American aid: trucks, machinery, equipment, supplies. The mission was invited to visit the Pasteur Institute where Dr. Sicé had carried out his studies and research on tropical diseases. A review of the troops was organized in the camp *Colona d'Ornano* where future officers of Free France were receiving their training. The Colonel also visited the port, the transport services and the region's depots, as well as the native part of the city. After being notified of Cunningham's visit, General de Gaulle sent him a telegram of welcome to which the Colonel replied immediately. He said that he was touched by the warm welcome and by the friendly and enthusiastic reception he had received since first setting foot on French soil, where "honor" and "homeland" remained viable principles and not just words. General de Gaulle sent a telegraph to U.S. Consul General Mallon in Leopoldville asking him to convey his deferential gratitude to President Roosevelt for sending this mission and to thank him for the great things America had already done and would surely continue doing to safeguard liberty.

Mr. Mallon himself was caught up in the feverish excitement and reported to Washington that Colonel Cunningham, an "excellent orator," had a way with people, understood the temperament of the French, and "spoke their language well."

The New York press reported this piece of good news on the secret mission, which outraged Vichy's embassy in Washington: it filed an immediate protest with the Department of State.

On October 16, 1941, the *New York Times* published an interview with Colonel Cunningham that disclosed the results of his meetings with the French as well as his hope for close cooperation with them. There was no longer any doubt. The United States was on the point of recognizing General de Gaulle. The Vichy embassy in Washington protested vehemently. Cordell Hull, furious, sent a telegram to the Colonel on October 23 reminding him that "you had no mission" but that he had been sent instead to French Africa to familiarize himself with and to investigate the situation, not to grant interviews to the press. Cunningham replied that he had in fact only granted one interview to a journalist from the *New York Times*, a Mr. Sedgewick, whom he had known for a long time and in whom he had complete confidence. He reminded Cordell Hull that he had been recognized right away as "head of the mission" and that as the most senior member he quite naturally was the spokesman for his two younger colleagues.

Cunningham sent a long telegram to de Gaulle, reporting his observations and making suggestions for aid and for the dispatch of American supplies. Cunningham also informed him of the political situation in Chad and made recommendations for the other territories controlled by Free France. The General, delighted to be in contact with such an understanding and friendly leader of an official U.S. mission, sent him a cable on November 8, 1941, inviting him to come to Syria and Lebanon to meet Generals Catroux and de Larminat, "who will view your coming with a great deal of pleasure." De Gaulle also invited him to visit London to answer questions about armaments, and proposed meeting him in person either in the Middle East or in Africa. The General felt that the United States had finally come to understand reality and was going to send him considerable assistance.

The State Department in Washington as well as the U.S. embassy in Vichy meanwhile received protest after protest. Vichy feared that because this mission was dealing with Free French authorities it would not stop before recommending the recognition of their official sovereignty over the African territories they occupied. Sumner Welles replied to Vichy that this small group of Americans had gone to Africa on a fact-finding mission, and that this trip could not in any way be construed as a sign of official recognition. To this, Vichy responded that the whole episode had obviously been an unfriendly gesture, "aggravated by the participation in this mission of officers and officials on official duty."[2] Meanwhile the American administration, already annoyed at the publicity accorded this affair, hesitated to recall Colonel Cunningham so as not to prove Vichy's protests correct.

Colonel Cunningham forged ahead enthusiastically with his investigation until he saw his mission assuming global proportions. On December 12 he sent a telegram to the State Department reporting that de Gaulle was planning a landing in Madagascar. The question might well be asked whether such rumors were really circulating and how Cunningham could have taken them seriously, knowing how weak the Free French military and naval forces really were. He informed the State Department that in this event Hitler "would demand something of Spain" and that Portugal would find itself in the same situation as Spain. Cunningham therefore concluded that the Allies must take all the necessary precautions to prepare for the anticipated occupation by the Free French of Spanish Guinea and Cabinda to forestall the Germans. The English should then occupy Fernando Po and San Tomé; the Belgians and the South Africans, Angola (then a Portuguese colony). All these strategic moves were urgent and Cunningham suggested that in order to facilitate operations the State Department should designate him liaison officer to the Free French, the English and the Belgians. He also needed the Signal Corps' secret codes and $1,000 in confidential funds to be sent by the next Clipper. The Colonel also thought it highly possible that these events would require occupying Martinique and Guadeloupe, in which case he recommended "that a representative of Free France, for example de Sieyès, whom he had met in New York, be named High Commissioner of the islands for Free France."[3]

One can well imagine how these telegrams, filled with details and suggestions concerning a worldwide war strategy to be employed against Hitler and Vichy, were received in Washington. Furious, Cordell Hull sent the following telegram to Cunningham: "Your December 12 telegram was received. Return to Washington by the first available transportation. You are not authorized to make any suggestions of military or diplomatic moves to any foreign representatives."

The Colonel was indignant at this response. How could anyone doubt the value and importance of his suggestions? He retorted at once by telegram that he would not comply with the order and requested "that your peremptory order be reconsidered and revoked. I know that it was issued under pressure of work and was based upon a misunderstanding."[4]

Still in the same vein, the Colonel added that his efforts to comply with the instructions he had received regarding the brevity of cables had evidently made his cables ambiguous. He claimed that he never expressed any opinion that was not purely personal when responding to questions posed him. He had never participated in any official conference. His suggestions concerning Africa were only the disclosure of certain projects of which "he knew the existence." If anyone asked him a question directly, he could hardly answer, for example: "'I am not authorized to have any opinions or to make suggestions to representatives of national groups who are aligned with us in a common effort to combat the common enemy.' That would imply that either I am an ass or that my country participates in the war only half-heartedly. I will not admit to either of these two suppositions."[5] And he added: "The suggestions that I made are due to the grave menaces that threaten American shipping and my recommendations concerning Martinique and Guadeloupe were addressed confidentially to the State Department alone."

He pointed out that he was the sole military representative in Equatorial Africa of the leading power in the world. As a result, thanks to his travels he knew Equatorial Africa better than anyone else. He couldn't refuse to respond to invitations and to contribute to the common cause. He added that he had been invited to three important conferences, one of which was with General de Gaulle himself! How could the State Department possibly expect him to refuse to participate in these important conferences that had been carefully prepared and involved important officials? He was enjoying "the total confidence of the Free French to such a degree that my English colleagues envy me, regretting their inability to equal me."[6] How could the State Department ask him to give up the acquaintances he had made, the fruit of three months of work? Lastly, he added that General Sicé, High Commissioner, considered his departure "a catastrophe that threatened to render null and void all the efforts of the Free French."

The Colonel symbolized Free France's hope in America. If he left, he insisted, general despondency would set in. Cunningham hoped that the order would be rescinded "in the interests of the final victory of the free people."

In fact the enthusiasm generated by the Colonel was not unanimous; Pierre Denis, Chief Financial Counselor for Free France, reported from Brazzaville to London that he'd met Cunningham, "a man of tall stature, exuberant, and a great traveler,"[7] who was on the best of terms with General Sicé. The latter was in conflict with the Governor General of Chad, Felix Eboué, regarding their authority over the Free French territories and concerning numerous administrative questions. However the governor was supported in these disputes, not by the Americans, but by the English consul, Parr. Poor Denis, caught between Parr and Eboué on the one hand and Sicé and Cunningham on the other, was having difficulty trying to carry out his mission in that chaos. The most extraordinary rumors were flying around Brazzaville concerning the role of these five characters who were fighting among themselves![8] It was said that "Sicé was leading Africa into chaos." Cunningham espoused the cause of General Sicé and treated Denis as a Judas, the worst of traitors. The people and the administration in Brazzaville chose sides, some supporting Sicé, others Eboué. Showing his support for his friend Sicé, Cunningham wrote a scathing letter to Denis, warning him that he had written to General de Gaulle asking for Denis' recall and that he had also asked the governor of the Cameroons to stop sending supplies to French Africa until Denis had been recalled. Moreover, he had recommended to the South African government that it adopt the same attitude. Denis telegraphed London asking General de Gaulle to confirm his mission and to reconfirm his confidence in him.

A short time later, Denis took ill and was hospitalized. The American consul visited him and in the course of their conversation, questioned him about Colonel Cunningham's famous letter. Needless to say, the consul reacted immediately, reprimanding the Colonel and immediately notifying Washington. The following day, Cunningham came to the hospital and asked Denis' forgiveness. Denis replied that he would not accept his apology unless the Colonel wrote to General de Gaulle and the governments of the Cameroons and South Africa, retracting his earlier messages. A bewildered Cunningham admitted that he had indeed written these letters but had not yet sent them.

In the midst of all this, an exasperated State Department sent Cunningham a comminatory telegram in the name of the Secretary of

State directing: "Your information will eventually serve our ends. A consultation is desirable. It is mandatory that you *return immediately*. You are no longer qualified to fill the role of foreign observer. . . ."[9] The American consul alerted French authorities of the termination of Colonal Cunningham's mission. He returned to the United States, and one can well imagine the reception that awaited him at the State Department.* In this very tumultuous situation, de Gaulle did not rebuke the Americans, but rallied on behalf of Governor General Eboué whose authority and functions he confirmed. He also had General Sicé recalled to London and put in charge of health services for the Free France military.

Following these extraordinary events, Washington's official attitude towards Free France continued to be restrictive so as not to offend the Vichy government, whose embassy protested even the slightest action on behalf of the Free French. I met General Sicé in New York after his dismissal from his post as High Commissioner. He recounted the whole Cunningham episode to me, adding that he considered it the "Saint-Pierre-et-Miquelon of the Americans." The whole story seemed so extravagant that I decided to check the American archives for myself, and have quoted from them at length to satisfy the reader that I have not embellished the story.

Luckily the extraordinary adventures of Colonel Cunningham did not have a lasting negative effect on American–Free French relations. Despite their unusual character, the reports of the Colonel's mission served as a confirmation of the strategic position of the Free French territories in Africa and the willingness of the local governors and population—natives and settlers alike—to cooperate with the United States. It became obvious that Free France was a valuable friend and that she needed help and support. Free French Africa badly needed equipment to build new roads and improve port facilities. It also needed transportation, health supplies, and other commodities. It would require military equipment in the event war spread to that area. The Colonel's reports, exuberant as they surely were, may still have influenced plans at an early stage in Washington to provide help through a lend-lease agreement.

---

*I have not found in the Department's Archives any information concerning what happened to Colonel Cunningham after all these events. General Sicé later confided to me that he himself was ignorant of the Colonel's fate.

❈

CHAPTER XIII

Sumner Welles: The Man to See

The many unresolved problems between Free France and the United States nevertheless did not prevent them from getting closer to a de facto acceptance of our Movement, swept on by the momentum of public opinion.

By the end of July 1941 the American government had considered the possibility of taking a first cautious step forward and authorized the "Lend Lease" program which allowed Free France to purchase equipment, supplies, and goods of a non-military nature indirectly for the free colonies. This Lend Lease program required that Britain act as transfer agent for the Free French.

On November 11 President Roosevelt declared: "I hereby proclaim that the defense of the territories under the control of the volunteer French forces is vital to the defense of the United States." De Gaulle's name was not mentioned in this declaration.

The State Department was courteous enough to inform me that I could speak directly to the American media before the official publication of the text. I therefore assembled the press in the Delegation's office, much to the astonishment of several who knew Washington's official restrictive policy of caution towards the Free French, and I briefed them on the letter written by President Roosevelt to Edward R. Stettinius, Lend Lease administrator. The reporters who were present noted this news with satisfaction. They knew that until this time, their government had gone out of its way to avoid offending the Vichy authorities. Laval's more active policy of collaboration with Hitler had probably provoked the American government into aiding Free France as a warning to Vichy. I was asked many questions. The one that most interested the public was, "Do you believe that the United

States is going to break off relations with Vichy?", to which I replied that this was a strictly diplomatic problem for the United States that I could not answer.

I was careful to point out on a map the strategic importance of the African and Pacific territories which were under General de Gaulle's control.

A year later, the State Department took another step towards recognition of Free France. On October 6, 1942, it granted Lend Lease directly to the French National Committee, this time with no British retrocession required. We were therefore treated as the representatives of a legitimate recognized government. Sending or selling arms would obviously not be done to an unrecognized committee, but only to a sovereign allied nation.

The Secretaries of State, of the Army, and of the Navy, as well as their officers, now cordially welcomed our military leaders at every opportunity when they were travelling through the United States. Admiral Father d'Argenlieu, General LeDantec, and General Sicé were only a few of the many who were warmly received. This fooled us into thinking that the prejudices against Free France had been forgotten by the Roosevelt administration. We soon found out, however, that the Department of State had not changed its position concerning political matters; we remained outcasts as before.

Relationships concerning military or economic matters with Free France were excellent and we were treated with trust. The U.S. Treasury was placed under the authority of Henry Morgenthau, who had been an unfailing supporter of Free France from the very beginning. The negotiations with his department were excellent; Pierre Mendes-France and Hervé Alphand were warmly received when negotiating with his department.

Donovan's department, the Office of Strategic Services (OSS), was in constant contact with the Free France delegations from Washington and from New York and often asked our advice on security matters. In some cases, they went so far as to submit to us applications of French candidates applying for entry into the United States. They asked our assistance in translating or deciphering intercepted messages or letters from France. They also asked advice on possible reactions in France to different projects of economic aid. I was personally on friendly terms with Allen Dulles, one of the founders of the OSS, and cooperated with him on many occasions.

The dramas of Saint-Pierre, Pointe-Noire, Tahiti, and New Caledonia were things of the past, and I had the impression that finally, despite their cautious policy of appeasement toward Vichy, the Americans considered the Free French to be their allies.

But the position of the State Department had not changed, in that it still wanted to avoid offending the Vichy government, with whom it hoped to maintain friendly relations. However, the Free French wanted help in their war against the Axis and were seeking a form of recognition that was against the policy of Vichy, which protested each time the Americans negotiated with the Gaullists.

Every State Department move dealing with Vichy or with de Gaulle engendered criticism. Whenever policy seemed to favor Vichy, the American press to our great satisfaction protested vigorously. When the administration leaned in the Free French direction, Pétain's vassal government complained no less vociferously. Dealing with the two Frances was indeed a "damned if you do and damned if you don't" nightmare. On April 8, for example, Henry-Haye, Vichy's ambassador in Washington, protested to Sumner Welles, the Assistant Secretary of State for all French affairs, over the sending of an American Consul General to Brazzaville in Free-French–controlled Equatorial Africa. Henry-Haye argued, in accordance with diplomatic tradition, that the Consul General's "exequatur" to act in that territory should have been requested of France's central administration—Vichy! Welles replied that, inasmuch as American policy was based on principles of "deep friendship" with the divided French people and a "sincere desire" to see them restored to their "independent position in the world," the State Department would deal with local authority. Welles added, ironically, that he was certain the Vichy government "was well aware that those territories were under the control of the Free French."[1]

Joseph Sumner Welles was a typical prewar gentleman. His outlook and personality were similar to that of the classic diplomat of the British Foreign Office. A man of great knowledge and distinction, he was author of many books on foreign affairs, and a career diplomat who had held important posts in Tokyo, Argentina, and Cuba. He was fluent in French and Spanish, and had been sent by Roosevelt in 1939 on a fact finding mission to Europe. Upon his return he had warned Roosevelt of the impending tragedy that he could foresee. The President trusted him and charged him, as Undersecretary of State, with European Affairs and especially with the thorny French problem. Everyone was aware of the personal rivalry between Welles and Cordell Hull. Hull, the Secretary of State, was a lawyer, judge, and former

Senator from Tennessee who was less well versed in international affairs than his subordinate.

During all this time, Free France had a sincere and active friend in Washington: Lord Halifax, the British Ambassador. He advised the French concerning their attitude towards the State Department and more than once informed them of the steps to take to improve their political situation. He used his influence to obtain a better understanding in Washington of General de Gaulle, because in the great disaster of June 1940 he was the only French general to join the British. He cautioned the Americans against extending their relations with Vichy. His interventions had to be discreet to avoid giving the impression that Free France, based in London, was merely a British vassal. His position was clear: Vichy under German domination was the enemy, while de Gaulle with all his faults was an ally. The ambassador was nevertheless aware of the serious shortcomings of the *Comité National Français* in England.

In May 1942, Cordell Hull and his State Department assistants became convinced that the Free French movement had to be made more democratic. Criticism of de Gaulle had been heard from a variety of French circles in the United States. Yet Hull was nevertheless contemplating the not-too-distant eventuality of an Allied landing in North Africa, or in France itself—an action that would force the U.S. to sever relations with Vichy and require it to deal with a French authority hostile to the Germans. The dilemma was clear.

Welles met with Lord Halifax and suggested that their governments jointly bring pressure on de Gaulle to transform the National Committee into a more democratic organization that would include a broader spectrum of French public opinion. Somehow, the special London correspondent of the *New York Times* learned of the meeting between Welles and Lord Halifax and was able to dispatch the complete text of their extensive and presumably secret discussions regarding a reorganization of the Free French movement under General de Gaulle. The *Times* published the text on May 26. De Gaulle was furious and made his anger quite clear in the press. He felt not only betrayed but (even worse) insulted, and he refused any comment on the subject that might make him appear a puppet of the two Anglo-Saxon nations.

Sumner Welles sent a highly critical note to the British government complaining that such publicity "completely defeated the constructive and desirable purposes which we had in mind when we undertook

these discussions." Lord Halifax tried to downplay the importance of
de Gaulle's public statements, replying that he "could not interpret
them as being so damaging as Sumner Welles believed them to be."
He argued that de Gaulle should be satisfied with being recognized as
"leader of resistance forces" within France. But Welles disagreed, contending that, while "certain elements within occupied and unoccupied
France might be responsive to de Gaulle, other equally important—if
not more important—elements of resistance were totally opposed to
General de Gaulle and would certainly be more so after his demand
for political recognition."[2]

The day the *Times* article appeared, Sumner Welles asked to see me
in Washington. I arrived at the State Department early in the afternoon and was astonished with the ease of access to the office of the
Assistant Secretary of State. My reception was very cordial. Welles
was physically an impressive man: tall, slim, and elegant, with a wide
forehead and brilliant eyes. He spoke slowly, in excellent French,
which he had learned as a child from his French nurse. He remained
amiable during the entirel conversation, which lasted almost an hour,
yet spoke frankly. After reviewing the world situation and expressing
his faith in the ultimate victory of the Allies over the Nazis, he said
he felt it imperative that the new world order be built on the principles
of liberty, morality, and justice. He voiced his distress at the numerous
divisions among Frenchmen. Why was this so? Since the fall of the
Third Republic, France had had no unchallenged legitimate and sovereign government. If some governments considered Vichy legitimate,
they obviously could not consider it sovereign since it was under German control. On the other hand, the National Committee in London
was also unelected; it was composed of men bowing before de Gaulle's
demands. Its authority was accepted by some Frenchmen but rejected
by many others. Even British recognition was very limited. Under
such circumstances it was inevitable that there be division. "You are
in a situation," he said, "where the principal of authority has been
substituted for the principle of legitimacy."

He then went on to affirm his great concern for France: "We will
do everything possible," he said, "to rebuild a strong France. I am
saying this not only sentimentally but politically. France is necessary
for the balance of power in Europe and the world over." He then
severely criticized the Vichy rulers, whom he did not trust: "Diplomatic relations with the Vichy group cannot last. But how can we
sever relations without giving the French people the impression that
the United States has abandoned them to their cruel Nazi masters?

The author (top left) as a member of the French legation in Cairo in 1939, where his principal responsibilities as attache concerned diplomacy with the Arab press. All of the members of the legation except him chose to ally themselves with the Vichy government.

The author (bottom left) in the uniform of the French Army in Beyrouth in 1940. After the defeat of the Army in France, he sought out officers of the British Army, but they would not allow him to fight alongside them against the Nazis. He finally put himself under the command of General Georges Catroux (bottom right), who had resigned as Governor of Indochina to become the first general to pledge his support to de Gaulle, whom he actually outranked.

De Gaulle was particularly effective at reaching out to the French people through radio, as shown in this photograph taken a year after his historic June 18, 1940 broadcast. Aglion was at Al Kantara, near Suez, in mid-June 1940 when he heard the faint but stirring broadcast of de Gaulle's voice, calling to Frenchmen everywhere with the words, "This war is not lost by the battle of France...join forces with me." Aglion set out to do just that.

Adrien Tixier (top left), whom de Gaulle named senior delegate in the hope that this "man of the left" would offset U.S. State Department fears that de Gaulle would become a military dictator. In fact, Tixier often had an agenda of his own, counter to de Gaulle's goals, which seriously confused negotiations with the American government. Raoul Aglion's (top right) responsibilities in New York were setting up the administrative apparatus for a French consulate in the city and dealing with the chaotic and often tragic plight of French refugees and their families arriving in New York. He attempted to develop the delegation's relationship with Undersecretary of State Sumner Welles and New York's Mayor Fiorello LaGuardia.

As a cultivated international businessman, René Pleven (above left) was among the most successful of the delegates in calming the Roosevelt Administration's fears about de Gaulle's ambitions. Nevertheless, neither Welles nor Secretary of State Cordell Hull ever granted him a personal audience. To correct this, de Gaulle sent André Philip (above right), economist and Socialist member of the French parliament prior to the war, as a special envoy. He actually met with Roosevelt in November 1942, but the meeting was a total disaster.

Diplomat Alexis Léger (left), famous as a Symbolist poet under the name St. John Perse and later a Nobel laureate, was the single greatest influence on American policy toward France. He convinced Secretary of State Cordell Hull and Undersecretary of State Sumner Welles (below, left, in dark suit) that de Gaulle was not the legitimate head of a government-in-exile because he had never been elected by the French people. Welles' particular responsibility was French affairs, and due to his tremendous admiration for Léger as a diplomat and as a man of letters, Léger's views resulted in the Roosevelt Administration's refusal to recognize de Gaulle's government until three months after the liberation of Paris.

Courtesy French Embassy Press and Information Division, Washington

"All the News That's Fit to Print."

The New York Times.

VOL. XCI...No. 30,681.

NEW YORK, THURSDAY, DECEMBER 25, 1941.

LATE CITY EDITION

THREE CENTS

FREE FRENCH SEIZE ST. PIERRE AND MIQUELON;
TWO MORE ENEMY LANDINGS MENACE MANILA;
WAKE LOST AFTER 14-DAY STAND BY TINY FORCE

WAR CASTS SHADOW OVER CHRISTMAS JOY THROUGHOUT LAND

Realization of the Job Ahead Expressed on Every Hand — Matters' Scan Skies

Heroic Defense of Wake Isle An Epic in Marines' Annals

Garrison of 400 With a Pacify of Guns Took Toll of Enemy Cruiser and Three Ships — Their Fate X

SEMPER FIDELIS

MAP SEA STRATEGY

The Roosevelt-Churchill Conference Centers on Moves in Pacific

VISIT CONGRESS M'ARTHUR AT FRONT

7 BEACHHEADS HELD

One Only 50 Miles From Manila, Which May Be Declared Open City

TAKE VICHY COLONY

Units From 4 Warships Occupy Islands in Half Hour Without a Shot

VOTE SET FOR TODAY

Withdrawal Promised if It Is Adverse—People Hail de Gaulle Force

The Free French invasion of St. Pierre and Miquelon made banner headlines in the *New York Times* on Christmas 1941. The very next day the *New York Herald Tribune* reported that the United States government had "initiated steps" to return the islands to Vichy control.

NEW YORK
Herald Tribune
LATE CITY EDITION
THREE CENTS

FRIDAY, DECEMBER 26, 1941

Vol. CI No. 34,739

Foe Presses Toward Manila; Hongkong Falls;
Army Plane Sinks Submarine Off California;
U.S. Moves to Void St. Pierre-Miquelon Coup

THE WEATHER
Today: Light snow or rain and somewhat colder

$1,301,075,000 Non-Defense Saving Urged

d Committee Asks Cut Road W.P.A.

An Allied Observance of Christmas in Washington Church

U.S. Is Acting To Give Isles Back to Vichy

Asks Canada What It Will Do; Free French Win in Plebiscite After Seizure

London and Ottawa Are Also Surprised

Luzon, Where Japanese Press Philippine Attack

Fall of Baguio To Japanese Is Reported

U.S. Army Quite Summer Capital of Philippines, Enemy Tank Drive Gains

Foe 35 Mil d From J

Léger's charge that de Gaulle was irresponsible and ambitious was comically confirmed by the adventure undertaken by de Gaulle's tiny navy in "liberating" the islands of Saint Pierre and Miquelon west of Newfoundland in 1941. The incident was a disastrous embarrassment for de Gaulle's delegates in New York and Washington who were attempting to win the favor of the American government—now furious over this military foray into North America. Admiral Emile Muselier (left) had been on his way to Washington to announce that de Gaulle had placed Free France's bases in Africa, Tahiti, and New Caledonia at the disposal of the U.S. fleet to demonstrate that de Gaulle's government was a true American ally, when a telegram from de Gaulle instructed Muselier, instead, to lead this controversial mission.

Courtesy Myron Davis, *Life Magazine*, August 24, 1942, p. 87. © 1942, Time, Inc.

Shown here in a notorious and melodramatic *Life* magazine photograph (August 24, 1942), "a French leader of the Resistance" under the *nom de guerre* Pierre Durand (actually E. d'Astier de la Vigerie) purportedly discusses the fate of French collaborators with the Nazis, with members of the Free French delegation in Washington (from left, press attache Jean Baubé, senior delegate Adrien Tixier, military attache Colonel de Chevigné, and naval attache Commandant Gayral). Beneath this photo *Life* ran a list of "SOME OF THE FRENCHMEN CONDEMNED BY THE UNDERGROUND FOR COLLABORATING WITH GERMANS: SOME TO BE ASSASSINATED, SOME TO BE TRIED WHEN FRANCE IS FREE," naming high-placed officers of the Vichy government who were Vichy leaders and Nazi collaborators, as well as a host of sympathizers well-known to Americans—music hall star Mistinguett, boxer Georges Carpentier, film producer Marcel Pagnol, actor Sacha Guitry, and entertainer Maurice Chevalier. The list further aroused fears in American governmental circles that a future de Gaulle government would be a bloodthirsty lot bent exclusively on revenge and unworthy of postwar American support. But in fact, *Life* magazine's treatment of the issue was much closer to the sentiments held by most Americans than the Roosevelt Administration then realized.

At the Casablanca meeting in January, 1943 (top), Churchill and Roosevelt each sat next to his own French protege. Churchill favored de Gaulle, while Roosevelt, who thought de Gaulle was both ridiculous and dangerous, preferred General H. Honoré Giraud, primarily because Giraud was trusted by Alexis Léger and was reputed to be apolitical.

Mrs. Eleanor Roosevelt, however, in touch with popular American sentiment about Free France, was a whole-hearted but, of necessity, discreet supporter of de Gaulle's cause in America. The author and Mrs. Roosevelt (bottom) renewed and continued their friendship in their work during the founding of the United Nations in San Francisco and afterwards.

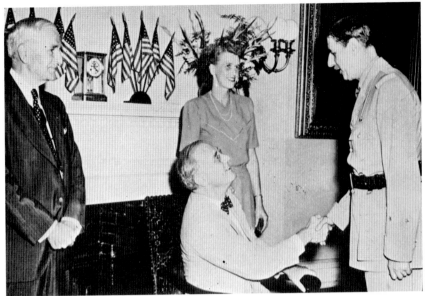

Courtesy F.D.R. Library

At long last, on July 16, 1943, Roosevelt and Secretary of State Cordell Hull agreed to receive de Gaulle at the White House (top), but with the understanding that he was there as a military leader in the fight against the Nazis and *not* as the French chief of state. The distinction was maintained to the last detail, including a 17-gun salute instead of the 21-gun salute accorded heads of state. The American press was appalled by such treatment of a now-admired ally. (From left to right, Cordell Hull; Roosevelt; his daughter, Anna Bettinger; General de Gaulle)

Courtesy F.D.R. Library

General de Gaulle, president of the French Republic, with Eleanor Roosevelt at Roosevelt's grave in April, 1945. When Adrien Tixier refused to allow the President of the Municipality of Paris to hold a special session in memory of the late American president, de Gaulle did not overrule him.

Nevertheless, the situation has reached a point where the United States administration cannot continue to deal with Laval. Severance is inevitable."

The conversation returned to the question of legitimacy. "The National Committee of General de Gaulle," said Welles, "would not be, and could not be, recognized as a government in exile. Governments in exile are legitimate governments that have fled invasion. Such is not the case of France, where the government did not choose to go into exile, but remained, and now is not free due to the pressure of the Nazis. De Gaulle's authority is based upon a small group of followers who sometimes fight each other, and on some territories overseas. Here in America, the majority of Frenchmen, even those who are opposed to Vichy and Laval, do not recognize de Gaulle's authority. . . . Frenchmen of international stature living in the United States—Alexis Léger, Jacques Maritain, Jean Monnet, Saint-Exupéry, Maurois—are keeping their distance from him. Eighty-five percent of the French living in the United States are not for de Gaulle. . . . What can we do? How can we help to create a rallying authority?"

I replied that de Gaulle, unlike Pétain, did at least enjoy a limited sovereignty as a trustee for France's interests. He had a small force fighting alongside the British, and (perhaps most important) he served as the symbol of resistance for the captive people in France. I did not think any other symbol in the resistance could now be substituted for his. Welles countered that many eminent Frenchmen who had been contacted—such as Édouard Herriot, speaker of the House, or Jules Jeanneney, the Senate President, had refused to leave France to form a free government abroad. "But," he said, "the question will remain under study."

We also spoke of the Free French delegation which was headed by Tixier in Washington and of its difficulties. The Secretary of State was quite aware of its internal dissensions. This was not unlike the situation in France where a large majority still favored Marshal Pétain. "You have learned by bitter experience," he said, "that the Navy and the Army are strongly against de Gaulle. Remember your failure at Dakar,* in Syria. . . . " He then concluded: "Have you seen Alexis Léger? He is a man of great knowledge and integrity. Mr. Cordell Hull and I consult with him on many occasions. The President holds him in great esteem."

---

*See Chapter VII, p. 56.

He ended by stating that he had read the articles of de Kérillis in
Pour la Victoire with great interest.

I learned later that negotiations had continued between the Americans and the British to strengthen or reorganize the French National
Committee in London and to make the Committee a body capable of
unifying all Frenchmen in the war against Germany and of representing the permanent interests of France throughout the world.

While the State Department was in an embarrassing position and
was trying to find a new solution to the French problem, public opinion was more than ever on our side. The press was always favorable
towards Free France. The courage and brilliant feats in Africa of Generals Leclerc, de Larminat, and Koenig, with their small bands of
heroes, were in most cases given front page coverage in the New York
press. During the months of May and June 1942, the heroic resistance
of the First Brigade of Free France at Bir-Hakim, under the command
of General Koenig, who had succeeded in blocking the advance of the
Italians and of Rommel's famous Panzerdivision, generated tremendous enthusiasm. General de Gaulle's comments in this regard, *"La
France vous regarde et vous êtes son orgueil"* (All of France is watching you and you are her pride), appeared everywhere in the American
newspapers. Bir-Hakim represented the restored honor and the fighting spirit of the French army.

Occupied France swelled with pride. (On June 24, 1942, the underground newspaper, *Libération,* printed a moving article on this battle
in its fourteenth edition: "This is only one episode in the war, only
one fight in the battle for Libya, but for France, it spells resurrection.")
No longer could it be said that the French were neutral and didn't
have the will to fight. Meanwhile, the State Department kept on its
own course and soon an incredible event took place. On May 30,
1942, six months after Pearl Harbor, the American government organized a solemn ceremony in Washington to commemorate Memorial
Day and invited military attachés from Vichy's embassy to attend.
These Vichy officials strutted about during the ceremony and were
congratulated on the fierce resistance of the Free French at Bir-Hak-
eim; the Free French officers, however, had not been invited.

This was, to say the least, an affront to the Free French fighting
men, and did not escape the notice of the American press. The Free
French perceived the event as an absurd and flagrant manifestation of
hostility toward them.

Several days later, I met our friend Fiorello La Guardia, Mayor of
New York, and told him of my disappointment over this incident. La

Guardia felt the same way but explained that if he protested to Washington now, it would be to no avail. I asked him in that case to invite a delegation of Free French fighters and veterans to New York for an Army Day celebration. La Guardia immediately agreed and kept his word. Thus in July 1942 I was able to organize under the Mayor's sponsorship an official Free French Week in New York.

On July 13, the day before Bastille Day—the national day of France—the Free French war veterans, the France Forever Association, the Free French war relief, and members of American war veterans' organizations came to City Hall in great numbers with their flags, and applauded a fiery speech delivered by the Mayor: " . . . That was not the first time that the French National Holiday . . . has been celebrated in New York City. What I had to decide was who would celebrate it, and to whom we would pay honor. The choice was very easy; we in America, in celebrating Bastille Day, are paying honor and tribute to the people of France. We have naturally selected not those who are in friendly negotiations with the Nazis, but Free France who is fighting the Nazis." A large crowd of sympathizers gathered with tricolor ribbons and flags, sang "The Star-Spangled Banner" and "La Marseillaise," and cheered itself hoarse.

CHAPTER XIV

Vichy's Embassy in Washington

Vichy representation in America was as riddled with intrigues and mistrust as most French organizations at that time. It was not supported by all the French in America, it was criticized relentlessly by the American press, and distrusted by the United States' administration.

To understand the importance of the Vichy embassy it is necessary to return to June 16, 1940, when Paul Reynaud resigned as Premier and a makeshift government was created with Marshal Pétain at its head. On June 17, the old Marshal asked Hitler the conditions of the Armistice and immediately ordered the French Army to lay down its arms, thus betraying France's alliance with Great Britain. The conditions of the Armistice were unusually harsh. Two-thirds of France including Paris were to be occupied or controlled by the Nazis. Nothing was prescribed for the return of the nearly 2,000,000 French war prisoners who surrendered to the Germans. The heavy costs of the occupation were to be borne by France. Alsace and Lorraine were annexed to Germany. The French police were ordered to cooperate with the Gestapo.[1]

Pétain proclaimed that he *incarnated* France, then moved his government to Vichy, a resort in central France. There he illegally abolished the French Republic, its constitution, and its laws, and created a French State (*État Français*) of which he was President for life, empowered to name his successor. Pétain, with full powers, created a puppet state in imitation of Hitler's Reich. He met Hitler on October 29 at Montoire to organize full cooperation with the Nazis. He declared the next day: "It is in order to maintain French unity . . . that I adopt today the policy of collaboration [with the Nazis]."[2]

Domestic legislation similar to the Nazi's was adopted; racial laws were enacted; French and foreign Jews and their children as well as other refugees were delivered to the Nazis to be sent to death camps in Germany. A "National Popular Legion" and a special militia—the SOL *(Service d'Ordre Légionnaire)*—were created on the Nazi pattern. And, with the express blessing of Pétain, a special French Legion was recruited, equipped and sent in German uniform, under the German High Command, to fight on the Russian Front.[3] Two-thirds of France was occupied, and the other third, an officially unoccupied zone under Vichy, became a German satellite.

It was the instructions of that puppet government that the French Vichy embassy in Washington was carrying out.

The Count de Saint-Quentin, whom I had occasion to meet many times in Paris, was a diplomat of the old school: very distinguished, very learned, capable of negotiating delicate affairs and quoting French classics. He was the French Ambassador to the United States in June 1940 at the time of the Armistice. A diplomat of great prestige, he had many friends in the United States and was personally on very good terms with President Roosevelt. He refused to answer de Gaulle's call. Instead, he obeyed orders to return to Vichy France. Had he joined de Gaulle, one can very reasonably assume that the course of Franco-American relations would have been completely different. Free France would have had a diplomat of exceptional prestige to represent the real France that was at war. He would have maintained the best and most cordial relations with President Roosevelt, whose relations with General de Gaulle might then have been mediated. Unfortunately, de Saint-Quentin believed that his duty was to obey blindly, and he returned home, leaving his prestigious post to Henry-Haye, a Vichy propagandist who was going to preach his master's credo.

Henry-Haye had been the Mayor of Versailles and had met many Americans in France before the war. He thought he could persuade his friends, some members of the government and of the press of his brand of isolationism, and of the justice of his viciously anti-British doctrine. He was also entrusted with explaining to Americans the benefits of neutrality for everyone and the importance of a Franco-German rapprochement to world peace.

His duty also was to wage anti-Gaullist propaganda and to keep in line all Franco-American associations such as the French-American Chamber of Commerce, the *Alliance Française,* the American Society of the Legion of Honor, the French War Veterans, etc.

When Henry-Haye arrived in the United States as the new Vichy ambassador, Vichy had a strong tactical position, because although the United States certainly did not approve of the dishonorable

Franco-German Armistice, it at the same time was making every effort possible to prevent Vichy from going further and yielding more to the Nazis. Vichy France had of course two trump cards: the strategic location of its loyal colonies, and its powerful fleet, which was still intact, while the British, the German, and the Italian fleets had all seen battle and suffered damage. The French fleet, one of the most modern of the time, included 238 warships: 11 battleships, 101 submarines, cruisers, and a number of mine sweepers and torpedo boats, among others. Not only had it been physically modernized by Admiral Darlan, but the technical skill, loyalty, and discipline of officers and crews were considered among the very best.

The danger that the French fleet would go to battle for and with the Germans was far from unreal. It is a fact that after the American landing in North Africa, for example, Admiral Darrien at Bizerte, carrying out the orders of French Admirals Platon and Estéva, delivered fifteen warships and nine submarines to the Nazis, who made good use of them against the Allies.

Henry-Haye had been highly recommended by William Bullitt, the American ambassador in Paris. He was warmly greeted by the President, who said it was his wish that Henry-Haye be cordially accepted in Washington, that he count on official American cooperation in his efforts to solve problems, and that he develop relations as cordial as those that fortunately had always existed between their two nations.[4]

Henry-Haye arrived with unusual officers who were not regular members of the French Foreign Service. His principal assistant was Col. Bertrand Vigne, who had an impeccable record in World War I. They arrived on September 6, 1940. Charles E. Brousse, who had the title of Press Attaché, came later.

On the day of his arrival the new ambassador made a long declaration to the press, to whom he stated that he did not come as the "Ambassador of Germany." He thought it a witty remark. The press commented on it with a great deal of criticism. A year later he would commit a serious indiscretion by disclosing to the press a confidential conversation that he had had at the White House. It did not endear him to the Department of State.

His pacifist and anti-British propaganda to the isolationist members of Congress finally irritated the press, which pointed out that all this vicious propaganda was made possible thanks to the State Department.[5] In fact, at the beginning of the war France had deposited a part of her gold stock, roughly $250 million, in the United States. The

Treasury was remitting every month $1 million to pay the personnel of the Vichy embassy and consular services and to finance the exports of certain merchandise to the French Antilles (Martinique, Guadeloupe, and French Guyana). The Embassy received for its own expense the sum of $100,000 each month, a considerable sum at the time.

The Ambassador was also accompanied by a bodyguard, Mr. J. Mussa,[6] about whom the FBI had certain suspicions; he lived sumptuously and spent large sums of money, despite a modest salary. After searching his home, a large amount of Nazi propaganda was uncovered. He was invited to leave the country. Finally Henry-Haye, with the help of his consuls, organized a perfect system of surveillance to monitor the opinions and the activities of the French in the United States. Reports were sent to Vichy and non-Vichyites were punished (they were stripped of their citizenship). In France, it would lead to seizure of their property and pressure against members of their families. The Vichy consuls pressured all Frenchmen in their constituency. They cajoled and threatened, announced that they would lose their pensions, that news of their families would be withheld. The FBI inquired into the complaints of the French refugees, and the press published many articles on the abuses of the Vichy French Embassy.

Since the American government greeted him so warmly, Henry-Haye thought it was opportune to make an extended trip to the areas of the ancient French settlements in New England, New Hampshire, Maine, and Massachusetts, where descendants of the early French pioneers, the Acadians, lived at that time. He wanted to revive their national sentiment about the country of their ancestors. The ambassador travelled in a beautiful limousine with a French flag, escorted by a motorcade. The trip thus had considerable prestige. Many local residents came to hear his speech in which he not only elaborated on the France of their ancestors, but also about oppression by the English who, two and a half centuries before, had chased their ancestors out of Canada. The aggression and the disloyalty of the English was the theme of all his speeches: England had been the real enemy of France throughout the ages. England had abandoned France at Dunkirk, had treacherously sunk her fleet at Mers-el-Kebir, was starving French women and children with her merciless blockade. It was British pressure, intrigues, and propaganda that had dragged France into this war. Germany had been generous. Germany made lenient conditions for the Armistice. Her army was helping the population that now trusted the German soldiers.

Everywhere his audience listened to him respectfully and with a revived sense of distrust and hostility toward the British—an attitude which was not entirely new for the descendants of the Acadians.

This trip had so many repercussions and led to so many comments that the Department of State finally let him know that the President did not approve of his speeches, did not uphold the policy of collaboration with Germany, or favor anti-English propaganda throughout the country.

Upon his return to Washington the Ambassador learned—to his astonishment—that a press agency had announced his departure from Washington "to go to England" to join General de Gaulle's Free French Forces. The Ambassador, violently shocked, became apoplectic. After inquiry, it was learned that a not-too-intelligent French reporter, who probably did not know his geography, had believed that Henry-Haye had gone either to New England or England, which were one and the same place as far as he knew, and if so, his purpose in going there could only be to join de Gaulle.

Amusement at the Ambassador's violent rage was the subject of endless jokes both in Washington's Vichy France and in Free France circles. It was a rare, unanimous feeling.

The press—the *Washington Post, Baltimore Sun, New York Daily Mirror,* and *New York Herald Tribune,* to name a few—published many stories unfavorable to Henry-Haye. The *Herald Tribune* on Sunday, August 31, 1941 exposed the spying activities of the Vichy Embassy under the headline, *"Vichy Embassy in U.S. shown as heading a clique of agents aiding Nazis."* The ambassador was openly accused of operating a secret intelligence service organization under the diplomatic cover of the French Embassy.[7] He was checking the arrivals and departures of British ships in American waters, endeavoring to obtain blueprints of military arms and equipment, and had made surveys of the preparedness of the American army and navy. Henry-Haye called a press conference where he informed the newsmen he was going to lodge a protest with the Secretary of State. "What is the aim of this campaign?" he asked. It is to try to realize the ambition of certain Americans and Frenchmen to break up or erode diplomatic relations between the French government and the United States. He said the "French government," because he insisted that there was no other French government than the one he represented.

The Department of State, despite its open criticism of Henry-Haye, decided nevertheless to try to improve relations with Vichy, and therefore soon after announced the appointment of Admiral Leahy, a personal friend of the President, as Ambassador to Vichy. It was a gain of great prestige for the Vichyites all over America. The Free French felt humiliated. A few days later, the Department of State, to create further confusion, officially announced that five Free French delegates of General de Gaulle had now been accredited to the United States, and that from then on they would enjoy a privileged status. The Vichyites were furious and protested, while Gaullists could not conceal their joy and their pride.

The American press was not long in taking a position advocating the severance of diplomatic relations with Vichy and the closing of its embassy and consulates. They considered de Gaulle their ally, and concluded that he should be recognized officially as such.

The State Department's dual policy created not only chaos but deep division within the French colony, which no longer knew whom to believe, whom to trust, or whom to follow anymore. The anti-Vichy French were all divided, as we have seen. There were those who did not like Marshal Pétain and did not like de Gaulle either. Others were for de Gaulle during the war, and with many reservations for the future. Finally, there was a committed group which considered itself unconditionally behind him.

The pro-Vichy group was not united either. Some were for Pétain as a temporary leader but were anti-German. Others considered the Marshal as the leader of France for eternity and followed his *Révolution Nationale*. Finally, others were for Pétain, for the Armistice, for the end of the war, and for collaboration with the Germans. Some even were pro-Pétain, pro-Laval, while others were against Laval and for Darlan. There was also a considerable number of them who did not want to express any opinion and waited to see who would win before making any choice. At the embassy there were also some who were secretly Gaullists, who were waiting for the proper occasion to resign and join de Gaulle. Vichy's confusion fully matched our own.

If the French were divided among themselves, most of their associations (registered in the United States) remained under the influence of the Embassy of Vichy. On the whole, the great majority of Frenchmen were not for de Gaulle.

Some people laughed at de Gaulle for having five delegates while England had only one, Lord Halifax. It is true that some people admired the organization of Pétain while not liking what he did, because at least he had just one representative. But this, of course, did not last. As early as December 1941, the press announced that Marshal

Pétain had sent another representative, Camille Chautemps, who had been Prime Minister of relatively liberal French governments. Chautemps had been responsible for manipulating the vote of the last Cabinet of the French Republic when it was divided on whether to seek an Armistice. Instead of seeking an armistice he suggested that they "simply ask for the conditions" of an armistice. This finally led to capitulation. Chautemps was unquestionably a man who had had great prestige. He was entrusted by Pétain with the extraordinary mission of finding out what was going on in the United States, because in some quarters of Vichy it was felt that Henry-Haye did not accurately report the political situation in America. Camille Chautemps was awarded a fine salary, was able to meet people at the highest level, and had the privilege of corresponding directly with the old Marshal—not through the pouch of the Vichy French Embassy, but through American diplomatic channels.

The fights between the two official Vichy representatives were known to everyone in Washington. Finally, Henry-Haye won this little war. Chautemps lost his fine salary. He then thought it was time to change his political position; he offered to join de Gaulle. De Gaulle refused. He asked to be a member of the France Forever Association in New York, and was turned down. In 1942, when General Giraud opened his recruiting office in New York, Chautemps offered to join, and this time was refused because of his age. He also tried unsuccessfully to join the American Army. Powerful as he was before the war, nobody wanted the ex-premier now!

As for the Embassy's staff, it remained loyal to Vichy but some had misgivings. The first to leave, as we have seen in Chapter II, was Garreau-Dombasle; but no one followed him. Francois Charles-Roux resigned very soon after and had a brilliant career as Attaché to General de Gaulle, and was later French Ambassador to various countries.

Another member of the staff was an economist and financial adviser of great standing, Hervé Alphand, who had never concealed his contempt for Vichy. He was a man of great charm, an excellent negotiator highly respected for his knowledge of financial matters. When I met him before his resignation his contempt for Vichy was readily apparent. He finally decided on June 14, 1941 to hand his resignation to Henry-Haye. In it he stated, "I have heard some of my colleagues, who believe that Germany has already won the war, argue that in that case a sort of natural charm of the French, their talent of invention and organization—which unfortunately was not revealed in the course of the last few years—will make our country indispensable at the creation of the new Europe. Consequently in the future grouping of nations, France will be called upon, with the agreement of Germany, to play a role equal to its past and to its genius."

After having refuted that policy, Hervé Alphand continued: "Even if we are certain of German victory, our duty would be to resist foot by foot, and accept none of the demands of the conqueror, and not to accept association to any of its plans. . . ." And he concluded, "It is because I realize the obvious results of the spirit [of collaboration with Germany] that I am certain that the very existence of our nation is in danger." Therefore he decided to resign from the embassy and refused any other post offered by the Vichy government.[8]

This resignation was commented on by the whole press because Alphand's personality had considerable impact. This written notification, by one of the highest officials of Vichy's Embassy in Washington explaining the motives of his departure, was widely commented on by the staff of the Embassy. Regrettably no one followed his example.

The return to power of Pierre Laval, imposed by the Nazis in mid-April of 1942, was followed in November by the recall to Washington of Leahy, United States Ambassador to Vichy. This finally provoked many resignations at the Embassy: Léon Marshal (Counselor), the Baron James Bayens (First Secretary), Fiot (Consul), and Benoit (archivist). However, they did not all join de Gaulle. While Marshal went to London to the Free French, the Baron Bayens and Levis Mirepoix enlisted in the American Army. De Gaulle was not appreciated by everyone, and the Delegation of Free France in Washington did not have a very brilliant reputation.

Paul Guérin, special envoy of the French Vichy authorities in North Africa and of General Weygand, went to the Department of State to find out what would be his status in case diplomatic relations between the United States and Vichy were severed, because he wanted to remain in Washington. One can wonder what persuaded him to remain—he was neither Vichyite, Giraudist, nor Gaullist. After all these events, the junior members of the Vichy consulates joined the Free French in wholesale numbers while the consuls general and high officials remained faithful to Vichy.

The former Vichy personnel when they joined us were astonished to learn how modest the salaries of the Free French were. Vichy propaganda had assured them that we were bribed and highly paid, while in reality our salaries were half those paid by Vichy and we worked seven days a week.

In March 1941, soon after my arrival, I received a visit from one of the vice-consuls, M. Breffort. He wanted to join the Free French Movement. I immediately consulted our headquarters in London, which answered that it would be preferable if he stayed where he was, where he could be of great service to our cause. Very soon thereafter, at my request and without the Vichy Consul General's knowledge, he delivered visas, passports and documents to our allies. In many cases he issued visas that were used by Free French secret agents who went to occupied France through Portugal and Spain. In some cases at London's request, he delivered a large number of blank passports to me along with the requested visas. Strangely enough, five years after the war an inspection by the restored French government uncovered the missing passports in the former office of Vichy, now officially a branch of the real French government. He was summoned to explain. I testified in his favor, thus saving his reputation.

To the dismay of the French and their distinguished friends, who had followed Vichy in New York with enthusiasm, the State Department ceased having relations with Vichy near the end of 1942, after the Americans landed in North Africa. Our delegation from Free France thus became the only French authority in America. I did my best to make all Frenchmen understand that we would extend to them whatever authority the State Department had granted us. They had, however, been so thoroughly brainwashed that they considered it impossible to join "a gang of adventurers, rebels, deserters, and traitors," as Vichy officials had labeled us.

They had to find another solution. The French Chamber of Commerce, which during the past few years had been fanatically anti-Gaullist and pro-Pétain, requested on November 13 to be recognized by the State Department as the authority representing the French people in America. The Department rejected their request, not wanting at that time to create further division among the French residents.

The high Vichy French diplomatic and consular services had an inglorious end. The American authorities ordered the closing of all Vichy offices after the total occupation of France by Germany on November 11 and after the decision by Marshal Pétain to sever diplomatic relations with the United States. Many officials, counselors to the Embassy as well as consuls general, refused to resign and maintained their allegiance to Marshal Pétain. The FBI invited them to leave their homes and to be transferred to one of the best hotels of Hershey (Pennsylvania) pending the negotiations for their exchange with American diplomats in occupied France.

More than one hundred of them led leisurely lives in Hershey during three whole months. They were housed and fed at the cost of the American taxpayer. They were not allowed to travel, but could take walks through the park. It was rumored that they had quarrels among themselves accusing each other of causing their misfortune.

The American government generously offered to set free all those who did not want to return to France, and who promised they would in no way oppose the American war effort.

Finally there remained eighteen diehards, whose love for the old Pétain was unflinching and whose respect for his New Order was unbendable. Together with Nazi officials captured in North Africa, they were exchanged for American diplomatic personnel who had been interned by the Germans.

It must have been a great joy for them to return to France—accompanied by their Nazi friends, on the *SS Gripsholm,* a Swedish freighter—to show their complete devotion to Marshal Pétain, Pierre Lavel, and their policy of collaboration with Nazi Germany.

❧

CHAPTER XV

A Disastrous Meeting with Roosevelt

While everyone in Washington and London was making plans for the day when the United States would sever diplomatic relations with the government of Pétain and close its embassy and consulates, de Gaulle decided that it was imperative to improve his relations with the State Department. He hoped that the Free French Movement would then be officially considered the only legitimate French authority. He was aware of the little prestige his representation had in Washington. In order to succeed Vichy's embassy, he had to gain the confidence of the State Department and the loyalty of the French residents and exiles. De Gaulle knew that Tixier had been unable to meet the President, even a year after his appointment. He had also failed to win Alexis Léger or Jean Monnet to our cause. He had acquired no influence with the State Department, which remained under the influence of Vichy and was steadfastly hostile to Free France. But de Gaulle, of course, was unaware of Tixier's real attitude, or that he was, as we have seen, complaining to the State Department about "this general and his entourage who were out of touch with reality."

The General thought instead that the Americans had not been convinced by Tixier because he had been out of France for too long to accurately report the most up-to-date feelings of the French people. The best way of correcting this, he concluded, was to send an active member of the internal French Resistance to the United States. This delegate, preferably a member of the left, could speak from first-hand experience and testify that de Gaulle had support in both occupied and non-occupied France.

The arrival of Emmanuel d'Astier de la Vigerie in London provided de Gaulle the opportunity. D'Astier was the perfect choice. He was a talented man of action, a liberal, well known for his impeccable reputation within the Resistance. (He was responsible for an important branch of the Resistance known as *Libération.*) He was also fluent in English. Shortly after d'Astier's arrival in London in April 1942, de Gaulle filled him in on the project. On June 10, 1942, de Gaulle sent a telegram to Tixier in Washington telling him of d'Astier's imminent departure for the United States, and told him that the mission should be considered top secret. The General also thought that d'Astier could convince Tixier, if it were necessary,[1] that the French trade unions were on de Gaulle's side. Tixier was, however, unsuccessful in organizing any of the meetings that d'Astier had been anticipating. He had been unable to interest either President Roosevelt, Secretary of State Cordell Hull, or Sumner Welles, the Undersecretary. Tixier was finally able to set up a meeting between d'Astier and Harry Hopkins, an intimate friend of the President, who must not have been terribly impressed with this newcomer. No account of their interview appears in the American national archives. Tixier arranged two additional interviews for d'Astier, one with Léger and one with Maritain, but these yielded no results as each remained firm in his anti-Gaullist convictions. Tixier was no doubt frustrated by this lack of success. Since the President had not agreed to receive d'Astier's message confidentially, Tixier decided to force the issue by granting an interview to *Life* magazine so that the President would have to read about it anyway. Tixier also believed that his belligerent attitude would please de Gaulle. *Life* then published an article on the French Resistance, complete with a dramatic photograph. D'Astier, who was using the assumed name of Pierre Durand, was photographed with his back to the camera so as not to be recognized. (Among the French in the U.S., he often used yet another name, "Bertrand.") Facing "Durand" and the reader was a solemn group composed of Tixier with the Free French military, naval, and press attachés.

Richard de Rochemont, a talented American reporter and President of France Forever, interviewed "Pierre Durand," who declared that the underground had excellent information about all major events. He was one of the "few men in France who knew that the bombardments of the Renault factories came just 24 hours after M. Louis Renault, notorious Paris collaborationist, and the Nazis had celebrated the delivery by his factory of its thousandth tank for the German army with a luncheon in his board room. Present . . . were German officers, French and Nazi overlords . . . as well as an observer sent by the underground. . . ."

"Pierre Durand" also firmly stated that "General de Gaulle has grown greater and greater in the eyes of the French. He is the only possible leader for France that fights and he has claimed no other right or authority. . . . Our organizations gave full and official adherence to de Gaulle. He did not ask for it. We gave it to him in response to our rank and file, and to that of the French labor movement." After having reflected a moment he continued: "The underground would like to have America recognize the Fighting French diplomatically."[2]

Before concluding he gave a summary list, a black list of "some of the Frenchmen collaborating with Germans." Remarkably, he added that some were to be assassinated and others to be tried when France was to be free. Among them were the actress Mistinguett, the former pugilist Georges Carpentier, the playwright Marcel Pagnol, Marshal Pétain, Count René de Chambrun, General Weygand, Admiral Darlan, Sacha Guitry, and even Maurice Chevalier. There were thirty-eight names in all.[3]

Roussy de Sales, who was on vacation in Connecticut, did not take long to send me a sarcastic letter. He did not think it was a good idea to publish a sensational article about a mission that was supposed to remain "top secret," in an American magazine that enjoyed a large circulation. If the mission were really secret, then it should have remained so. The article gave the obvious impression that Free France was bypassing the American administration and was instead making a direct appeal to the American public. Roussy added the following postscript: "Looking once more at that photo, I see that the only conclusion that the average *Life* reader can draw from it is that those solemn gentlemen pictured here are the tribunal and perhaps even the firing squad that will execute Marshal Pétain and Mistinguett." De Sales was certainly right that the article was another black mark against us at the State Department. Whether it was effective propaganda for the public, I still don't know.

De Gaulle's attempt to persuade Roosevelt of his support among the Resistance movement within France did not succeed. Despite this de Gaulle tried again by sending another emissary to Washington to convince the President of his popularity. André Philip, an old friend of mine, was a new member of the French Resistance, a prominent member of the socialist party, and a well-known economist and former Cabinet Minister who had arrived in London. De Gaulle appointed him to the French National Committee in London.

Philip had recently escaped from France and after countless adventures had arrived in London on July 25. The following day I received a telegram: He was bringing with him a message from the French underground to the effect that it recognized General de Gaulle as its only leader.

When he arrived in New York, Philip filled me in on the whereabouts of my friends; some had gone underground, others were now prisoners of war, and still others, tragically, had been sent to concentration camps. But Philip was bubbling with enthusiasm and expressed an unmitigated support for de Gaulle that charmed those who were already on our side but did not always win over the others. Especially heartening was the news he brought of the resisters in France, who engaged in an underground and very dangerous battle.

Philip had boundless energy. He gave press conferences in French and in English as well as lectures in many Protestant churches and to many American associations. His English was excellent and he impressed everyone with his courage and sincerity. He declared: "I know, and am authorized to say as much, that all the Resistance movements recognize General de Gaulle as the legitimate representative of our country. The majority of the democratic elements, especially the socialists and the trade-unionists, have maintained this from the outset and have in the last six months been joined by conservative elements who had previously felt some initial hesitation. The French National Committee in London is therefore the sole responsible authority who can give instructions to the Resistance groups, especially in military matters. We believe that, when the Allies land in France, General de Gaulle will be the only one with the authority and prestige necessary to prevent the massacre of all those who have collaborated with the Germans or with the Vichy government."[4] This served to calm the anxieties of those Americans who feared that after the Germans left, France would be plunged into a state of terrible chaos that would degenerate into civil war. At the very least, they had feared there would be terrible vengeances enacted, followed by the massacre of untold numbers of Vichy collaborators.

André Philip was also the bearer of a very important message from General de Gaulle to President Roosevelt, which he delivered to our delegation on October 27, 1942, and was to deliver to Sumner Welles, the Under-Secretary of State, without delay.

This letter arrived at a very crucial time. De Gaulle had just learned that preparations were under way for a gigantic Allied military operation on the northern coast of France. He had had before leaving London a long discussion with John Winant, U.S. Ambassador to the Court of Saint James, during the course of which de Gaulle outlined the possible contributions that could be made by the Free French forces, as well as the support they could lend to the landing of the Anglo-American forces. He also pointed out to Winant the direct relations that should be established between the French National Committee and the Allies.

De Gaulle knew that Sumner Welles had once warned Lord Halifax not to recognize the French National Committee as it now stood. Welles cautioned Halifax to insist upon a complete reorganization of the National Committee to include members of Parliament as well as elected representatives who were influential in France. The letter that Philip brought responded to these problems and to certain criticisms from the U.S. State Department and from a large number of French exiles who were residing in the United States. It was dated October 26, and it said:

> Mr. André Philip will deliver this letter to you. It will set out the conditions existing in France when he left. As to the information he brings on the development and cohesion of French Resistance groups and, more generally speaking, on the spirit that exists now in France, I would like to add . . . France is feeling a profound sense of humiliation because of the injustices she has been forced to undergo. This is why it is imperative that France take her place once again in the combat before the war is over.

Then de Gaulle went on to say:

> I was not a political leader. All my life I had kept strictly within my profession. It is true that before the war I had tried to interest the political leaders in some of my ideas, but it was only to bring to realization some military project for the benefit of the country. Likewise at the time of the Vichy Armistice it was primarily along military lines that I appealed to the country. When we observed, however, that larger and larger groups responded, that whole territories adhered or were joined to the Fighting French, and that we alone were in a position to act with any form of organization, we saw that larger responsibilities had fallen to us. We have seen in France the growth of a sort of mystical conception directed toward us, and bit by bit uniting all the elements of resistance. Thus we have become, by force of circumstance, a French moral entity. This has created for us duties for which we feel deeply responsible and which we could not avoid without betraying the respect of the country and the hopes placed in us by the French people.

After having outlined France's situation following the Armistice, including the failure of the civil and military leaders, de Gaulle explained that he had "undertaken what seemed to him to be the necessary action so that France would not give up the fight." He maintained:

> We consider ourselves and have proclaimed ourselves as an authority that is essentially provisional, responsible until the next elected government and biding by the laws of the Third Republic . . . I am not a political man. All my life I had kept strictly within my profession.

The General felt compelled to assume a greater responsiblity following a rallying of vast territories and the response of Frenchmen within as well as outside of France. "We have become a moral entity. . . . " Following a justification of his politics, he added:

> I have been told that persons who have access to you [*de votre entourage*] may be fearful lest in recognizing our existence one would prejudice the chances that certain elements, particularly of a military character, now attached to the Vichy Government, might again take part in the war. But do you believe that by ignoring those Frenchmen who are fighting, and by leaving them in a discouraging isolation, you would attract others for war service? Think of the risk to France, on the other hand, in the fact that her allies seem to be promoting the disintegration of the country by favoring the formation of several factions, some of them neutralized by agreement with the Allies themselves, and others trying to fight separately, but for the same cause. After all, have not the two years of bitter experience demonstrated that every element which separated itself from Vichy either found its way to the Fighting French or, if left apart, remained in ineffectual isolation? In the tragic situation in which the French people have been placed they see things very simply. They see that their only choice is between war and capitulation. If the choice is to be war, then it means naturally the Fighting French, and the national instinct rallies them around those in whom they see the symbol of their war effort. In this we have the real explanation of the fact that in spite of the extreme difficulties under which the Fighting French have kept going in the last two years, they have held fast and gained in solidarity.
>
> Notwithstanding the capitulation and the Armistice, France still represents a power in the world which must not be ignored. We must find a way for her to return as a participant in the war along with the United Nations while preserving both her susceptibilities and her unity. This is one of the most important problems of the war, and it is for this reason that I ask you to agree to undertake a general and direct examination of the relations between the United States and the Fighting French.[5]

This detailed letter fully exposed for the first time the complete historical account of the movement that the General had founded in June

1940 as well as his moral and political justifications. It refuted all accusations of personal ambition and outlined very clearly the major interest that the United States had in closely examining its relations with the Fighting French.

Ray Atherton of the State Department's French desk, who had never been very favorable to Free France, commented on this letter in a memorandum to Sumner Welles:

> "If this letter had been written at the outset of the de Gaulle movement it would have been a great asset in our relations with them but it is two years late and takes some ten pages of introduction to get down into the very little meat there is in it. . . . Unhappily General de Gaulle seems to have no conception of the reasons for our relations with Vichy . . . or that our information from France thereby is possibly as good as his and we have been able to maintain our contacts with the French people both in unoccupied France and North Africa. This blindness of the General is more tragic in view of the fact that our ever-increasing collaboration with him we have fully explained to his representatives here, and even later, obtained the agreement of many of them that our policy was based on the best hopes for preserving the French Empire [sic]."[6]

Unfortunately, de Gaulle's letter did, in my opinion, come too late. Many misunderstandings had already arisen and many untimely interventions had been made by Frenchmen with different and sometimes hostile attitudes to de Gaulle. Atherton had surely not forgotten the incidents of St.-Pierre-et-Miquelon or of Pointe-Noire. The General's belated attempts to explain his doctrine, his policies, and his goals had no effect whatsoever.

General de Gaulle's letter to President Roosevelt was never even answered. Within days, however, on November 7, 1942, Roosevelt spoke in French directly to the French people, in a message broadcast by all American radio stations and beamed at North Africa. The French community in America was electrified by it—Roosevelt was announcing a landing and preparations for a massive offensive that would ultimately liberate France. For two years, how many had impatiently waited for this moment! The president said:

> My friends, my friends. . . . We will be arriving in your midst to repulse the cruel invaders who would like to deprive you forever of the right to self-government and the right to worship God as you please. We would like to restore to you the means of living in peace and security. We are coming amongst you for the sole purpose of annihilating your enemies. Rest assured that we wish to do you no harm and that once the Italian and German threats have been removed, we will leave your

territory immediately. I am appealing to your reason and to your ideal of the French nation. Please do not hamper us in this noble objective. Lend us your help wherever you can, my friends, and we will witness the return of the glorious day when liberty and peace will once again rule the world. Long live eternal France!

The exiles telephoned one another, and gathered in the streets where they shouted and waved their arms, screaming with joy, and weeping. They were finally going to see an end to their anguish.

On November 9, the overseas broadcasting station called me very early in the morning to tell me it was addressing numerous appeals to North Africa and France. Could André Philip broadcast an urgent appeal at this crucial point in time? I hurried over to see Philip, who was very excited by the news that American forces were landing in North Africa. When he arrived at the studio, with a pipe in his mouth, his hair tousled and his eyes dancing, he was greeted with applause. Then and there he delivered the following impromptu speech, which I reproduce from my personal notes:

> On Saturday evening, President Roosevelt made an appeal to the French people asking them not to offer any resistance to the American army that would be landing in North Africa to liberate our country. I do not know whether this will take place in North Africa or what will be the attitude of the Vichy administration and of its army. . . . The Free French forces will do all they can to help . . . . Everyone in occupied as well as in non-occupied France sends you their best wishes for success at this historic moment. . . . Let us avoid a fratricide between French and Americans with French blood flowing merely to profit the enemy. . . . Everyone unite behind General de Gaulle. We must do so. . . .

The Free French were ecstatic. The Americans were finally joining them: the mass landing of troops in North Africa, code-named "Operation Torch," would provide a springboard for a later European offensive. At the Free France Delegation, the feeling was one of incredible excitement. Stacks of congratulatory letters and telegrams poured into my office. We also had visits from American friends of Free France and from some of those who had withheld their support until now.

Suddenly the bubble burst. General de Gaulle had not been informed of the operation, which meant that the Free French forces would not be taking part. De Gaulle was incensed. The American press, which had been exultant, became quite concerned, and began interrogating the State Department about the nature of any agreement the United States may have made with Vichy to facilitate the operation. In response to the American landing the Germans immediately seized the remaining portion of France to forestall any American attempt on the south of France.

The announcement that the Germans were now occupying all of continental France quickly put an end to the myth of the legitimacy, sovereignty, and independence of the Vichy government. What did this mean for the French living outside of France? Not only had the United States, Great Britain, and many other countries accepted all passports, visas and other documents issued by the National Committee of Free France for the past year, but now neutral countries would begin to accept them as well.

Vichy's supporters in the United States were losing their embassy and all their consulates. They were devastated, especially the so-called elite who had lost face, particularly with elegant New York society.

Several days later, Saint-Exupéry, who had continued to treat supporters of de Gaulle with exasperating reserve if not downright hostility, joined General Giraud. On November 15, he published an open letter recommending a general mobilization of all Frenchmen under one flag and concluded the letter by announcing that he had volunteered to serve with a French squadron in North Africa under the orders of General Giraud and not de Gaulle.

Official telegrams were received from France that presented a confusing array of apparently contradictory information. Roosevelt appealed one last time to Pétain not to offer any resistance to liberating forces and received the following reply: "That he [Pétain] was astounded and very saddened . . . that he could not believe what he was hearing and had accordingly given his men orders to resist any American military landing of troops . . . " and that Laval had informed the American *chargé d'affaires* of the severance of diplomatic relations.

At this point, on November 12, André Philip and Tixier asked Sumner Welles for an interview, which was immediately granted. They protested the unethical agreements drawn up by the United States with such Vichy representatives as Admiral Darlan, and stated that the National Committee would not collaborate with the High Commissioner in North Africa. Sumner Welles replied that Darlan had been used "for military ends only," and in order to avoid a senseless bloodbath between American and French soldiers, since the real enemy was still Germany. After the meeting Tixier told me that Philip had vehemently protested but did not succeed in convincing Welles.

On November 18 we learned that Pétain, still referring to himself as Chief of State, had nevertheless turned over all his power to Laval. Furthermore, he had denounced on the radio all the Vichy Army generals that had joined forces with the Allies. Meanwhile, in Africa, confusion reigned. Admiral Darlan was giving orders to the army in the name of the Marshal and they were reportedly being obeyed.

In view of those events André Philip asked for an interview with President Roosevelt. This meeting might well have marked the turning point in the history of Free France's relations with the U.S. I heard two slightly different versions of this meeting—one from Philip and the other from Tixier.

The State Department archives also contain a fairly complete version drafted by Sumner Welles, who was the only other person in attendance.[7] There had been one previously scheduled meeting that had been cancelled when Tixier and Philip arrived more than four hours late. This unforgivable delay made a bad impression in Washington. Foreign dignitaries naturally are very careful to be prompt when they are granted an audience with a head of state, and certainly Tixier and Philip, who enjoyed only semi-official status, should have been on time. As a result of their tardiness the meeting had to be postponed until November 20. President Roosevelt received them very cordially and from the outset declared that he would enjoy having General de Gaulle come to Washington to discuss an overall view of the situation with him. Roosevelt asked Philip to extend this invitation to de Gaulle. The President was also aware that General de Gaulle had refused to send a delegation from the National Committee to Algiers to confer with General Giraud because the latter had been appointed by Admiral Darlan. Roosevelt stressed once again the stance he had publicly assumed three days earlier with regard to Darlan. Roosevelt insisted that Free France subordinate her interests in North Africa to the more important goal of a victory for her and her allies. Nothing whatsoever was to delay this. France must be liberated at the earliest possible date. The President insisted that the appointment of Darlan as High Commissioner was based solely "on considerations of a military order," and that the moment Darlan stepped out of line, he would be immediately recalled, and this would apply to anyone in command in North Africa. Roosevelt added that as long as the United States remained "the dominant force [of occupation] in North Africa, they would have the final word. . . . "

As far as France itself was concerned, it was too early to make any decisions, said the President. "It is impossible at this time to predict how and where the initial operations for the liberation of continental

France might be carried out." The President added that his policy was that "until the whole of France was liberated, it would be his government alone that would determine which Frenchman would eventually administrate the free territories." André Philip and Tixier vehemently protested, assuring the President that they were in contact with the Resistance within France, which would recognize no one but General de Gaulle and the National Committee as their rulers.[8]

"I pointed out to him," Philip told me later in anger, "that this war was a major moral conflict between two diametrically opposed types of institutions—dictatorship and democracy—and that one could not base a policy on strictly military needs." According to Tixier, Philip monopolized the conversation and didn't allow him to get a word in edgewise. Tixier said he was even forced to interrupt in order to explain Free French objectives in the conflict. He added that for military operations the Commander-in-Chief would naturally be in charge, but that he should be precluded from dealing with matters of civil administration. Philip concluded by bluntly stating that the National Committee "would not permit any portion of French national territory to be administered by a foreign power."

The conversation, which grew heated at times, lasted for fifty minutes. Welles, according to U.S. documents, seeing that they were far from reaching any understanding among themselves, concluded by suggesting it would be better if "General de Gaulle, himself, came to Washington where he could discuss these important political questions with the President himself.[9] According to Philip's version, the President acted in an "imperious, abrupt, and superior manner that resembled that of Louis XIV on his throne. I responded 'tit for tat' as if we were engaged in a tennis match. We had a real rally going. . . . "

It was quickly learned in Washington that de Gaulle's two envoys had made a bad impression on the President and Sumner Welles, both of whom had probably been forwarned against them. Neither Philip nor Tixier thanked the Americans for their efforts and sacrifices in liberating North Africa. They did not let the President finish his thoughts without interruption. Roosevelt found them to be "selfishly ambitious and totally incomprehensible."[10] Despite all this, the President repeated his invitation for General de Gaulle to come to Washington.

Thus, the first meeting between the President and representatives of de Gaulle, which the General had tried to arrange for so long, ended in a political disaster of serious consequences.

Tixier confessed to me upon his return to New York that he was concerned about General de Gaulle meeting President Roosevelt because, as he put it with uncharacteristic understatement, "the atmosphere is not a good one!" He shared his feelings with Roussy de Sales and also with several Americans. Philip, on the other hand, thought that de Gaulle's sincerity was such that Roosevelt couldn't help but be impressed by it. Philip felt it was "inevitable" that the two men would meet sooner or later.

François Charles-Roux, at that time an attaché in de Gaulle's cabinet, recalled that on December 10 Philip, who had just returned from Washington, "reported some rather unfavorable impressions that he had received concerning Roosevelt's attitude with respect to the General and to Fighting France." Amazingly, André Philip testified that the President's objections to General de Gaulle were based on the three following points:

1. De Gaulle is a general and the President does not want to establish a precedent that could benefit another general, MacArthur, whose popularity the President envied.

2. General de Gaulle is too close to Russia and Washington fears the development of a type of "armed Jacobinism" for which a close agreement between the USSR and France would serve as a basis.

3. Roosevelt believes that the Allies should prevent the founding of a provisional government which might then be imposed on the French people. He couldn't see the necessity of a united resistance movement before victory was achieved. After the victory, France could, in all freedom, choose for herself her institutions and her own government.[11]

One might well ask whether André Philip's commentary was too theoretical and based on a misunderstanding of the interview. It seems curious that Philip had not warned de Gaulle about Léger's nefarious influence. Everyone in Washington knew how close the latter was to the President.

The idea that recognizing General de Gaulle would somehow increase MacArthur's prestige seems far-fetched. Roosevelt was aware of his own tremendous popularity which none of his generals would ever be able to rival. The fact is that Truman, who was a much less popular President than Roosevelt, easily controlled and even circumscribed the powers of General MacArthur, the hero of the war in the Pacific.

As to France's alleged alliance with the USSR, the idea was quite bizarre. At this point, Roosevelt saw France as a country in ruins with no army to defend itself, and he also knew that Stalin considered France of little importance and treated it with a great deal of contempt.

The third notion, that the various resistance movements should be united only after France's victory, seemed to reflect accurately the political views of the State Department, even though it was never noted in the American report of the conversation. Following the long meeting with the President, Tixier sent a long telegram to London.[12]

On November 28, 1942, Tixier met Undersecretary of State Adolf Berle, who asked him whether he had any news of de Gaulle. Tixier had asked Berle why "this invitation (from Roosevelt to de Gaulle) had been kept so secret." He confided his concern to Berle, saying "General de Gaulle considers himself to be the victim of a great injustice and consequently feels very bitter as a result. If the two men ever come face to face, there might be a confrontation." He insisted further, "There is no need for such a meeting to take place. Does the State Department want to spark a conflict between President Roosevelt and General de Gaulle? This idea would only lead to an explosion of temperaments. Perhaps the State Department would like General de Gaulle to come so that he could discredit himself once and for all."

An indignant Berle retorted that Tixier had lived in the United States long enough to know better. "Our government does not get involved in intrigues of that sort. We invite people to come to Washington for constructive, not destructive, purposes." Naturally, General de Gaulle could sabotage his chances by losing his self-control, but Berle doubted that he would do that. Tixier remained unconvinced and insisted that they do everything within their power to prevent the trip. He stated that he understood the policy of expediency Roosevelt had adopted for North Africa, and added "that he had advised de Gaulle to accept, on a short-term basis, the presence of Darlan as a strictly military one because, in view of the situation, there in fact was no other alternative." This statement, which contradicted what he said to the President in the presence of André Philip, was of course in conflict with General de Gaulle's policy. Tixier pointed out, however, that if Darlan were to land in France at the head of an American-equipped French army, a civil war would break out.[13] Berle replied that the French fleet at Toulon "had been scuttled [in 1942] on Darlan's orders given in 1940, so as not to fall into German hands. This was a fact. Regardless of what they thought of Darlan now, he had induced North Africa to come over to the American side and had brought the French army to fight alongside the Allies. These were military facts that couldn't be denied." Tixier replied that "he would be the first to recognize these military feats. . . . "[14] Tixier would have a new opportunity to change his views regarding Darlan's appointment.

Early in December, I was visited by Admiral Father Thierry D'Argenlieu. He was stern and ascetic in his dark blue uniform, wearing no insignia other than the stars of his rank, the gold leaves of his cap, and the badge of the Free French Navy. D'Argenlieu commanded respect. After having bravely served in the Navy during World War I, he had entered the very strict order of the Discalced Carmelites, of which he became the Provincial for France. At the outbreak of World War II he left his monastery to join the Navy again. Captured by the Nazis in Flanders on June 19, he escaped three days later and made his way to England in a small fishing boat. He immediately placed himself under the orders of General de Gaulle, who at first appointed him Chaplain, and then Captain, of the Navy.[15] It was D'Argenlieu who was credited with having suggested to de Gaulle that the Cross of Lorraine of Joan of Arc be made the symbol for all the Free French Forces. De Gaulle adopted the suggestion. D'Argenlieu accompanied de Gaulle on the ill-fated Dakar expedition, where he was wounded by the Vichy French. Later he became Rear Admiral and High Commissioner for New Caledonia and the French Pacific.

When I met him upon his return from New Caledonia he told me he had had considerable difficulties with General Patch of the United States Army, who had landed with American troops to defend the island against possible Japanese invasion. Patch wanted to negotiate directly with the Admiral as a *local authority;* the Admiral of course referred him to the Comité National in London, the central authority. The State Department refused to negotiate with the Comité National. Finally the conflict was resolved. Patch signed an agreement on February 28, 1942, with the Admiral *in his capacity as representative* of the *Comité National.* Thus the delicate problem of recognition was postponed to a later date.

During a visit which would occur later in December with Cordell Hull, Tixier, accompanied by the Admiral, heard the American position once again on the Darlan affair: The United States must use all available manpower, regardless of its origin, to win the war as quickly as possible and to liberate France at the earliest moment.

The Secretary of State stated that "General de Gaulle was regarded by all as an imposing military figure. For the Americans he held a very special position with regard to France. The Americans only hoped fervently that all the French who were able to participate in the battle to liberate France would put aside their political differences and put everything they had into this war against Hitler." At the conclusion of this meeting, Tixier thanked the Secretary of State, saying, "If General de Gaulle were to visit the United States, he [Tixier] would bring him directly from the plane to Cordell Hull's office at the State Department, so that he could explain the facts to de Gaulle in an identical manner." Surprisingly in light of his previous statements, Tixier said this was "the best response to calm the fears of the Fighting French."

One month later, Tixier asked Sumner Welles for an interview, during which he learned that General de Gaulle's visit had been delayed because of the situation in North Africa. This time Tixier protested, saying that "because General Giraud had been chosen as High Commissioner, it was vital that General de Gaulle's visit to Washington not be delayed." Tixier felt that "it was indispensable that General de Gaulle understand for himself the views of the President and of U.S. government officials because he [Tixier] no longer had it within his power to influence General de Gaulle's decisions."

Sumner Welles realized that Tixier had made a complete about-face concerning the General's proposed visit: in the beginning he opposed it; now he advocated it. The Undersecretary of State told Tixier that this matter depended on the President and that if Roosevelt had anything else to say on this subject, Tixier would be notified.

Tixier then admitted that he in no way disagreed with Sumner Welles' policies and he (Tixier) too felt that *all* the French in North Africa (including all Vichyites) who could be mobilized, should be used in the fight against the Axis powers. He concluded by saying that he did not agree with "the National Committee of de Gaulle in London who were opposed to this policy. . . . "[16]

Once more Tixier insisted on the fact that he did not approve of de Gaulle's policy. It was in contradiction to what he had said to the President in the company of André Philip.

As it turned out, General de Gaulle did not visit the United States during the entire period that he was represented by Adrien Tixier. The President later decided that negotiations concerning the General's invitation would be carried on by his embassy in London only, without informing Tixier.

CHAPTER XVI

❧

Walking with the Devil

In times of great danger, you are permitted
to walk with the Devil until you have crossed
the bridge.

—Franklin D. Roosevelt

While André Philip and Tixier were delivering de Gaulle's letter of October 26 to the State Department, the Americans were feverishly preparing the landing in North Africa. They landed on November 7. André Philip and Tixier met with Sumner Welles on November 12, while Darlan was abandoning Vichy and joining the Allies. Finally, the two Free French envoys met the President on November 20. All these dates coincided with political as well as military operations simultaneously carried out in Washington and North Africa.

The American landing was one of the most daring operations carried out during World War II. It was one of the most complex operations in military history. It presented considerable difficulties of logistics: the hazards of transporting an enormous army through an ocean infested with submarines, the difficulty of keeping such an operation secret, the strategic problems of an unknown land, the grave danger in facing a thoroughly trained and equipped enemy, and also the political divisions among the French themselves. General Marshall, General Eisenhower, Admiral King, the army, and the navy were against it. The risks were too great. Roosevelt, who had maintained the best possible relations with Vichy precisely for such an event, insisted that the vast operation should be carried out, and he was right.

To succeed, the military action had to be preceded by political preparation not only in North Africa, but with Portugal and Spain as well. Those two countries should remain neutral and not oppose the American landing. The military operation, even with the best strategist and the best army, would not succeed if the political operation went wrong.

Roosevelt also felt strongly that the initial attacks should be made by an exclusively American force. De Gaulle and the Free French could not be included because of the St.-Pierre affair, de Gaulle's fiasco at Dakar, and his unpopularity with the Vichy army. Roosevelt considered the British to be hated by the French population because they were suspected of wanting to annex the French colonies to their Empire, while the Americans, on the other hand, he thought were considered disinterested and would be welcomed.[1]

The American army had to land on the Northern coast of Africa, in Morocco and Algeria. It was essential to have the whole civil administration and the army in that region joining and fighting with the Allies. Any opposition would slow down the Americans, although of course they could fight their way through.

There was speculation that, though Marshal Pétain would not come over to our side, neither would he oppose the Americans; that he would declare neutrality instead. In fact, contrary to all expectations, he ordered his troops to fire on the Americans.

There was wishful thinking about General Weygand, hero of World War I, but responsible for the armistice and the capitulation of June 1940. He was approached by American officials who handed him a personal letter from President Roosevelt encouraging him to resist pressure from Vichyites. He immediately turned the letter over to Pétain, showing his loyalty to the Vichy regime. Everyone in Washington was on the lookout to find another suitable leader for the French. Various people were approached without positive results.

Then it was learned in Washington that Honoré Giraud, a French officer with a rank equivalent to five-star general, had escaped from prison in Germany. He was not welcomed when he went to Vichy. Pétain assigned him instead a residence near Lyon. He was secretly approached by the American embassy in Vichy and was asked to lead the French army in North Africa and support the insurrection. He was smuggled out of France and met General Eisenhower at Gibraltar but he proved to be difficult and stubborn. An agreement was finally reached with him just as the Americans were landing on November 8. They met with fierce resistance from the Vichy army and suffered fifteen hundred casualties. It was urgent to stop the useless fighting, so Giraud made an immediate appeal over the radio.

Nobody responded to Giraud, the officers having sworn allegiance to Marshal Pétain. It became necessary that someone else be found immediately. Robert Murphy, the American envoy, learned that Admiral Darlan, a Nazi, heir to Pétain's Vichy government, was in Algiers. He contacted him secretly and convinced him to join the Allied side. Darlan gave orders to the Vichy army in the name of Marshal Pétain, and was obeyed. It was a successful covert operation. Darlan was then made High Commissioner in North Africa, and commander-in-chief of Vichy's naval forces. Under Darlan's orders, Giraud was chief of ground and air forces in an agreement approved by President Roosevelt and Eisenhower. When Pétain found out about the agreement he cabled Darlan to cancel it. Darlan then argued that Pétain was a prisoner of the Germans and no longer free in his decisions. He continued to give orders in the name of Marshal Pétain and was always obeyed. (One of my friends, Louis Vallon, who represented the Resistance in Algiers, told me that the prestige of the name of the Marshal was such in the army that if it was decided to shoot Pétain it would be done in the name of the Marshal.)

The French army then ceased to fight the Americans, and joined them in their offensive against the Nazis. It was different at Toulon, where the large French fleet, the trump card of Darlan, was at anchor. Admiral de Laborde refused to join the Allies in North Africa but would not let the Germans take the fleet, and ordered it scuttled. That day France lost a total of sixty-two modern warships.

Once the secret agreement with Darlan was made known in the United States, a general outcry followed: the public considered that one must never allow the end to justify the means, however important or noble the objective. The entire American press lashed out against the Eisenhower-Darlan agreement which, it believed, resulted from Cordell Hull's underhanded policy of appeasement vis-à-vis Vichy, which had been in effect since the 1940 armistice. Frida Kirchway, editor of the *Nation,* wrote that this was not a reasonable military expedient but rather a grave political error. Africa had produced a historical conflict between two political principles: that of opportunism versus that which followed the straight and frank. Walter Lippmann also protested vigorously and Dorothy Thompson wrote that the war had a moral foundation, that one could not justify making agreements with enemies such as these without disgracing oneself.

Influential political figures such as Vice President Henry Wallace, Secretary of the Treasury Morgenthau, and Archibald MacLeish, among others, protested to the President along with such congressmen as Sol Blum and Claude Pepper. Even more importantly, Wendell

Willkie, the Republican who had run against Roosevelt in the last election, issued a public statement to reporters of the *Herald Tribune* denouncing "the American government who had promised liberty to the French people and who had instead put their oppressors in charge of them." Navy Secretary Stimson barely managed to calm him down, but the American press, particularly in New York, continued to protest: "Are we going to have to deal with Laval for Paris and with Quisling for Oslo? Are we making war just to keep the Nazi agents in control? What liberty are we promising to bring to a people once they have been liberated from the German yoke?"

The British press was even more outraged in its reactions than the American press. In the beginning, Roosevelt had believed himself solely responsible for the human lives engaged in the conflict and wanted to achieve the landing as quickly as possible. He did not stop to consider, however, the political dangers of the operation and he now strove to give public explanations. He gave assurances that his policies had been only a "temporary" expediency and that he would get rid of Darlan as soon as he no longer had need of him. Roosevelt reiterated, in different ways, the famous "Bulgarian, or Serbian, or Rumanian ... or Orthodox Church proverb" that said it was "permissible in times of grave danger to accompany the devil to the far side of the bridge." Roosevelt, who appeared to like this proverb, also quoted the following version: "A saint, in order to safely ford a stream, can perch on the devil's shoulders.") Churchill—fully aware of the exact terms and consequences of the agreement—was indignant, but he could not dissociate himself from Roosevelt, and now he found himself in an awkward position. Churchill cabled his anxiety to Roosevelt: "Let us not underestimate the political damage that has been done to our cause, not only in France, but in Europe, where it is now thought that we are ready to deal with Quisling. Darlan had a heinous past.... Darlan is a turncoat."[3] As for Stalin, he approved wholeheartedly of the Eisenhower-Darlan agreement and echoed that one could use "the devil himself and his grandmother" if indeed it was necessary.

In Vichy, one of Marshal Pétain's staff members of Laval's clique, who was not a friend of Darlan, commented, "We live in sad times when we cannot trust our own traitors anymore."

In Washington President Roosevelt issued the following statement to the press on November 17:

> I accept General Eisenhower's political arrangements made for the time being in Northern and Western Africa.

I thoroughly understand and approve the feelings . . . that, in view of the history of the past two years, no permanent arrangement should be made with Admiral Darlan. People of the United States would never understand the recognition of a reconstitution of the Vichy government in France or in any French territory.

We are opposed to Frenchmen who support Hitler and the Axis. No one in our army has any authority to discuss the future government of France or of the French Empire.

The future French government will be established—not by any individual in metropolitan France or overseas—but by the French people themselves after they have been set free by the victory of the United Nations.

The present temporary arrangement in North and West Africa is only an expedient, justified solely by the stress of battle . . . The present temporary arrangement has accomplished two military objectives . . . (saving American, British, and French lives) and to save time. . . . Temporary arrangements made with Admiral Darlan apply, without exception to the current local situations only . . .[4]

General de Gaulle flew into a violent rage when this statement was made public. He dashed off a scathing note to Admiral Stark, who was Roosevelt's representative to the Free French Movement in London: "You can pay off the traitors, but not with France's honor." Admiral Stark was wise enough to avoid an incident—he refused to accept this note, and sent it back indicating to de Gaulle at the National Committee in London that it must have been sent by mistake. Palewski, chief of de Gaulle's civilian staff, attempted to file it away, but Free France's press and information bureau, headed by the fiery Jacques Soustelle, National Commissioner of Information, leaked its contents to the American and British press. Needless to say, once again Roosevelt was infuriated and the State Department felt slighted by the language de Gaulle used in his note.

Darlan without question had rendered a great service to the landing forces. The facts proved that the army of Vichy accepted his orders, and his orders alone. He stopped the absurd fight against the Americans, and turned the army against the Germans. However, his Vichy past, and his active collaboration with the Nazis during two years, could not be forgotten by the Free French or the underground forces in France. It was inconceivable that he could return to France at the head of a victorious Franco-American army.

There was no political solution in sight. Roosevelt had no way of forcing him to resign without risk of losing the support of the Vichy French army in Algeria.

CHAPTER XVII

The Reluctant Bride at Casablanca

Prima donnas do not always like each other.
—Palewski

An extraordinary event occurred that suddenly changed the complicated setup in North Africa. Admiral François Darlan was shot dead at 3:30 p.m. on Christmas Day in 1942 by a twenty-year-old man, Fernand Bonnier de la Chapelle. He was designated to carry out the murder by a group of young royalists of which he was a member. The Admiral, hit twice in the chest, died instantly. Bonnier was arrested on the spot, gun in hand. He acknowledged the crime and admitted to its premeditation. He was brought to a military court the same night and sentenced to be shot the next morning. General Giraud categorically refused a stay of execution. At midnight, he gave orders that the sentence be carried out. Bonnier was executed at 7:30 a.m. on December 26 and buried in an unmarked grave.[1]

It is curious that General Giraud was in such a hurry to have Bonnier executed. Was he afraid that he would reveal some truth, that he would talk? To this day the full story of Darlan's assassination, or the real motives for it, are still unknown.

In fact Darlan's assassination came as a great relief to everyone—especially to Roosevelt, who was badgered by a press that reproached him on the immoral aspect of his policy towards France. He succeeded in having the Imperial Council created by Darlan name Giraud High Commissioner for North Africa and Chief Commander of the French forces (the council was composed of Boisson, Chatel, Noguès and Bergeret—former Vichy officials). Roosevelt, believing that he had brushed aside de Gaulle for good, cabled to Churchill: "Why does de

Gaulle not go to war? Why doesn't he start for north, by west half west from 'Brazzenville'? It would take him a long time to get to the 'Oasis of Somewhere'!" In his preparatory telegrams for the conference at Casablanca, Roosevelt, seeing that de Gaulle was unwilling to come, wrote to Churchill and made de Gaulle out to be the "bride" whom he was trying to pawn off on Giraud, the "bridegroom."[2]

Nevertheless, de Gaulle thought that since Darlan no longer posed a problem, it would now be possible to unite all the French forces and all the liberated territories. He telegraphed to Giraud asking him for a rendezvous at either Algiers or Chad. De Gaulle wanted that meeting to take place before his personal visit to Washington on December 26 to meet with Roosevelt.

Giraud responded negatively, and by an extraordinary coincidence, Roosevelt postponed de Gaulle's invitation to Washington. De Gaulle was not unaware of Roosevelt's opposition to him. He clearly understood that he was being put off by Roosevelt, who meant to be done with him once and for all. De Gaulle made a statement to the American and British press in London on January 2, 1943, stating that North Africa was in total confusion because Fighting France, which was the sole French authority outside of Vichy, was being excluded. He stated he had suggested in vain a meeting to Giraud with a view to establishing a provisional French authority.

The American papers, which had kept up their constant criticism of the State Department's position with regard to Darlan, had been more or less mollified following his assassination. De Gaulle's press release, however, roused the critics once again. The press campaign against Roosevelt and Cordell Hull's policy resumed more strongly than before. They would ask: "How can we have nothing to do with the Free French, who are the only Frenchmen who fought alongside us since 1940?" The immorality of an American policy that dealt only with traitors, Vichyites, or those who had rallied at the last minute was causing a scandal. What did the United States hope to accomplish by this war? Did it simply want to put the former collaborators back into power or keep them in place, or did it wish to install a new government—one that had fought alongside them in this struggle?

Cordell Hull received telegrams and letters of protest that were unpleasant reminders of those he had received when he interfered in the Saint-Pierre-et-Miquelon operation.

To placate public opinion, Roosevelt tried to explain his policy towards France: he said he was attempting to unify all Frenchmen involved in the struggle to liberate their country, and place all French forces under a single command. He thought that when he passed through Casablanca en route to the conference at Teheran to meet with Stalin he would attempt to reunite the two generals and put Giraud in charge with de Gaulle reporting to him, or at least in a less powerful position. This way, Roosevelt could show the moralists of the American press that he had had a farsighted policy with respect to France, and had in fact succeeded in uniting the French.

Roosevelt asked Churchill to invite de Gaulle to come to Casablanca for a meeting where everything could be arranged.

Before leaving London, de Gaulle had a long meeting with Admiral Stark, who listened carefully to what he had to say. De Gaulle gave him an account of the history of France and her tragedies. Even in her darkest moments, France was somehow always able to rise again, thanks to the leadership of various previously unknown personalities. Such was the case with Joan of Arc, Bonaparte, Clemenceau, and a host of others. Joan of Arc was a peasant, the daughter of illiterate peasants, but she had saved the kingdom.

Stark was very impressed by this historical account. He thought that Roosevelt, who saw France only in relation to her defeat, the Armistice, and the collaboration, would now see an everlasting France, rejuvenated and rising up from the flames like a phoenix. The Admiral urged de Gaulle to repeat this account to President Roosevelt when he met him at Casablanca. What de Gaulle did not know, although he suspected as much, was that Roosevelt and Churchill had agreed to dispose of him before the liberation of France. W. Averell Harriman, the President's friend and advisor at Casablanca, said: "It is obvious that we were mistaken in supporting Giraud, just as the British were mistaken in supporting de Gaulle. It's a pity that no Frenchman has come forward with the courage of de Gaulle but none of his egoism."[3] These remarks by Harriman summed up the atmosphere that prevailed in Washington with regard to de Gaulle, as well as Roosevelt's attitude towards him. It was not going to change.

Upon his arrival at Anfa, close to Casablanca, in January, Churchill had a long meeting with de Gaulle and advised him to remain calm and above all to listen to the President, not to impose any conditions, and to do all he could to get along with General Giraud. "As for me," he said, "when I formed my cabinet, I included political adversaries, even those who favored the Munich agreements, which I opposed. . . ." De Gaulle retorted: "I am not a politician who picks from different parties in order to have a balanced cabinet which is acceptable to the Parliament."[4]

Overshadowing the conflict of personalities there was also a conflict of doctrine between the President and de Gaulle. Roosevelt considered that France, in capitulating to Germany, had accepted the status of satellite state and had lost her independence. Furthermore, due to the complete occupation of France since November 1942, she had lost even the semblance of existence as a nation; therefore there was no civil authority left, and the Allied military commander had full power of administration of freed territories until victory and liberation of the captive nation, when elections could take place.

De Gaulle, on the contrary, strongly held that the French nation had never left the battlefield, that if the land of France was occupied, its soul, represented by him, had not died and instead fought with the Allies. This, the true France, was still at war, had retained its democratic institutions, and had never died. The Republic had not ceased to exist. According to those institutions the civilian government ruled its military. The consequence of this doctrine was that de Gaulle and the National Committee in London represented a civil government and the continuation of a republic entitled to rule and command its military. De Gaulle, its president, being the civil authority, had to have power over General Giraud, military commander of the French Forces.

This doctrine of the transfer of legitimacy of an occupied nation to its free citizens fighting abroad was a new concept. Roosevelt refused to accept it. Of course General Giraud opposed it because it placed him, a five-star general, under one of lesser rank.

The long-awaited meeting between Roosevelt and de Gaulle took place on January 22, 1943, in a magnificent villa prepared for the President's visit at Anfa, and although it was customary for chiefs of state to use interpreters at their meetings, Roosevelt wanted to put the general at ease by speaking to him in French.

He greeted de Gaulle with a smile and a *si content de vous voir.** The President's knowledge of French was not very good and de Gaulle's French—classic and sophisticated—was not easy for him to understand. As a result the interpreters who were in attendance had to interrupt and to participate in the discussions. This of course created much confusion. It seems that Roosevelt had stated that he could not recognize de Gaulle's committee because de Gaulle "had not been

---

*"So happy to see you." It has been repeated to me that to show his friendship he called de Gaulle by his first name. One can only wonder about the reaction of the solemn general.

elected," to which de Gaulle replied that Joan of Arc, who had saved France, had not been elected either. Other historic examples fell on deaf ears and Roosevelt later recalled only the name of "Jeanne d'Arc," about whom he was to make many malicious remarks. He was already immensely enjoying making fun of this towering general with the austere and solemn demeanor. The jokes and ridicule that Roosevelt considered to be witty were repeated often and in many versions that made the rounds in Washington and even in foreign capitals. Roosevelt would be saying to de Gaulle: "The other day you told me that you were Joan of Arc, now you tell me that you are Clemenceau. Who are you?" And de Gaulle would reply: "I am both." Roosevelt then would say: "You must choose one or the other because you can't be both."[5] Those who were closest to the President embellished the stories: de Gaulle would have supposedly claimed to be Joan of Arc one time, Colbert the next, or Bayard or Bonaparte or Foch . . . and undoubtedly Louis XIV as well. Churchill, who had his moments of violent disagreement with de Gaulle, was asked by Roosevelt if it was true that de Gaulle saw himself as Joan of Arc. To which Churchill was said to have replied: "Yes, Mr. President, he thinks he is Joan of Arc, but unfortunately my bishops won't let me burn him." Someone later asked Churchill if he had made this statement, to which he replied: "No, but it's so witty, I'm sorry I didn't."

De Gaulle was not unaware of these sarcastic remarks, but he never responded to them or indicated whether or not he was hurt by them. In his *Mémoires,* he spoke of Roosevelt with respect. He noted, however, that during his meeting with him, although "his interlocutor pretended to be alone," de Gaulle detected "shadows at the far side of the upper gallery and he noticed the curtains stirring slightly in the corners."[6] Harry Hopkins later disclosed that several secretaries were listening in and that armed security men were watching over the President. Because of these shadowy presences, a most unusual atmosphere prevailed during the Roosevelt–de Gaulle conference at Anfa.

Harry Hopkins would write about this interview: "I noticed that a whole secret service detachment was hidden behind the curtains and above the gallery of the salon. I caught a glimpse of a 'tommy gun' that was held by one of these men. . . . One could not risk the possibility of an accident happening to the President. None of this transpired when Giraud saw Roosevelt."[7] He added: "That evening we were most amiable to each other, but we both agreed to be very vague on the French question." In his *Memoirs,* Churchill noted that "contrary to all expectations, they got along very well but very little could

be done to bring them into accord."⁸ De Gaulle remarked with regard
to Roosevelt at the end of that evening that it was "without goodwill"
that Roosevelt looked upon him.⁹

One could say that the welcome was less warm. The next day, they
met in the same place, and had a talk which was friendly but
restrained. The President told de Gaulle how sorry he was that there
had been no understanding reached between him and Giraud. With
American public opinion uppermost in his mind, Roosevelt asked de
Gaulle if he would consent to be photographed with him, Churchill,
and Giraud. "Of course," replied de Gaulle. Roosevelt then asked if
he would go so far as to shake Giraud's hand in front of the camera.
"I shall do that for you," de Gaulle answered in English. The President
was delighted. He would have photos to prove to the American press
the extent to which his policies had succeeded, now that he had a hand
in fostering French unity. Roosevelt, however, would not go so far as
to soften his stand in the slightest with respect to Free France.

Shortly afterwards, on May 8, Roosevelt wrote to Churchill:

> I am sorry, but the conduct of the BRIDE continues to be more and
> more aggravated. His course of attitude is well nigh intolerable. . . .
>
> The war in North Africa has terminated successfully without any
> material aid from de Gaulle, and the civil situation with all its dangers
> seems to be working out well. . . .
>
> However de Gaulle is without question taking his vicious propa-
> ganda staff down to Algiers to stir up strife between the various ele-
> ments including Arabs and Jews. He is expanding his present group of
> agitators who are working up counter demonstrations and even riots.
>
> Unfortunately too many people are catching on to the fact that these
> disturbances are being financed in whole or in part by British govern-
> ment funds.
>
> De Gaulle may be an honest fellow but he has the Messianic com-
> plex, further he has an idea that the people of France itself are strongly
> behind him personally.
>
> This I doubt, I think the people of France are behind the Free French
> Movement; that they do not know de Gaulle and that their loyalty is
> to the fine objectives of the movement when it was started and to the
> larger phase of it which looks to the restoration of France.
>
> This is why I become more and more disturbed by the continued
> machinations of de Gaulle.
>
> In my judgment there should be a reorganization of the French
> National Committee, removing some of the people we know to be
> impossible such as [André] Philip . . .
>
> Furthermore I am inclined to think that when we get to France itself,

we will have to regard it as a military occupation run by British and American generals. . . . I think that this may be necessary for six months or even a year after we get in France. . . . If they [the people of France] only knew what you and I know about de Gaulle himself, they would continue to be for the movement but not for its present leader in London.[10]

Roosevelt suggested naming General Giraud to the top post and dismissing General de Gaulle. As for the French Committee of National Liberation, the President believed that it should not act as a provisional government, but rather in an advisory capacity.

It must be added that General Giraud was full of illusions regarding his own prestige; he wanted top command, with de Gaulle in second place. "After all, de Gaulle served as a colonel under me."[11] Besides, Giraud believed that he had favorably impressed Roosevelt and Churchill. (I later met General Giraud at the United Nations and must confess I was not at all impressed. He seemed to me precisely the kind of officer who had assured the defeat of France: reactionary, self-important, arrogant, racist and dull. His only claim to military fame was that he was captured by the Nazis and escaped.)

The meeting at Anfa did nothing to modify Roosevelt's position. As for de Gaulle, he was in a better state of mind. When he left the first meeting, he said to Palewski: "Roosevelt is a patrician. . . . " De Gaulle had been seduced by Roosevelt's attitude and refinement, this man about whom so much ill had been said to him. He confessed to having been "strongly impressed by the inverviews that they had had, and convinced of their great usefulness."[12] Moreover, Palewski noted that "Roosevelt felt that he had in front of him another 'prima donna' and 'prima donnas' don't always like each other. And then there was the political conflict. The French residents in the United States, especially Alexis Léger, were determined to convince Roosevelt that France no longer existed, which justified their own attitude, and that it was up to him, Roosevelt, to decide anything that concerned France. . . ."[13]

The impression de Gaulle made on Roosevelt is clearly stated in Eleanor Roosevelt's autobiography. Upon his return from Casablanca, Roosevelt said to his wife: "General de Gaulle is a soldier, patriotic, devoted to his country, but on the other hand, he is a politician and a fanatic and there are, I think, in him, almost the makings of a dictator."[14]

She added: "It was not altogether a happy meeting."

In any case de Gaulle, who did not harbor any illusions, held a press conference on February 9, where he revealed what had taken place at

Anfa. His report did not concur with the communiqués published by the American press. The General pointed out the ulterior motives of the Americans, who reproached the Fighting French for getting involved in politics, hoping that in this way they could "prevent France from having [a policy] of its own."[15]

> President Roosevelt cabled to Churchill on June 17: "I am fed up with de Gaulle and the secret personal and political machinations of the Committee. These last few days prove that there is no possibility of our working with de Gaulle. . . . I am absolutely convinced that he has been and is now injuring our war effort and that he is a very dangerous threat to us. . . . The time has arrived when we must break with him . . . . We must divorce ourselves from de Gaulle because first he has proven to be unreliable, uncooperative, and disloyal to both our governments. Second, he has more recently been interested far more in political machinations than he has in the prosecution of the war and these machinations have been carried on without our knowledge and to the detriment of our military interests. One result of this scheming on the part of de Gaulle has been that Eisenhower had to give half of his time to a purely *local* political situation which de Gaulle has accentuated. The war is so urgent and our military operations so serious and fraught with danger that we cannot have them menaced any longer by de Gaulle.
>
> Our two countries have solemnly pledged that they will liberate the French Republic and when we drive the Germans out, return that country to the control of the sovereign French people. This pledge we renew."[16]

Meanwhile, Roosevelt persisted in supporting General Giraud as "the only French leader" in North Africa. Earlier he had also helped him to establish military bureaus in Washington and New York, to bolster his forces. The one established in New York would compete with the military bureau of my own delegation and create further confusion and division among the French.

CHAPTER XVIII

❖

The Sailors of "Le Richelieu"

Never has France had a more powerful and more efficient navy.

—Winston Churchill

It was shortly after the Americans landed in North Africa that General Giraud's delegation opened its own military recruiting office in New York, in a lavish building on Fifth Avenue, not far from Free France's military recruiting office. With America now at war, and the Neutrality Act no longer in force, it became possible to recruit volunteers for Allied armies. The proximity of the two French recruitment offices, both of which were seeking volunteers to work towards the liberation of France, caused a new source of confusion to all. Sailors who wanted to sign up with de Gaulle saw the tricolor flag outside both offices and unwittingly signed up with General Giraud's forces. Some discovered this too late, after having signed their enlistment papers; the Free French delegation was unable to renegotiate on their behalf. The Free French office advised them to remain where they were and to continue the fight for the liberation of a single united France.

Giraud's military delegation protested loudly when the number of sailors leaving their ships to sign up with the Free French naval forces reached significant—and for the Giraudists, alarming—levels.

One such ship lost 60 percent of its crew. Another, the *Richelieu*, a magnificent modern battleship completed in 1940, berthed in New York on February 15, 1943, to undergo emergency repairs for damage it had sustained when it helped repulse the British and Free French fleet at Dakar. The *Richelieu* lost 350 members of its crew to the Free French recruiting office in New York.

Henri de Kérillis came to my office in a state of indescribable agitation: "It's scandalous! Your press agent is luring sailors from Giraud to de Gaulle. I am the son of an admiral, a patriot and a Gaullist.* I cannot permit such deplorable desertions to take place. You must put an end to this scandal immediately. Sailors cannot abandon their ships. Behavior that runs contrary to discipline should in no way be encouraged." I replied that my office had not engaged in any propaganda efforts with respect to crews from the *Richelieu,* that the pay in the Free French Naval Forces was less than what they now earned, that we were offering neither bonuses nor special promotions, and that I would never encourage defections from one navy to the other. "I think," I told him, "that if men wish to leave their ships to come over to our side, it is because they are convinced that the liberation of France is not far off. They prefer to return home after having fought with a unit distinguished by its great actions to crewing on a ship immobilized by its neutrality while others were doing the fighting." I also told him that I had learned that many of the sailors had lost confidence in their officers, who had been brainwashed during the past two years with anti-American, pro-Vichy, pro-German, and most certainly, anti-Gaullist propaganda. "In any case," I continued, "I am not authorized to give instructions to refuse volunteer enlistments. Any complaints should be addressed to Captain Gayrald of the FNFL, naval attaché to our Washington delegation, or to Adrien Tixier, head of the Free French delegation in Washington." I concluded, "I will inquire into this matter myself."

A furious de Kérillis telephoned Washington, and our delegation immediately sent telegrams to London, where Admiral Auboyneau and General de Gaulle himself decided that in principle we could not turn away Free French volunteers, regardless of where they came from. That had been the very basis of the Free French movement since its inception on June 18, 1940; we were a movement of volunteers.

It should be noted that Admiral Fénard, General Giraud's representative, with whom I had a short meeting, refused to make any inflammatory comments on the matter and did his best to avoid increasing

---

*Many people at that time considered themselves "Gaullists" while rejecting de Gaulle himself.

the tension that existed between the two recruiting offices. Nevertheless, General Giraud's delegation believed that this problem not only
put the future of his fleet in doubt, but also had the appearance of a
genuine plebiscite—with political overtones. Giraud felt that an
appeal should be made to the American authorities, who had never
displayed an excess of sympathy towards the Gaullists. Accordingly,
Giraud on March 3 obtained an important decision from the Navy
Secretary, the text of which was published in all the newspapers:

> The American government is of the opinion that the friction that exists
> between French factions imperils the war effort. It [the American
> government] will do all that is necessary to suppress it. It should be
> pointed out that the United States will help with the repair of the
> French ships to enable them to put out to sea as soon as possible and
> take part in the liberation of their country. The French ships now in
> the ports, once rearmed, will be very useful in operations to come, and
> the desertions impair the usefulness of these ships.
>
> These quarrels between Frenchmen only serve to hinder the military
> projects of the Allies, and the United States government wants them to
> come to an end.
>
> The arrest of the sailors who deserted has been coordinated by the
> Departments of Justice and of the Navy and as of today, twelve French
> sailors are being detained on Ellis Island. The deserters will be consid-
> ered as undesirables and will be exposed to the sanctions of the Immi-
> gration Authorities.

The Navy Secretary's decision was obviously motivated more by
political than military considerations. It violated the August 2, 1941,
agreement between the Free French National Committee of London
and the American government, which agreed to treat the FNFL crews
passing through the United States in the same manner as crews of
Allied ships, who were granted automatic residency permits.

The *Richelieu* conflict reached the President, who was told all manner of untruths. Agents from my delegation as well as women from
Free French committees were allegedly visiting bars in order to entice
sailors, offering them money to win them over to our side. The President, who understood the political consequences of such actions, was
furious. He bitterly reproached Churchill, accusing him of complicity
if only because de Gaulle's military operations were bankrolled by
Britain.

Admiral Stark in London lodged an official protest with General de
Gaulle, who replied that these defections were "totally spontaneous"
and stemmed from deep-rooted and serious discontent. French sailors

who had been forced to fire on British and Allied ships, and who had been fed Nazi propaganda during the last three years, no longer trusted their officers. Vichyite propaganda was so intense that Pétain's portraits could be found all over the ships and, shocking as it may seem, most of the officers openly declared that they were hoping for a German victory. To the argument that the warships would be immobilized by the lack of sailors, De Gaulle replied that most of the crews would be unemployed anyway during the lengthy repairs. These remaining sailors could replace the ones who had left for the Free French navy. De Gaulle also offered crews to replace the ones which Giraud had lost.

The American press, often critical of its government's decisions and hostile to any action that threatened the principles of liberty and freedom of choice, was quick to side with the twelve sailors, who, in spite of the propaganda to which they had been subjected, still preferred to fight with the Free French.

Tixier was summoned to the State Department, where he was requested to obtain a resolution from London against the so-called deserters and to order the recruitment bureau of Free France to refuse any enlistment of sailors. He replied that the orders from London were categorical: volunteers could not be turned away. He telephoned me asking if I would see to the defense of the twelve sailors being detained by American authorities. To this end, I contacted the famous trial lawyer Arthur Garfield Hayes, who had been very active for the American Civil Liberties Union and whose specialty was trials involving human rights. Hayes considered it his duty to defend these sailors and therefore refused to accept a fee for his work.

Needless to say, these events only served to divide the French colony even further. Henri de Kérillis came to see me again to read the vindictive words that he had written in his notebook on this matter: "In June of 1940, I had rallied enthusiastically to de Gaulle's cause which called all Frenchmen in France and throughout the word into lofty combat at the side of the Allies, putting aside politics, and practicing self-denial, sacrifice, and honor. Today, I renounce forever a Gaullist movement whose intrigues divide Frenchmen and infuriate our Allies. . . ."[1]

That same day, the *New York Post,* which was very sympathetic towards the sailors, described how Immigration agents had arrested the French seamen who had left the *Richelieu* and joined the Free French Navy: "at least twelve of them have been sent to Ellis Island for deportation or internment. All of them had been carrying papers

stating that they had signed up with General de Gaulle's forces." Once
again the point was made: "These sailors had no confidence in their
officers. . . . They were not deserters but rather wanted to fight under
officers whom they trusted."

The following day, other newspapers, such as the *New York Herald
Tribune* and the *New York Times,* spoke out on this sensational event.
In the March 11 edition of the *Herald Tribune,* Walter Lippmann
wrote an article entitled "General Giraud and the Rubicon."
Lippmann did not openly confront the problem of the sailors' predi-
cament but rather studied the general problem of French policy in
North Africa, and of the Republican constitution. He made it clear
that "it was unwise to supply weapons and war material to armed
forces whose leaders might not have the same ideology as the
Americans."

On March 18, in a widely read editorial entitled "Why?" the *Herald
Tribune* analyzed the sailors' plight in a sympathetic fashion and
reduced the entire problem to one of principles. It emphasized in particular the importance of rejecting the ideology behind Vichy's
national revolution. It concluded by stating: " . . . but it seems that, in
certain circles in Washington, the feeling is that General de Gaulle
deserves to be punished for having been stubbornly right all along."

Radio commentators were also quick to intervene in the debate on
Free France's behalf: Johannes Steel, of radio station WMCA; Lisa
Sergio, station WXQ12; Hans Jacob, station WOV.

In the face of a defense presented by Arthur Garfield Hayes, Attorney General Francis Biddle decided that no more sailors who had
shifted camps would be arrested for illegal entry into the United States
until the twelve who were already being detained on Ellis Island were
judged. He announced that a test case would be made of those twelve
internees.

What was the administration actually trying to prove by all this?
The press was quick to publish its findings: If the sailors were allowed
to leave their ships, massive desertions would ensue. Half, if not two-
thirds, of the *Richelieu*'s 1,500 men would leave. The battleship, even
after being repaired, would still be unable to take to the seas again.

American naval authorities hoped that the arrest of the twelve seamen would serve as a deterrent powerful enough to prevent a similar
action by the rest of the crew.

The *New York Times,* strongly influenced by the State Department's views, printed an editorial on March 17, criticizing the actions
of the twelve sailors, declaring that General Giraud had "reestablished

the laws of the Republic and that, to date, these laws had never permitted crews to choose either their officers or the moment when they would do battle. Sailors who choose their own officers commit acts of military insurrection punishable by the laws of the Republic." The *Times* added that these acts were also punishable by American law. It was undoubtedly the harshest article ever to have been written by the New York press with regard to Fighting France.

Radio commentators such as Johannes Steel and Waverly Root leveled specific accusations at the captain and the officers of the *Richelieu*. They reproached them for, as their own sailors had put it, their "fascist behavior." In reply to these accusations, the *Times* published a letter that Captain Deramon of the *Richelieu* had sent to Admiral Fénard to be delivered to Navy Secretary Knox. In this letter, he stated "that he did not have the slightest desire to collaborate with the Germans," a declaration that became the source of ironic commentaries by other newspapers.

The case was brought before the New York Supreme Court, where defense lawyer Hayes described in detail the moral dilemma the sailors were facing. These men, he said, had not wanted to desert but, having lost confidence in their officers, were asking to be allowed to enlist with the Free French navy to fight under leaders they could trust. The crew of the *Richelieu* served one of the most powerful modern battleships afloat. Early in 1940 when it took to sea, the Germans were the enemy to be fired upon. After the armistice of June 1940 they docked at Dakar (West Africa) and had fired on British and Free French warships. On September 24, 1942, they received orders to fire on the Americans. After being repaired in American dockyards in 1943 they took to the sea to combat the Germans again.

It is quite amazing that the *Richelieu*'s officers, by a blind twist of discipline, under the orders of turncoat Admiral Darlan, were changing enemies at least once a year. First the Germans, then the British and the Free French, then the Americans and finally the Germans again were the enemy. No doubt the crews were confused and wanted to join the Free French Navy, for whom the enemy, the Germans, had always been the same.

The American judicial system has always acted in an independent manner and allowed the plea of conscientious objection. Hayes won his case on April 2, 1943. The sailors were set free and were allowed to set sail for London, where they joined the Free French navy. They participated in the war in the Atlantic and in the landings in France a year later.

The acquittal of the sailors was hailed in the press on April 2 as a welcome gesture. It was followed by the expression of relief in all the newspapers.

The sailors reported to the journalists that while they were being detained, they had been unusually well treated by Immigration authorities, who were openly sympathetic to their cause. Moreover, they had received a considerable volume of mail from unknown Americans who wanted to show their support for the sailors' cause.

In many cases, these letters contained more than mere moral support; they often were accompanied by financial assistance as well. The Free French delegation in New York received countless letters, some of which contained checks in amounts as large as $250. These contributions were an attempt to brighten the lot of the prisoners, who had become the focus of widespread public interest. The other sailors, those who had not been arrested, waiting for the results of the case before the court, were enthusiastically welcomed by the people of New York. The public applauded and hailed them when they appeared in the streets wearing their French uniforms and their berets with the red pompom. The French naval beret became incredibly popular; a chocolate manufacturer of Fifth Avenue even sold round blue boxes of candy with a red pompom on the top.

It should be pointed out that, for the most part, the press and radio commentators had once again taken the side of Fighting France in 1943, as they had done once before in 1941.

Finally, on April 24, an article in the *Times* attracted a great deal of national attention. "An agreement," it said, "was reached between the National French Committee's delegation in Washington and General Giraud's mission under whose terms a combined commission composed of Fighting French officers, Giraud's North African former Vichy officers, and U.S. Navy officers would in the future judge the case of every sailor who wished to leave his ship to rally to de Gaulle's cause. Authorization would be granted only under extenuating circumstances."

The aggressive campaign waged by the press from February 22 through April 2, 1943, reflected a public opinion that also strongly opposed the United States government's decision against the sailors. In the case of the *Richelieu* as with the seizure of the islands of Saint-Pierre-et-Miquelon, the American public sided with de Gaulle against

---

*This, however, was not the position of most of the French refugees in the United States, who remained hostile to de Gaulle.

their own government. In both cases, Frenchmen outside of France, who were free to express their opinion, overwhelmingly rallied to Free France's side.* In the case of Saint-Pierre the figure was 98 percent. Had the American government not intervened, a very large percentage of sailors, without question a majority of them, would have done the same.

The case of the *Richelieu* was not an isolated one. At the same time crews of the *Montcalm* and the *Fantasque* left their warships to join de Gaulle's navy. Across the Atlantic in Greenock, Scotland, seven of Vichy's ships were immobilized by the departure of almost all of their sailors. The United States Marines actually boarded a French ship, *La Jamaique,* to prevent the departure of all of its crew, who refused to remain under the orders of Vichy officers. When it became clear that the men could not be forced to stay on against their will, the vessel was placed under the leadership of General de Gaulle's navy and was allowed to leave with its jubilant crew flying the Cross of Lorraine. These incidents were repeated many times.

The press, the radio, and American public opinion, so often critical of their government's stance, had a field day. The State Department, which had been outspoken in 1941, was more careful this time and let the Navy Secretary issue the public statements. Washington authorities by now had to take into account the overwhelming evidence: neither Pétain, Darlan, nor Giraud had ever obtained a plebiscite in their favor. People began to ask themselves whether this situation would be repeated in France once the country was liberated. As for de Gaulle, he had already won his case. . . .

Hervé Alphand, who later became ambassador of France to Washington, was in the United States at this time. He had met with many sailors from the *Richelieu,* the *Montcalm,* and the *Fantasque* and concluded that "they were living proof . . . of the impossibility, so many times proclaimed by us, of subjecting men to the discipline of leaders whom they hated." Alphand testified that the sailors left their ships to enroll in the naval forces of Free France because they could not serve under and obey orders from officers "intoxicated by Nazi propaganda." These officers were even ready to fight the Americans, whom they considered to be very reluctant allies. One such officer declared: "We are fighting to liberate our leader, the Marshal." Another officer, in a drunken state in a bar, was heard crying: "Long live Germany!"[2]

In view of the misinformation circulating at this time, I myself undertook to conduct a thorough inquiry into the matter. I interrogated many sailors and drafted several reports, which I sent to London. I discovered without a shadow of a doubt that none of the sailors of the *Richelieu* had been influenced by Free French propaganda to leave their ships in order to join de Gaulle.

The existence of the two separate French recruiting offices finally ended when Giraud resigned his co-presidency of the *Comité* (CFLN) in Algiers. De Gaulle was then formally appointed its only President on October 3.

The division among the French thus finally came to an end. There was now one single army, one single fleet, and one single leader for the first time since June 1940. This union of all French people was of major importance in view of the great events that we could foresee.

CHAPTER XIX

❧

C'est la Guerre

It was as early as January 1944 that our office was hearing rumors of the impending Allied invasion of Europe. The news excited us. We were enthusiastic and hopeful for its success. The long awaited Allied attack would surely be the beginning of the end of Hitler, and it renewed our faith that France would reclaim its sovereignty. But no sooner had we learned the news than new conflicts were brewing between Free France and the United States.

We were informed by the Department of State, for example, that France's Gaullist government was not recognized as a "government in exile" like the governments of Norway, Belgium, or the Netherlands, and, as a result, France would be liberated by American forces and governed by an American military administration. We were going to be treated as an enemy nation even though we did have an active and Allied established provisional government in Algiers. A military school under the name of Allied Military Government of Occupied Territories (AMGOT) had been established since early May 1942 in Charlottesville (Virginia) and was training American military officers to act as civil administrators of occupied countries, France included. We were going to be treated like Italy, an enemy nation. Members of AMGOT would replace or work side by side with former Vichy officials. Norway, Belgium, and the Netherlands, whose governments in exile were officially recognized by the United States, would avoid this humiliation.

The Department of State also informed us early in 1944 that they intended to print French currency, French francs, for use by the Allied forces in France. De Gaulle was indignant. This policy of denying any French sovereignty was an affront to the Free French Forces and to the French underground, which was fighting with the Allies. De

Gaulle decided that he would print his own "francs." On June 12, 1944, Roosevelt sent Churchill a letter concerning de Gaulle's currency, explaining that he did not mind any statement made by de Gaulle in its regard "provided it is clear that he is acting entirely on his own responsibility and without our concurrence he can sign any statements on currency in whatever capacity he likes, even that of the King of Siam . . ." Roosevelt added, "It seems clear that prima donnas do not change their spots."[1]

I accompanied and assisted Pierre Mendès-France when he was sent by our government in Algiers with the mission to protest the American plan and to offer the use of a French currency to be printed by the CFLN (the provisional government of the French Republic). Though the Treasury was sympathetic to our cause the Department of State was adamantly opposed. Despite continuous protests from de Gaulle, the American "francs" were printed in the United States and the liberated French population accepted them.

It was in this atmosphere of suspicion and hostility that de Gaulle received, in Algiers, Churchill's invitation to come to London immediately. When de Gaulle arrived in London on June 4, two days before D-Day, he was informed for the first time of the momentous landing operation. Considerable forces would be sent to capture bases, ports, and bridgeheads. An important American army was already in England ready to strike; a much greater one was on its way from the United States.

What happened during the two crucial days that preceded the landing in Normandy is, in my opinion, vital to a true understanding of the explosive force of de Gaulle's character. It is for this reason that I include it here. The General at first expressed to the Prime Minister his admiration for the overall planning of the gigantic operation ahead. In his *Mémoires* he states that Great Britain,

> . . . after so many ordeals so valiantly endured and thanks to which she had saved Europe, should today be the base for the attack on the Continent and should engage such tremendous forces in it, was a striking justification of the courageous policy which [Churchill] himself personified since the darkest days. Whatever continuing events were still to cost France, she was proud . . . to be in line at the side of the Allies for the liberation of Europe.

Churchill then suggested that they might talk about "political matters." That was obviously the last thing to say to the general, who replied: "Political matters? What for?" Churchill said that he had been in correspondence with President Roosevelt, who now wished to have a meeting with him concerning important matters, such as the equipment of the French Forces, the administration of France.... De Gaulle, who was faced by a fait accompli, angrily replied that there was no hurry and that he "considered that at this moment it was better that he would be here than in Washington."[2] The Prime Minister insisted that it was necessary to discuss the question of the future administration of France. De Gaulle replied again that there was no hurry, and added in French, "C'est la guerre, faites-la, on verra après." (This is war, get on with it, we will see later.)

Again Churchill insisted; after the battle it was important that General de Gaulle go to America, where he would discuss questions concerning the currency, and the administration of liberated territories. He was sure that the President could be convinced. De Gaulle again repeated: "C'est la guerre, faites-la, on verra après."[3]

The Mémoires of de Gaulle show that Churchill made matters worse when he insisted once again. De Gaulle then thundered:

> Why do you think I have to submit my candidacy for authority in France to Roosevelt? The French Government exists. I have nothing to ask in this respect of the United States nor of Great Britain. This being said it is important for all the Allies that the relations between the French Administration and the military command should be organized. Nine months ago we proposed as much. Now since the armies are about to land in France, I understand your haste....

After protesting again concerning the currency that would be used by Allied armies in France, he concluded ironically:

> I expect that tomorrow General Eisenhower, acting on the instructions of the President of the United States and in agreement with you, will proclaim that he is taking France under his authority. How can you expect us to come to terms on this basis? Allez faites la guerre avec votre fausse monnaie (Go ahead, wage war with your fake currency).[4]

This was repeated to me by General Bethouard, who was present at the meeting. Churchill answered that whether or not de Gaulle would visit the President was a matter for the General to decide, but he strongly advised him to do so. He also concluded that he would not ask the President to give to de Gaulle the title deed for France. He considered however that the Comité de Libération Nationale should be the principal political group with whom the Allies should deal in France.

Time was of the essence. In the afternoon of the same day, Churchill and de Gaulle went to the headquarters of General Eisenhower, who explained his plan for the landing in France. De Gaulle states with admiration in his *Mémoires:* "I could see that in this extremely complex and hazardous operation the Anglo-American gift for planning had been exercised to the maximum degree."[5] The conversation was friendly until Eisenhower told de Gaulle that on the day of the landing he would broadcast a proclamation to the French people. De Gaulle, angry, shouted, "You! Broadcast a proclamation to the French people? By what right? And what will you tell them?" Eisenhower handed him the typewritten proclamation, prepared in Washington urging the French nation to carry out his orders. It declared "that in the administration, everyone will continue to fulfill his functions unless contrary instructions are received. Once France is liberated, the French people themselves will choose their representatives and their government." De Gaulle considered that Eisenhower appeared to be "taking charge of our country" though he was merely an Allied general entitled to command troops, but not the least qualified to intervene in the country's government.[6] De Gaulle saw there a repetition of the Algerian problem, where the Allies did not recognize a French civil government. Obviously he felt that Roosevelt wanted to maintain whoever Vichy had appointed until general elections would finally allow the creation of a new French government. This proclamation did not mention General de Gaulle, the Free French, or the *Comité de Libération Nationale* of Algiers, and, of course, it did not mention de Gaulle's provisional government. It maintained the same political position that President Roosevelt had held for the past four years.

Eisenhower replied to de Gaulle's protests by saying that it was only a draft and that he could present his own version. The next day, on the morning of June 5, de Gaulle sent Eisenhower his corrected version of the proclamation. It was too late—the original proclamation that had been printed in the United States was already in the planes and ready to be rained upon France a few hours later.

De Gaulle was furious. The invasion of France that he had expected for years would be done without him, and finally the strategy of Roosevelt was going to eliminate him at the last hour.

At 4 a.m. on June 6 General Eisenhower made the decision to launch the great invasion of Europe. De Gaulle was informed that the Allied leaders (the King of Norway, the Queen of the Netherlands, the Grand Duchess of Luxembourg, the Prime Minister of Belgium) would broadcast to their people. Eisenhower then would speak and finally de Gaulle was invited to speak to the French people.

De Gaulle refused. He said that by speaking after the American general he would appear to sanction what he had said, of which he disapproved. "If I were to broadcast," he said, "it could be only at a different hour and outside the series."[7]

De Gaulle took further action to make his opposition clear. Despite the protests of American and British military officials, he withdrew the two hundred French liaison officers who were to embark for France and assist the Allied armies in the landing. Thus France would not participate in the operation because there was no agreement between the American and British governments and General de Gaulle concerning the future administration of France.

Finally, however, de Gaulle at 6 p.m., long after the landing had taken place, decided to make his appeal to the French people through the BBC. "The decisive battle has begun. . . . Of course it is the battle of France, and it is France's battle. . . . For the sons of France, whoever they may be, the simple and sacred duty is to fight the enemy with all available means. . . . *The directions issued by the French Government* and by the French leaders who have been delegated to issue them must be followed to the letter . . . " De Gaulle did not mention his Allies, the Americans or the British. He directed the French to obey *his* authority alone, and precisely he omitted to mention a *provisional* government. He thus proclaimed himself the Government of France. Needless to say, Roosevelt and Churchill were furious. They could not reverse the situation and found themselves in a delicate position. They had no alternative but to negotiate with de Gaulle's committee for the civil administration of liberated France.

That same day, June 6, a gigantic American, British, and Canadian army was landing on the coast of Normandy, in order to battle German forces, at a time when there was no agreement between General de Gaulle and the future liberators of Europe. We at the Embassy were appalled when news of the clashes between the Allies reached us through coded telegrams from London. I remember our press attaché, Jean Baubé, commenting that his job had become a very difficult, if not an unpleasant, one. At this crucial stage of the war we had believed that we were all united in the ultimate battle to liberate Europe.

Those unfortunate quarrels between Allied leaders at that very moment were not a secret. They shocked French and Americans alike. The discord would never end! In Washington, the press did not hesitate to express their misgivings. Important American individuals, in particular some military men who were alarmed by the situation, were going to intercede on de Gaulle's behalf.

William J. Donovan, whom I had met several times before, was an energetic and charismatic officer. A World War I hero, former American public prosecutor, eminent ambassador and jurist, creator and founder of the Office of Strategic Services (later the C.I.A.), he was going to play an important role in Franco-American relations. He felt a deep sense of friendship toward France which he had acquired during the course of World War I. Donovan felt, and rightly so, that this war could be brought to a satisfactory conclusion only if the person presiding over America's destiny worked in harmony with the leader of the French Resistance. The agencies working for Donovan were quick to inform him of the scope of the French Resistance and of the importance of the role it could play by severing German communication lines and by liberating portions of France's national territory before the advance of the Allied armies. In his reports, he emphasized the sacrifices and risks that these freedom fighters had taken. In his conversations with Roosevelt, Donovan explained that not all of these underground groups approved of the make-up of the Committee (CFLN) in Algiers. However, the majority, regardless of their attitude toward de Gaulle, were convinced, in the interest of their national insurrection movement, that it was necessary to consider de Gaulle as the only symbol of the Resistance.[8]

Later on, during de Gaulle's visit, in the course of preliminary discussions with the representatives of Dewavrin (Colonel Passy) in Washington, Donovan declared that he was "in favor of establishing a civil and military representative of the General, under the auspices of the Allied government . . . and that these Free French forces of the Interior, the FFI, should form part of Eisenhower's command. This was agreeable to the French because that would ensure that General de Gaulle would be in almost uncontested control of France at liberation."[9]

Donovan remarked that if the U.S. did not support de Gaulle's movement in France, it would be the FTP (*Franctireurs et Partisans*), the tough communist groups, who were well-organized, well-disciplined, and well-armed, that would benefit. This was a major argument used with many senators. Donovan suggested to the President that he recognize de Gaulle.[10] The President agreed that Donovan should go to Algiers, where he had a meeting with General de Gaulle, who approved the dates of June 6–8 as the date for his trip to Washington. That date was postponed.

Meanwhile General Eisenhower, now in liberated Normandy, who for a long time had understood how popular de Gaulle was in France, sent his Chief of Staff, Bedell Smith, to London in order to ask the President to invite de Gaulle to Washington to settle once and for all a situation that was becoming embarrassing. Luckily, at that time General Marshall, who was also in London, was aware of the de Gaulle–Roosevelt conflict and supported Eisenhower's demand. In the midst of all this, France's Admiral Fénard arrived the following day from Washington with a message from President Roosevelt proposing different dates for the future meeting.

De Gaulle did not want to see a replay of the situation of Anfa, during which Roosevelt had not listened to him. This time, de Gaulle wanted to arm himself with internationally recognized credentials. Between June 8 and 20, we received telegrams informing us that the exiled governments of Belgium, Luxembourg, Yugoslavia, Norway, Poland, and Czechoslovakia had all recognized the provisionary government of the French republic. However, this was not enough for de Gaulle. He intended to appear with French credentials. The General set off on the destroyer *La Combattante* and on June 14, 1944, arrived at Bayeux (a small fishing village in Normandy) where he received a triumphant welcome from an enthusiastic populace. Thus it was France itself—a liberated France—who had demonstrated her political choice. This small village, the first to have been liberated, substantiated the claims of de Gaulle and of those who had supported him during the war's darkest hours.

The American press was unanimous in their reporting of the population's enthusiasm: "Everywhere, he was welcomed by cheers, tears, and hastily organized demonstrations," reported *Newsweek* on June 26, 1944, under the caption "The Hurrahs of the French for de Gaulle Rang Hollow in the Allies' Ears." The situation was the same at Isigny in the midst of the still-smoking ruins. The photographs of the crowds cheering de Gaulle appeared in all the newspapers. The General returned to London in order to see Churchill on July 16, and then continued to Algiers. From there, de Gaulle went to Rome, where he was received by the Italian Minister of Foreign Affairs. De Gaulle then continued on to an official visit at the Vatican. Everywhere he had been hailed as France's head of state. He thus believed that he had attained a rank that would permit him to speak to Roosevelt as a full-fledged Allied head of state rather than with the status of an unrecognized leader.

De Gaulle, who wanted to leave nothing to chance, decided to personally make preparations for certain aspects of his trip. First of all, he wanted this trip to be viewed as an homage to the president of the most powerful state in the Western world, whose war effort was a pledge of success, and also as a demonstration of the former Franco-American friendship. The two heads of state would be discussing general questions that concerned the future of their respective countries as well as the future of Europe and the world.

CHAPTER XX

De Gaulle at the White House

I was disappointed by the unworthy reactions of many Frenchmen. . . .
—Franklin D. Roosevelt

I was amazed by the strange preparations at the Embassy for de Gaulle's trip to Washington, made in an atmosphere devoid of trust on both sides. The issuance of the invitation itself from the outset posed incredible, even absurd, problems of protocol. President Roosevelt, a head of state, believed it beneath him to extend an invitation to an individual whose rank he did not recognize. For his part, de Gaulle did not want in any way to appear to be soliciting an invitation. Finally, some vague contradictory statements that responded to the wishes of both Roosevelt and de Gaulle were drawn up in a fairly confused fashion.

In fact, de Gaulle's London office received a message from Roosevelt on June 6, proposing a date for de Gaulle's visit. The General answered on June 14 that he hoped the situation in Europe would allow him to make the trip and that "he accepted the invitation." The President then officially answered that he was pleased General de Gaulle had "expressed a desire to visit America for the purpose of having conversations with the President."[1] De Gaulle, however, felt that he had not asked to see the President, but rather he had finally been invited to do so.

For all Frenchmen, and especially for all Free French like me, the meeting of General de Gaulle with President Roosevelt was of major importance. I had prepared twice for de Gaulle's arrival when I was head of the delegation in New York, and twice the project was cancelled due to political difficulties.

The meeting between the two statesmen was of major import since it would influence the future of our country and our very destiny. We were hopeful that the two leaders would overcome their prejudices and work instead for the establishment of friendly relations between the United States and Liberated France. The Free French had not fought this war against Germany to find their country on unfriendly terms with America, who was saving us by sacrifices of men and matériel in North Africa and in Normandy.

I had to leave Washington on July 1 for the United Nations monetary and financial conference at Bretton Woods in New Hampshire, as I was appointed to be the assistant delegate for the CFLN (*Comité Français de la Libération Nationale*). Suddenly I was treated like all official delegates of other nations. I was housed in a sumptuous hotel overlooking the peaceful hills and woods of New Hampshire. I had been officially greeted by United States officials and by the officials of Great Britain, Belgium, the Netherlands, Norway, and felt that by my attendance my country had been "recognized" as the great nation it had been in the past. At the conference, the Allied countries discussed very complicated financial matters that would face a liberated Europe. While the debates among us heated up, my mind was in Washington, where I knew General de Gaulle was due to land on July 6.

Before my departure for Bretton Woods, I had asked the *Comité's* press attaché, Jean Beaubé, who was a friend since the days we called ourselves the "Free French," to keep me informed on a daily basis about events in Washington. I had also asked Gaston Palewski, who was accompanying de Gaulle on this voyage, to inform him that I was sorry not to be able to greet him upon his arrival, but that I would be in New York on July 10 to see him.

Beaubé telephoned me quite often from the Capital and many press correspondents kept me up-to-date, especially Serge Fliegers, a particularly bright young man who worked for Reuters, the British news service. I was therefore quite well informed about General de Gaulle's historic arrival in Washington. The reception he was accorded shocked us and must have shocked the General all the more: he was given a seventeen-gun salute. American protocol required that military men of very high rank were to be greeted with a seventeen-gun salute; chiefs of state were greeted with a twenty-one-gun salute. This American gesture was not without an intended message: the president was setting the clock back and informing de Gaulle upon his arrival that despite all his efforts he was not being considered a Chief of State, but rather merely a distinguished military officer visiting the United States.

After leaving the plane, de Gaulle was introduced to a large group of American military men, the glory of United States power in the war: General Marshall, Admiral King, General Arnold, and General Vandergrift—but there were no civil or diplomatic dignitaries. Again, Roosevelt seemed to be warning him that it was only as a military leader that he was greeted, not as a chief of state. It seemed evident that American foreign policy toward him had not changed, and that he was not invited as the President of the provisional government of France.

Later, when he arrived at the White House, he was welcomed in French by a smiling and friendly President Roosevelt: *"si content de vous voir,"* he said once again. He was then introduced to the diplomatic leaders of the country who had in the past opposed him: Cordell Hull, Secretary of State; Sumner Welles, Assistant Secretary of State; and Admiral Leahy, the former U.S. Ambassador to Vichy. Tea was served to the guests and it was said in Washington that Roosevelt offered some to General de Gaulle and, turning to Admiral Leahy, who had been his ambassador to Vichy, quipped, "For you, Admiral, Vichy [mineral] water would be more appropriate." The very word "Vichy" must have stung de Gaulle. He had never appreciated Roosehvelt's wisecracks; now he got up and would have walked out had he not been kept from doing so. Later the atmosphere became more relaxed.

On the next day, July 7, the President gave a state luncheon at the White House and made the following moving speech:

I think we will all agree that this is an historic occasion we will remember all the rest of our lives. A great many of us know France personally. A great many of us were there in our childhood, or in our young manhood. There is something about France that doesn't exist anywhere else in the world. I think you know what I mean. It is the spirit of civilization that endears itself not just to us but to all the world, all the people who ever go there, and that includes the people of France.

During these past four years a great many of us—all of us—have been thinking about what France has gone through. And so time has gone on, and we have seen the dawn of the new day for France, the complete liberation of that civilization which will go back not just to what it was before, but to something even more appealing, something even greater than before this war.

We are enlisted in this country in the great task of bringing that great day, the liberation of France, even closer. When that day has come and the government of France is restored to its own people, a great many of us will want to be there and see France, see the rejuvenated France, taking its rightful place among all the nations.

After drinking the toast to France, Roosevelt turned to de Gaulle and addressed the following words to him:

Now I want to say, shall I call it a personal word. A year ago last January, at Casablanca, General de Gaulle and I met for the first time. I am glad this has been the second time, and most assuredly there will be a third time and many other times ...

There are a lot of troublemakers in the world. I won't refer just to certain elements of the press in Algiers, and in Washington. That is with us always. But after all, the professional lives by stirring up controversy. That is an inherent part of our public information, which is not always correct.

There are all kinds of problems, most of them what might be called technical, or detailed, or local, which can be resolved by the meeting of the leaders—the old idea that if you get around the table with a man you can solve anything.

There are no great problems between the French and the Americans, or between General de Gaulle and myself. They are all working out awfully well, without exception. They are going to work out all right, if they will just leave a few of us alone to sit around the table. . . .

General de Gaulle and I have been talking this morning about all kinds of things all over the world. We have talked about controversial things—controversial to the press, but really not controversial at all—things that we are in complete agreement on, things for the future of the world, to disarm Germany, to see that this kind of thing that has been happening for the last five years shall not happen again for the next fifty. . . .

And, therefore, it has been a great privilege to have General de Gaulle come over here to talk about things, quietly, and to work out plans not just for the future of France but also plans for the future of the world, the cause of our objectives, our common objectives on which we are all agreed.

Therefore, it seems that at this meeting even now—and it isn't over yet—we will do even more.

I call it historic because it is going to have a great influence on all of humanity, on a great many countries and a great many continents. We can work these problems out if we keep on meeting the way we are meeting now.

It is a real pleasure to have him with us, and as I said before, something is being done for the good of the world. And that is why I think we can all tell the General from the bottom of our hearts how very happy we are to have him here in this common effort. The liberation of France is, of course, the most important of all. Every German boot we want out of France, once and for all. And when that day comes, we will all breathe much more happily and much more safely, not only during our lifetimes but the lifetimes of our children.

So I propose to the health of General de Gaulle, our friend.[2]

This most amicable toast to the liberation of France and to his "friend" General de Gaulle was carefully prepared not to present him in any way as the President of a provisional government of France or as the head of all French fighting forces or even as the head of the civil administration of France. Roosevelt's position remained the same.

In her autobiography, Eleanor Roosevelt states that on July 7 "De Gaulle lunched with Franklin in the White House. We wondered whether this visit would soften his [Roosevelt's] feelings about the General. Their meeting was evidently completely formal but pleasant and I saw no difference in Franklin's attitude," she stated.[3]

Roosevelt was determined not to discuss any substantive matters. He had taken all the necessary precautions to avoid misunderstanding. De Gaulle had to know by now that he was being received as a distinguished military leader and not as a chief of state. Despite reports from General Marshall, Eisenhower, and the OSS, the President had a *hunch* that a leader of the French underground, unknown to the outside world, would emerge from completely liberated France and would be proclaimed by the French people as their legitimate President. This event he believed would put aside de Gaulle and his exiled supporters in London and bring an end to their ambitions.

The conversations to take place the next day with de Gaulle therefore did not cover any substantive questions. The two men spoke very freely of general problems concerning Franco-American relations and the organization of the world of the future. In the second volume of his *Mémoires de Guerre*, General de Gaulle described in great detail the objectives and the content of their conversations.

He listened with interest as well as some anxiety to the President's description of the world of the future. De Gaulle reports that he cautioned President Roosevelt against his vision of a world controlled solely by four policemen—the United States, Great Britain, the USSR, and China—and the relegation of Europe to second place. De Gaulle remarked, "By assigning Western Europe a secondary role, is not Roosevelt going to repudiate the cause that he wants to defend, that of civilization? By backing the Soviets, he risks sacrificing the Poles, the Czechs, and the Baltics. Can he be sure of China's stability, who is his ally for the time being?" He raised the great importance of practical political problems and drew the President's attention to their urgency.

Finally, after having expressed the necessity of granting Europe the status that would restore her as a world power, the General pleaded on behalf of France, which was currently fighting with all her might to achieve a victory. Was she not entitled to regain the status and the prestige that were formerly hers? A strong France, he stated, was indispensable to a balance of power in Europe.

President Roosevelt, at the end of their conversation, could not help saying how upset he was by the disastrous Franco-German Armistice, and how disappointed he had been by the "unworthy" reactions that such a disaster "had raised among many Frenchmen, notably among those whom he knew personally."[4] The President could scarcely make a broader criticism to a French leader concerning the behavior of his compatriots in exile in the U.S.[5] As we have noted, the elite among French exiles as well as 85 percent of the French residents had stubbornly opposed General de Gaulle during the entire war, and their attitude had not been without influence on the President and the Department of State. For his part, de Gaulle did not point out that the misunderstandings between Roosevelt and himself and between the United States and Free France were due to the fact that the American President had listened to these opponents far too willingly.

Although these conversations continued for two more days, one is surprised to find not a single mention of them either in State Department archives or in the notes of the President's personal secretary. Only in General de Gaulle's memoirs are these friendly talks recorded. In any case, it is amazing that the President—at the height of his power, leader of the most powerful country in the world—would spend his time giving General de Gaulle long lectures outlining his vision of the world to come. One may well ask if Roosevelt was only avoiding discussing matters that were more immediately pertinent.

During these meetings, de Gaulle, for his part, thought of nothing but the problems faced by a France exhausted by war, whose role would be relatively insignificant in the dazzling world mosaic that Roosevelt was painting for him.[6] Once again, each man spoke at, rather than to, the other and made no effort to understand the other's point of view.

The press conference that Roosevelt held immediately following these talks at the White House on July 11 proved that the President still had the same attitude towards de Gaulle and his party: "Until such time as the French are free to choose their own government," Roosevelt accepted the Committee as "the de facto authority for the civil administration of France." "General Eisenhower [is] Commander-in-

Chief with all the necessary authority . . . in other words, the seat of the civil administration, the territories to be considered non-military, will be determined by General Eisenhower alone."[7]

When questioned on this matter, Roosevelt specified that "De Gaulle's Committee was not considered as France's provisionary government" and that General Eisenhower was free to deal with other French authorities and to choose or himself name the local authority capable of maintaining the peace.

There is no better way to sum up the results of the encounter between the two men than to quote from a letter written by President Roosevelt, about which de Gaulle was to learn several days later. Roosevelt, alluding to an obscure American agreement with the French General Transatlantic Company, warned his correspondent to be sure to keep de Gaulle in the dark about it, for if de Gaulle were to find out, he would get rid of the company's director. Roosevelt concluded by saying, "De Gaulle and I have lightly touched on matters of current interest. But we have spoken much more seriously about France's future and of that of her colonies, of world peace, etc. When it comes to dealing with future problems, he [de Gaulle] seems completely 'accommodating' as long as France is viewed as a world power. He is very sensitive when it comes to dealing with France's honor. But I believe that he is essentially an egoist."[8]

Before leaving the White House, de Gaulle presented the President with a large model submarine[9] built by the specialists of the Bizerte Arsenal.*

General de Gaulle, before leaving Washington, visited General Pershing, a World War I hero, who was incapacitated and was recovering at Walter Reed Hospital. Photographs of the two generals appeared in the press with articles describing their encounter. Pershing, who had certainly aged and whose memory was, shall we say, less than perfect, asked de Gaulle for news on the health of Marshal Pétain, whom he had known in 1917. A disconcerted de Gaulle replied that he had no news of him. "It's been a long time since I've seen him. . . ."

---

*A few months later, at Christmas time, it was said in Washington that the model submarine was on Roosevelt's desk. His grandson Curtis asked if he could have it. The President acquiesced, but Eleanor pointed out that it was a gift from a foreign Chief of State and that as such could not be given away. The President replied, laughing: it was not given by a Chief of State but by "General de Gaulle, president of some French committee or another."[13]

The next day, July 10, in New York, Mayor Fiorello La Guardia, friendly toward Free France as usual, gave de Gaulle a warm welcome at City Hall. A large reception held for the General at the Waldorf Astoria attracted a considerable crowd. Naturally, all of de Gaulle's supporters were present, as well as Giraud's supporters, those who had been lukewarm, those who had been undecided, and, finally, former Vichy supporters. For the first time in years, all Frenchmen were being united after the long tragedy of war and exile. De Gaulle's appeal for the union of all Frenchmen was met with a lengthy round of applause.*

I had a personal interview with General de Gaulle later that same day in his suite at the Waldorf Astoria Hotel. I had seen de Gaulle briefly at a meeting in London a year earlier. This time I was able to have a longer interview. He appeared to me taller than I remembered and, as usual, was icily calm. His elegant suite contrasted sharply with the simply furnished office he kept in London at Carlton Gardens, his headquarters. And he seemed oddly out of place in such a luxurious setting with his neat khaki uniform devoid of even a single decoration. He asked me to take a seat beside him, lit a cigarette, and began in an informal yet tense way a series of questions about the current situation. He asked me what I thought of the attitude of the American press towards him, whether public opinion was really favorable to him. He asked me questions about the monetary and financial conference at Bretton Woods, which I had just left, and wanted to know the positions of the different delegations. I told him that the occupied countries had taken more or less the same position regarding currency and credits. There was an important difference, however, between the position of the American delegation led by Harry White and that of Britain led by Lord Keynes, I said. De Gaulle responded that the differences would be resolved "because Britain will always accede to America."

He lit another cigarette, walked to the window and looked at the stream of cars rushing along Park Avenue. "C'est énorme," he said, "this country has not built automobiles for three years and look at all the cars ... what a capital they represent ... and what a powerful industry!"

In a firm voice he described the enormous power the United States

---

*De Gaulle, however, refused to meet with Alexis Léger, Labarthe, Tabouis, de Kérillis, Giraud, and Chautemps, all of whom had opposed him throughout the course of the war.

now had and would have for years to come: her industrial might and her agricultural production gave her an overwhelming superiority over all her allies. He concluded, "It will be the wealthiest and best-equipped country after the war is over" and said that the United States was "already trying to rule the world."

He later had an interview with Pierre Mendès-France, who was the president of my delegation at the Bretton Woods conference.

At the end of his short stay, on July 11, the General gave a press conference at the embassy in Washington, which I attended and which attracted a large crowd of French and American journalists. Admittance had to be strictly limited. When de Gaulle entered the room, he received a standing ovation and was frequently applauded in the course of the conference by a press that, for the most part, had never stopped supporting his movement and urging recognition of his government. De Gaulle appeared to be very relaxed, and spoke calmly (in French, of course) about the liberation of France as well as the great problems facing Franco-American friendship.

The conference began with these words: "Good morning, ladies and gentlemen," and then continued in French with a prepared text. The General spoke of "objective" talks with the President on important questions of mutual interest:

> ... I believe that we attained the principal object which President Roosevelt and I had fixed for this journey, namely, frank and objective talks on the grave questions of common interest to the United States and France in this great war and after the war. I am sure that, henceforth, the settlement of all the common problems which face, and will face, the American government and the French government as the Allied armies advance, and, later, in the course of world reorganization, will be easier because now we understand each other even better.

The journalists who were present were astonished to find themselves in the presence of a cordial man who was dignified and reserved. They asked many questions.

"Have you reached an informal agreement with the United States similar to that worked out by the British, for your participation in the administration of liberated areas of France?" The General replied that this was not one of the goals of his trip. He hoped however that the atmosphere that he had created would have "results along those lines."

He was asked if he would establish a temporary capital at Rennes in Brittany. "The capital of France is Paris," he replied.

"Are you satisfied that the United States has no designs on French territory?" The General exclaimed: "I am convinced that the American President, the American government, and the American people have no such designs."

He was asked whether he and President Roosevelt had discussed when a plebiscite would be held in France to determine whether the French Committee would be recognized. "No," he replied. "That is purely a French question."

"Do you expect the French empire to be returned intact?"

General de Gaulle said he was certain that France "will find everything intact that belongs to her," and that France "is also certain that the form of French organization in the world will not be the same."

"Does France want additional territory after the war?"

General de Gaulle said that as far as Africa and the Far East were concerned, France wanted nothing more than was hers now. Europe was a different matter. . . . A questioner wanted to know if France regarded itself as a great power.

General de Gaulle answered that "France not being great was too ridiculous to consider."

"It is so obvious that there could be no real world organization without France on the first plane. . . ."[10]

France again was a world power.

What reaction was there in American public opinion as a result of General de Gaulle's trip? It is true that this trip to the United States was preceded in almost all the major American newspapers by a series of articles favorable to de Gaulle and advocating recognition of the Committee in Algiers as the provisional government of the French Republic.

To this end, Walter Lippmann wrote a lengthy article which appeared in the *New York Herald Tribune* on June 28, 1944:

> The grave question of our French policy, which may yet involve our relations with Europe and the settlement of the war, has become a personal matter to a degree which the American people have not yet realized, to a degree which responsible and informed American journalists feel constrained to touch upon with great reserve.
>
> One may judge how serious they are by the fact that four European governments, all of them deeply concerned to retain the good-will of the President and of the American Nation, have openly separated themselves from Mr. Roosevelt by recognizing the French provisional government. That would have not happened, that could not have happened, if they were not profoundly convinced that General de Gaulle

is the leader of the French nation and that as Europeans they cannot and dare not enter the period of their own liberation without a working partnership with France.

On July 29, after the General's trip was completed, Drew Middleton wrote in the *New York Times:* "The attitude towards the future government of France is in a way astonishing. The majority of Frenchmen in this area are waiting for the French Committee of National Liberation to be recognized as the provisionary government of France. They were surprised to learn that there was some discussion on this point."

Harold Calendar wrote a series of articles advocating recognition "without further delay." He compared Great Britain's position with that of the Soviet Union, which was that the American attitude towards France should be improved and that United States reservations should be lessened. He concluded: "The British government has virtually given recognition to 100 percent of the French Committee of National Liberation."[11] Several days later, he wrote further, "The reason why the Committee has not received formal recognition is because the American government refused to join with Great Britain and the USSR in granting recognition to the Committee . . . . The State Department is not particularly to blame [for this situation]. The President is the major stumbling block in Franco-American politics." He concluded: "One thing is certain: If the American government pursues its present policy toward France, it will alienate friends who have been remarkably patient in tolerating American gaffes and it will end in a result opposite to what the Americans wished to achieve."[12]

Later, Geoffrey Parsons added: "The continual delay of the State Department in recognizing the French Committee of National Liberation is causing embarrassment and irritation among United States allies. The British and Soviet governments have clearly communicated to us their wish for immediate recognition."[13]

The General's trip, even though it did not alter President Roosevelt's opinion of him, at least attracted the attention of the press and of the American public to the thorny issue of recognition. This, in turn, triggered an unremitting campaign in de Gaulle's favor, which was backed by such powerful arguments that once again the White House was forced to reconsider its position, although it did so cautiously and with the greatest reluctance. Roosevelt, who was still listening to Alexis Léger, insisted that the "recognition" of the Committee be strictly limited.

CHAPTER XXI

L'Éminence Grise

Can the persistence of Roosevelt's suspicion of and hostility towards de Gaulle be explained solely by events described so far in this book, or is there a more compelling explanation? There is, in the person of Alexis Léger, who provided an ideological and legal structure to Roosevelt's already profound misgivings about de Gaulle.

After my first meeting with Alexis Léger early in 1941, I paid him a few other visits, between 1942 and 1944, in the same small and sparsely furnished room he maintained in Washington, D.C. Our visits lasted for hours, allowing him ample time to discourse on the war and its political significance. He never met the General. His antipathy towards him during the intervening years had not diminished. On the contrary, his feelings deepened with the passage of time, and, by the time we had our final meeting, Léger could no longer utter de Gaulle's name, but referred to him instead as *"l'homme"* ("that man").

Discussions about the war deteriorated into Léger's tirades against de Gaulle. Their theme was always the same: France no longer had a legitimate government and could not, as a result, legitimately express the political will of the people. He felt that no single person had the right, under these circumstances, to assume that he could lead the French nation or direct its foreign policy. De Gaulle of course was doing both.

Léger had established himself, long before the war, as a competent and knowledgeable diplomat. He had, as Secretary General of France's Foreign Office, sent numerous unsolicited but welcome reports to the State Department on subjects ranging from the external affairs of Poland and Rumania to Italy's action against Ethiopia. It is not surprising that at the State Department his views carried the weight of considerable authority on matters pertaining to the war effort in general, and to France in particular. It is also apparent that he wished to wield this authority, since he chose to make Washington, D.C., his home during those years and not, as he might have, New York, where a community of nearly 100,000 of his compatriots, many of them the leading French intellectuals of the time, had sought refuge from Hitler. Among them were Professor Henri Laugier of the Sorbonne, Nobel laureates Jean Perrin and Jacques Hadamard, and also Antoine de Saint-Exupéry, whom he had known in Paris.

But how did Léger manage to exercise such considerable influence over Roosevelt and his administration? Part of the answer stems from the fact that Léger had arrived in the United States immediately following the collapse of France—which he had foreseen. Since Léger was part of no political group, neither Gaullist nor Pétainist, he seemed at once removed from and above the fray. Roosevelt felt that Léger was the only Frenchman he could trust to remain impartial and who also had exceptional experience in diplomatic matters.

To Roosevelt, Léger seemed the ideal advisor: independent and discreet, and knowledgeable about all of France's and Europe's problems. He also demonstrated the integrity of his views by refusing to join either Vichy France's offers of collaboration or de Gaulle's offer to head his Free French Delegation in Washington. When his personal charm and the intellectual virtues he had as a poet are added into account he must have seemed an irresistible advisor.

Léger's influence was known by the French community and confirmed to me at least on one occasion by Sumner Welles, who told me that Léger was influential because President Roosevelt held him in "high esteem."

Hervé Alphand, the future Secretary General of France's Foreign Office, who had met Léger on several occasions, had told me more than once how concerned he was about Léger's hostility towards de Gaulle. Later in his memoirs he recalled that Léger had "loudly declared the necessity of not allowing de Gaulle to engage in any French diplomacy whatsoever." He believed that de Gaulle's personality was such that "no meeting, no cooperation whatsoever [between the two] is possible. . . ." And Alphand added: "Léger is well heeded here and his opinion carries tremendous influence on many occasions."[1]

Léger's influential status in Roosevelt's administration was also noticeable in the kind of knowledge he had about American policies. To my astonishment, Léger always seemed able to foresee the stance that the American authorities would take with regard to de Gaulle, the non-recognition of Free France, the Lend-Lease Act, the Darlan affair, and AMGOT.

I recall one day when Léger said to me: "There are plans to take a high-ranking general out of a German jail. We are thinking of a 'real' general who was a hero in the war—someone, more importantly, who does not get involved in politics. There will also be a separate civil committee or an office to administer French civil affairs, until there is total liberation and free elections." Only later did I learn that he of course was referring to General Giraud.

The naming of a politically non-ambitious five-star general such as Giraud who would comply with the elaborate procedures of the Third Republic was desirable to Léger, and the fact that the United States contemplated the same goals is a telling example of his influence. Léger's most profound political conviction was that France had to be resurrected from its defeat by the Nazis by the reestablishment of the political system of the Third Republic. His consuming hatred of de Gaulle was due in part to his observation that de Gaulle was pursuing his own personal vision of the way France was to be resurrected and of the political structure it would later adopt.

De Gaulle, although aware of Léger's attitude, was also aware of his influence and had endeavored on several occasions to win his support. He approached Léger first through René Pleven, who visited Léger in Washington in June 1941. Having no success with this attempt, de Gaulle sent a succession of envoys—Pleven once again, Adrien Tixier in 1941, d'Astier de la Vigerie in 1942, André Philip and then Henri Hoppenot as late as 1943—in an effort to win him over. Each attempt failed. De Gaulle eventually understood what Léger had done during the war, and when he visited President Roosevelt at the White House in July 1944, de Gaulle made it well known that he did not wish to meet with Alexis Léger.*

That Léger's hatred of de Gaulle also stemmed from personal reasons is clear. Paul Reynaud, who as Premier of the Third Republic had fired Léger abruptly in the days just before France's defeat, had also named de Gaulle as Undersecretary of State. In Léger's mind this raised suspicions as to de Gaulle's trustworthiness—he was afraid that de Gaulle might join with Reynaud after the war. When I told him

---

*Léger's intense hatred for de Gaulle was such that the well-known author de Bois-deffre, who had met with Léger in the mid-1960s, reported in *La Revue des Deux Mondes* in December 1984 that the hatred had not diminished at all even twenty years after the war.

that de Gaulle, who did not tolerate defeatists, would never again offer to work with Paul Reynaud, Léger became livid and cut me off with the following remark: "You know nothing about it. I have my reasons for believing that the friendship between these two still exists and that de Gaulle will call upon him."

Because of this profound distrust of the General, Léger quite openly deluged government officials and the press with an unremitting and violent anti-Gaullist propaganda campaign. Elsa Maxwell, one of the leading columnists at the time, wrote from Washington: "I fear that his [Léger's] influence has been detrimental to the Free French cause. He does not like de Gaulle who to him, I imagine, has been something of an upstart. . . . I am absolutely certain that it is the quiet persevering hand of Monsieur Léger that has advised against recognition of the French National Committee of Liberation as the Provisional French government. . . . That our government deeply desires to replace General de Gaulle with someone from within some mythical group inside France, is obvious. . . ."[2]

Following the American landing in North Africa, Churchill also called upon Léger's wisdom, early in 1943. Churchill offered Léger, if he would come to Algiers, help in obtaining an important post—probably in Foreign Affairs on the National Committee, with de Gaulle and Giraud. Léger refused. He may have had greater ambitions. But Churchill noted: "I have just had a meeting with Léger . . . He has informed me that he would never want to work with de Gaulle and that he would not come to London as long as de Gaulle is our man. On the other hand, he is in agreement with the Gaullist movement [of French liberation] and thinks that if it got rid of de Gaulle, this would be a good omen for France." Léger was ready to become part of the National Committe in Algiers, according to Churchill, " . . . as long as de Gaulle was not part of it."[3]

At bottom, Léger's influence in Washington and his rejection of de Gaulle also had a more philosophical basis. Léger's political philosophy was juridical, whereas de Gaulle's was nationalistic. This difference had its effects: neither could agree on the method by which France's liberation could be achieved, nor could they agree on the political framework France would adopt after Liberation. Obviously, only one of these views could win acceptance in Roosevelt's administration.

That de Gaulle's principal driving political force derived from a

*See Chapter VII.

nationalistic vision of France is evident in his reaction to France's defeat and his declarations concerning her resurrection.*

De Gaulle *saw himself as the nation France,* a living and fighting nation. During the years of the defeat, Léger saw France as an occupied nation whose constitutive legal documents had been suspended by the occupation of a hostile enemy controlling its territory. The resurrection of France, to him, was the resurrection of its constitution, which had provisions for its reenactment in the event of a hostile takeover. This juridical view of France had a profound effect on the relations between Léger and de Gaulle and also between the Roosevelt administration and de Gaulle.

Léger's legalistic view of France enabled him, since the time of his arrival in Washington, to trust American policies. I remember one of my long visits with him concerning American policy with regard to Vichy or Free French liberated territories. Léger knew, of course, how hostile de Gaulle was towards the idea of the United States dealing directly with local authorities rather than through the Free French National Committee in London. Such a policy not only bypassed what de Gaulle considered to be the sole legitimate national authority but raised suspicions as to American intentions toward France. By dealing with local authorities, the American administration was establishing independent ties with French colonies, and he feared the United States was doing so to further her own interests. Léger saw otherwise: "It has long been a practice of the Americans to deal with local authorities in charge either of portions of or an entire foreign territory," he said. "This policy enables them [the United States] to deal directly with problems that affect the United States and is established without regard to the country's sovereignty. It is just a temporary expedient that will be formalized later, when there is a sovereign and legitimate government. . . . President Roosevelt has the aim of maintaining intact the rights of the French people. In the present situation he should be trusted and considered as the sole guarantor of French interests in the world."

This trusting and knowledgeable view of the United States strengthened ties between Léger and Roosevelt's administration. He must have seemed far more reasonable than de Gaulle. Léger exploited these feelings of mutual respect by constantly warning President Roosevelt against what he saw as the "dictatorial tendencies" of de Gaulle.

Léger supported his accusations with a logical set of arguments that had their basis in French constitutional law. Of the various letters and notes Léger sent to the President, his long memorandum of January

31, 1944, four months before the invasion of Normandy, outlines most clearly the position he advised Roosevelt to assume. Léger first states that the time is coming when the invasion of Europe will thrust weighty responsibilities upon the Allies with regard to the French people. "Whatever decisions the Allies might make, they must respect the Treveneuc Law, the constitutional law of 1872," by which the people of France safeguard their democracy. This is achieved principally by the calling together of the *conseils généraux* (county governments), which must meet immediately after being summoned. Each *conseil général* elects two delegates to a special provisional assembly that is charged with the task of preparing a general election.

"This fundamental law is required in the present situation. No provisional French administration can refuse to apply it without violating the French constitution.... The Allied Powers and particularly the U.S. cannot disregard its application...."[4] Léger annexed to this letter to President Roosevelt the short text of the Treveneuc law as well as an extremely long three-part commentary he had written.

Léger further accused de Gaulle and the Committee in Algiers of "making plans to *illegally* assume power in France just as soon as the country becomes liberated." This, Léger concluded, should not be allowed to happen, and the United States was responsible for seeing that the Treveneuc Law was applied. In a letter to the President on November 3, 1943, Léger insisted that the upholding of democratic freedom in France is "your responsibility." Any violation of that law "would have serious consequences and would be resented, in the future, by the French people."[5] The President, therefore, was to be the trustee of the democratic liberties of France.

Léger succeeded to such an extent in convincing Roosevelt of that role that in a letter to Ambassador Wilson in Algiers, Roosevelt stated in words similar to Léger's that "General de Gaulle and his associates have arrogated to themselves the credit for resistance to Germany, ignoring or belittling the efforts of other French and the enormous assistance rendered to the French cause by the United States and other Allies.... *We regard it as our duty to the French people for which we will be accountable in history ...*" to maintain the principles of democracy.[6] It scarcely deserves emphasizing here that further clashes and competition between Roosevelt and de Gaulle would be inevitable since each man considered himself accountable to the French people.

It can be said in all truth that until two months after the liberation of Paris the American President constantly did his very best, by enforcing a French constitutional law that dated from 1872, to thwart de Gaulle's initiatives. But this is not without some irony. Léger's influence in Washington was ultimately due to the fact this his legalistic views coincided with the American constitutional outlook. How persuasive Léger, who favored a constitutionally sanctioned solution to France's dilemma, must have been in Washington! To the Americans, whose constitution was nearly a century older than was France's at the time, such a solution must have seemed absolutely legitimate. To the Americans, the Constitution has always been and continues to be a fundamental and irrefutable document. To the French, constitutions change according to political imperatives. The Third Republic was the longest surviving constitution in French history. It lasted nearly seventy years. The constitution of the Fourth Republic, enacted under de Gaulle's leadership after the war, lasted only fourteen years, and although the Fifth Republic established in 1958 survives today, it may change should the French people find it no longer efficacious.

The entire policy of the President of the United States towards France was thus ultimately influenced by a foreign exile—a former civil servant and poet whose juridical views of his nation found receptive ears in an American administration that shared his constitutional views.

Léger did not, in the end, succeed in preventing the recognition of the *Comité Français de Libération Nationale* (CFLN), but he was clearly influential in drafting its strict limitations: the *Comité* could be considered a de facto authority, *but not a French government,* and the word "recognition" was used with the utmost circumscription. Indeed, the text read,

> ... the Government of the United States recognizes the French Committee of National Liberation as administering those French overseas territories which acknowledge its authority.
>
> This statement does not constitute recognition of a government of France or of the French Empire by the Government of the United States.[7]

It was signed with reservations and restrictions on June 9, 1943.

CHAPTER XXII

Recognition at Last

The Allies would no longer deal with any French authority other than the *Comité Français de Libération Nationale.* Vichy was definitely out. The Committee would have authority over all Frenchmen. The document stated, "The United States Government is in favor of the establishment of the French Committee of National Liberation.... We hope that the Committee will function according to the principle of collective responsibility for all its members for the active pursuit of the war. In view of the major importance of the common effort for the war, relations with the CFLN *(Comité Français de Libération Nationale)* must continue to be subject to the military necessities of the Allied leaders...."[1] It must be noted that while the de facto recognition by the Americans was cautious, entailing only limited sovereignty, recognition by the British was far more comprehensive. The Soviets went even further, recognizing the CFLN as the undisputed representative of the interests of the French Republic everywhere. This was a first step toward full recognition of a real government, of which it practically had all the power but not the name. It was for me and all Free Frenchmen the beginning of a dream come true.

I received telegrams and letters of congratulations from the Americans who had helped us during the dark days. Mayor La Guardia telephoned me and exclaimed, "You have won!"

The recognition of the Committee meant the end of Free France in America, England, and all the Allied countries. A new French administration had to be created, the staff enlarged. We had to build up new offices, blending the Free French with the former hesitants and neutrals who were now joining en masse. In North Africa, the Free French forces that had fought alone heroically since 1940 were merged on August 25, 1944, with others from the resistance and from some of the former Vichy segments. The Free French fighters, however, could wear the *Croix de Lorraine* on their uniforms, which had been their symbol in the darkest hours of our history.

The Free French Delegation in New York, which had existed for three years and whose statute was limited, was now transformed into an Agency of the CFLN. The head of the office in New York was no longer a delegate as I was, but an "agent." My functions with the delegation ended, and I was transferred to our future Embassy in Washington, where I was put in charge of legal and economic postwar conferences in the United States. I had become an official representing a nation. The years of anguish were over. I was no longer a man without a country, nor was I a man without a status. I was once again able to correspond with my family in France and was relieved to find out they were safe and had survived the Nazi occupation.

Although the CFLN was not recognized as the successor of the French Republic, the buildings previously occupied by Vichy personnel were now placed at our disposal. These included the important embassy building in Washington, and the consular offices in New York, Chicago, San Francisco, and other cities. I bade farewell to the renting personnel at Rockefeller Center and returned to them the offices they had rented to Frenchmen without credentials.

I found myself suddenly limited in all my activities by the strict rules of the Foreign Office. Life was less exciting. I no longer enjoyed the freedom of a Free French representative to innovate and act as I believed to be in the interests of my country.

I then went to the new offices, the former Vichy offices, and found documents that the Vichy diplomats had not destroyed in their hasty departure. To my disgust and indignation I read the papers and copies of reports that they had made to the government of Pétain against us, the Free French. They had given every possible detail of our actions, so that Vichy could persecute our families and confiscate our belongings. They were responsible for the denationalization decrees against most of us.

After the United States "recognized" the CFLN as a Committee (but not as a government), the status of the French abroad changed radically. We were no longer considered outcasts by the State Department. Our relations with the American agencies could now be conducted on a governmental level.

In the United States the attitude of the French themselves underwent a radical transformation. Now they had one single government—the one presided over by General de Gaulle. Not everyone liked it, but there was no alternative. Suddenly a great number of talented and experienced men joined us. We now had all the help we needed, especially since practically all the members of the French Civil Service put themselves at our disposal to help in the war effort and the plans for future reconstruction.

Of course, with American and foreign officials I did not speak in the name of a "Committee"; I always explained that I was instructed by the "Provisional Government of the French Republic." The stationery and documents we all used bore that heading. We were beginning to see the dawn of liberation and the restoration of our country's democratic institutions.

Roosevelt did not yet want to grant full governmental recognition because he still expected an unknown leader to emerge from the liberated territories of France and claim the legitimacy of the government of the Republic. Roosevelt soon learned that newly liberated Bayeux in Normandy had acclaimed de Gaulle and that Paris had given him an enthusiastic reception. The President still refused to recognize the Committee as a provisional government.

At that time I learned that the last enemies of de Gaulle had failed. The treasonous schemes of Pétain, Laval, and their Nazi collaborators were finally crushed. The well-armed communist resistance guerrillas finally joined de Gaulle's forces.

Throughout the rest of newly liberated France, de Gaulle rapidly established a nationwide network of able new administrators to replace those appointed by the Vichy government during the Nazi occupation. All over the country, de Gaulle was enthusiastically hailed as France's legitimate leader.

By the end of July Hitler's empire was crumbling. The success of the Allied Forces caused a real panic in Vichy; some collaborators of the Nazis fled to Germany, others went into hiding. At this time France was still without a government. The country was in a state of upheaval that neither the German army nor the police could control. On realizing that the German Reich had lost the war, Marshal Pétain sent a secret document through Admiral Auphan to General de Gaulle on August 11, 1944, offering to make an "agreement for all Frenchmen of good faith," transferring his powers to General de Gaulle "so long as the principle of the legitimacy which *I incarnate* is safeguarded." De Gaulle, who had always contended that "the Republic has never ceased to exist," and that the Government of Marshal Pétain at Vichy was illegitimate, did not respond.

Two days before General Eisenhower planned to liberate Paris, the capital became the scene of a popular insurrection against the Nazis. Eisenhower had to divert his forces from Normandy and ordered General Leclerc of the second Free French Armored Division, with the support of the U.S. Fourth Infantry Division and the U.S. First Army under General Hodges, to race to Paris to save it from destruction by the Nazis. The troops arrived in the capital on August 22.

Three days later, General de Gaulle, backed by the *Comité National de la Résistance* as well as by followers from London and Algiers, announced the liberation of France to an ecstatic crowd at Paris's Hôtel de Ville (City Hall). When Georges Bidault, President of the *Comité National de la Résistance*, urged de Gaulle to proclaim the Republic then and there, the latter answered it was not necessary: "The Republic has never ceased to exist." The Republic was in London under the name of the *Comité National Français*, then in Algiers as the *Comité Français de Libération Nationale* and then as the Provisional Government of the French Republic. Jacques Chaban-Delmas, leader of the Resistance, was now appointed military governor of Paris by de Gaulle.

The preeminence given by General Eisenhower to de Gaulle's Free French Forces was certainly not part of President Roosevelt's plans and did not conform to his policy. Eisenhower, however, acted independently of the President because he was convinced that only General de Gaulle could prevent disturbances by local factions and the communists and guarantee a calm population at the rear of his army.

Eisenhower, who had masterfully planned the whole invasion and whose men had borne the brunt of the fighting during the Normandy landing, decided to allow the Free French forces the honor of entering Paris first. General Eisenhower, whose tact before and during the invasion was credited by Allied officials with having paved the way for cooperation with de Gaulle, proved to be not only a master strategist, but a better diplomat than many officials and statesmen of that time. He won the hearts of all Frenchmen. Harold Calender wired the *New York Times* on September 9, 1944: "Affection of Paris goes to Americans—Eisenhower and Patton are its heroes. Paris, which in this and so many respects undoubtedly reflects all France, is visibly and enthusiastically pro-American today as it has not been since 1918 and it may not always be in the future."[2]

President Roosevelt now found himself in an embarrassing political situation vis-à-vis France. He was well aware that de Gaulle had not adhered to the terms set down by the French constitution in the Treveneuc Law of 1872 regarding the conditions for the formation of a provisional government. But he was considered by the French to be the president of a provisional government which was more or less self-appointed, composed as it was of Frenchmen from London and Algiers, and members of the Resistance. This government had been accepted by the underground Resistance Council of France and in many ways represented the consensus of a very large majority of Frenchmen.

Léger's persistent advice finally had to be disregarded, especially after Churchill complained that it would be embarrassing to conduct diplomatic negotiations with the Italian provisional government, a former enemy nation, while refusing to recognize the French provisional government, an ally. Roosevelt's position was rendered even more awkward when Stalin declared his willingness to recognize General de Gaulle as President.

The facts spoke for themselves and Roosevelt was finally forced to give in. In so doing he tacitly admitted four years of error in his foreign policy toward France.[3]

President Roosevelt's recognition of France's provisional government was brought about in large part by the actions and influence of Edward Stettinius, the new Secretary of State, and by Army Generals George Marshall and Dwight D. Eisenhower. They were backed by a free and independent press that had supported the Free French cause during the entire course of the war.

It was said in Washington that the State Department had prepared a formal declaration of recognition at the beginning of October, in which it outlined broader recognition of the provisional government of the French Republic. For a long time this document remained on Roosevelt's desk. The President continued to stall particularly because, it was said, Léger continued to discourage him from acting on the recommendation.

Roosevelt finally recognized the provisional government of the French Republic on October 23, 1944. De Gaulle, still smarting from past humiliations, received the news without enthusiasm. When asked in a press conference several days later for his reaction to official recognition, de Gaulle replied: "I can tell you the French government is satisfied to note that one is willing to call it by its name." ("*Je puis vous dire que le gouvernement est satisfait qu'on veuille bien l'appeler par son nom.*")[4] For de Gaulle, this recognition did not signify merely the acceptance of a legal reality or the reestablishment of

France's diplomatic relations with other nations; more important, he believed it would lead to France's admission into the Allied War Council. Free France, which was founded on June 18, 1940, came to an end on August 15, 1944. Two months later the Government of the Republic was recognized. De Gaulle, now in the Elysée Palace in Paris, was able to administer the country, organize the return of two million war prisoners, plan for the reconstruction of the devastated areas, and direct French foreign policy.

CHAPTER XXIII

❖

Unforgiving Memory

The persistence of phantoms arising from the
wounded pride of an unforgiving memory.
—Jean Monnet

De Gaulle, in his role as a recognized head of state, immediately extended an official invitation to Churchill and to Eden, who accepted and came to Paris on November 10. Invitations were also sent to President Roosevelt and Cordell Hull, both of whom declined. De Gaulle concluded that his personal relationship with Roosevelt had not improved at all, and that despite everything an unremitting hostility remained between them. However, shortly after this, without any diplomatic communication whatsoever, General de Gaulle learned that a conference was going to take place at Yalta (in the southern USSR), with Roosevelt, Stalin, and Churchill in attendance. De Gaulle was not invited, and this deeply offended him. Roosevelt was not the only one who wanted to keep de Gaulle out of Yalta. Stalin did too.

Although during the days of Free France I had become accustomed to sudden storms between Roosevelt and de Gaulle, I innocently believed that after the recognition of the French Republic relations would be normalized. Unfortunately, I was mistaken; it would take time for France to be treated as a full-fledged ally.

The conference at Yalta began on February 4 and ended on February 11, 1945. We learned later that, thanks to Churchill, France obtained as much as she possibly could have received even if de Gaulle had been in attendance. De Gaulle, however, resented his exclusion and considered it an affront to his sovereignty. In any case, de Gaulle felt that France had only been given what was due to her. He never forgot his exclusion from Yalta and refused to let his resentment die.

Roosevelt, to avoid the reaction he saw coming, decided to take the first step and sent his friend and advisor, Harry Hopkins, to Paris to ease the tense atmosphere. Georges Bidault, Minister of Foreign Affairs, warned him that the General would not let himself be cajoled. In fact, de Gaulle's response to these overtures was that if the United States sincerely believed that Franco-American relations were not what they should be, why was not something done to rectify the situation? France should have been invited to Yalta.[1] Hoping to smooth things over, Roosevelt sent his ambassador Jefferson Caffery on February 12 with three notes,[2] inviting France to attend the United Nations conference in San Francisco, to be an inviting power, and to discuss trusteeship (colonies). De Gaulle accepted only the first.

The American ambassador returned the same afternoon to see de Gaulle and to give him a personal message from Roosevelt expressing the latter's desire to meet de Gaulle in Algiers on his way back from the conference at Yalta. The President asked de Gaulle which date would be suitable for such a meeting: "I anticipated with the greatest impatience the pleasure of meeting him in Algiers 4 or 5 days hence. It is with a great deal of regret that I must inform him that I cannot possibly accept his most kind invitation to visit Paris at this point in time. I hope that Algiers as a meeting place will meet with his approval."[3]

On February 13, de Gaulle sent the following reply to President Roosevelt: "Regrettably, it is impossible for me to come to Algiers at this time and without warning. We [the French government] had invited President Roosevelt last November to come to Paris and greatly regretted that he could not do so at that time. We understand fully that it is impossible for the President to come to Paris. We would be happy to welcome him in the capital should he wish to make a visit at any time whatsoever. If he wished during his trip to make Algiers a port of call in spite of this, would he be so kind as to inform us of the fact, in order that we might give [orders for] everything to be done in accordance with his wishes."[4]

De Gaulle was outraged that Roosevelt's suggested meeting would take place following the conference at Yalta, from which he had been excluded. Moreover, de Gaulle felt that an American president had no right to propose meeting in Algeria, then a French territory. He took advantage of this opportunity to assert his independence once and for all and to take revenge for past snubs. This letter was approved by the majority of members of de Gaulle's cabinet. Bidault, the Foreign Minister, opposed it.

De Gaulle later complained vehemently that there was a certain opposition to his decision from organized political parties, businessmen, intellectuals, and also the communists. Nonetheless the majority of the French press was on his side.[5]

The American press, which had backed de Gaulle throughout the entire war, felt that an insult to their president was a slap in the face to the entire country. Journalists recalled the countless sacrifices of the American people and of their soldiers who had died in an effort to liberate France. They also pointed out that the rebuilt French army had been armed and equipped by the United States, adding that France could not possibly be rebuilt without many years of considerable economic and financial aid from America.

Roosevelt himself was deeply offended and upon his return to Washington issued a press release which made mention of this unfortunate event. Then, on March 3, the President presented a report to Congress on the achievements of the Yalta Conference and made a scarcely-veiled reference to de Gaulle, referring to him as a "prima donna" whose whim had prevented a potentially useful meeting from taking place.[6] De Gaulle bitterly resented the terms used by Roosevelt towards him. Relations between the two statesmen were at an all-time low and the attitude of the two countries towards each other reflected this situation.

Shortly thereafter, on April 12, after long months of illness, Roosevelt died. There had been no third meeting between Roosevelt and de Gaulle.

The day after Roosevelt's death, de Gaulle sent the following message to President Harry Truman: "Roosevelt ... was, from the first to the last, France's friend. France loved and admired him."[7]

De Gaulle went to Washington, where he attended President Roosevelt's funeral together with all the Allied and neutral Chiefs of State. He met Eleanor Roosevelt and President Truman.

At that time, Adrien Tixier, de Gaulle's delegate to Washington during the war, was now Minister of the Interior. In that powerful position, he flatly rejected a request from the President of the Municipality of Paris on April 23 to hold a special session to honor the memory of the late president. One may wonder whether a decision with such implications for a foreign power could have been made without the prior knowledge of de Gaulle. In any case, the General did not rescind it.

It is difficult to imagine worse diplomatic relations between two allied chiefs of state. The "prima donna" passage in Roosevelt's speech to Congress a few weeks before his death, and de Gaulle's tacit acquiescence in the face of Tixier's rebuke, summarized the feelings of both leaders toward one another. Needless to say, this state of affairs did nothing to improve relations between the United States and France.

However, General de Gaulle in his *Mémoires de Guerre,* written many years later, expressed respect and admiration for the President and stated that "if Roosevelt had lived longer, we would have had the occasion, once the war was won, to discuss the matter [of my policy] thoroughly. I think he would have understood and appreciated the reasons that have prompted my actions as head of France!"[8]

CHAPTER XXIV

※

Allies at War: The Military Incidents

Allies are strangers—they can become ene-mies tomorrow.

—Charles de Gaulle[1]

The tense relations between Roosevelt and de Gaulle were, as we have seen, a result of the President's unbending and often stubborn policy, which was fueled by Alexis Léger and other French exiles. It was also due in large part to de Gaulle's formidable character, his intransigence, and his vision of an eternal and superior France. He more than once boldly challenged the President's policy.

His strategy did not change when he was recognized as a legitimate chief of state, when France was free again, and when he had at his disposal a sizable army. He brought his confrontation with the United States to a near breaking point. He stood firmly by his position, with calculated risk, and finally gained with minor concessions what he had sought to obtain.

De Gaulle had always considered that the army was an instrument of domestic as well as foreign policy.[2] During the early years of the war, from 1940 to 1942, he had at his disposal only a small Free French Force that was used mainly in Africa and the Near East in close conjunction with British forces.

After the liberation of North Africa by American forces, the U.S. government, fearful of de Gaulle's independence, decided to arm and equip a powerful new French army under the command of General Giraud alone, whom they trusted. Giraud, however, soon had to resign from the co-presidency of the *Comité Français de Libération* and his power passed to de Gaulle.

He soon had three near-clashes with the American Army: the first for the defense of Strasbourg in December 1944, the second for the evacuation of Stuttgart in April 1945, and the third in June 1945 in the province of Cuneo, Italy. The first conflict started at the end of Roosevelt's lifetime; the two others occurred during the Presidency of Harry Truman. All three conflicts had political undertones and did not arise from disagreements of pure military strategy.

The first conflict arose when Field Marshal von Rundstedt, Supreme Commander of the German Army, suddenly launched a powerful offensive in the forest and mountains of the Ardennes in Belgium, in the area where the Allied Forces had advanced rapidly and were too thinly spread. At that time French General de Lattre de Tassigny, with his First French Army in northwest France, had captured Strasbourg after a fierce battle and was pushing ahead. General Eisenhower, Supreme Commander of the Allied Forces, considering the danger of having the Wehrmacht outflank the American and French armies between Alsace and Belgium, decided to shorten his line of operations and to fall back with all forces to a better line of defense. He ordered General de Lattre to evacuate Strasbourg. Eisenhower did not realize at that time that Strasbourg was for the French a real national symbol. That city had been captured and annexed by Germany after the Prussian war of 1870, recaptured by the French and returned to France after the victory of World War I in 1918, reconquered and reannexed to Germany after Hitler's victories in 1940, and had now just been retaken by the French in 1945. Strasbourg was the symbol of the honor of France. To surrender it now to the army of Von Rundstedt was to deliver to the Nazis the population that had greeted the allies. It would be a national humiliation and a real setback. General de Gaulle, now President of the Republic, sent an imperative order on December 30 to French General Vigier, who was the Governor of Strasbourg, to General de Lattre of the First French Army, and to the American General Devers not to evacuate but to defend the city at all costs. De Gaulle also informed General Eisenhower of his decision, explaining the political importance of Strasbourg to the French people. He also cabled President Roosevelt and Winston Churchill to that effect.

At first de Lattre hesitated to obey him, considering that he was under the direct orders of the Supreme Allied Command, but de Gaulle again cabled him imperatively demanding that he defend Strasbourg. On January 3, at the request of de Gaulle, a meeting was held at Versailles between de Gaulle, Churchill, and Eisenhower. The latter explained the strategic reasons for immediate withdrawal, to which de Gaulle replied that "armies are made to serve the policies of states" and that political necessities were more important than military ones. There followed veiled threats between de Gaulle and Eisenhower, who finally gave up and reluctantly ordered General Devers of the American Fourth Army to suspend withdrawal and defend Strasbourg.

Luckily for all the Allies, the powerful German Army's advance had been blocked during this time by the heroic stand of the American General McAucliff at the famous Battle of the Bulge, where, under siege, he refused to surrender. He was relieved just in time by the U.S. 101st Airborne Division from the north and by General Patton's Third Armored Divison rushing from the south. The Wehrmacht had to retreat on all fronts. Strasbourg was saved, and the incident was closed.

Shortly after, another serious incident once more placed General de Gaulle at odds with General Eisenhower.

De Gaulle with his limited forces wanted to establish them in a strategic position in Germany, where he would have a bargaining position with the Americans concerning the delineation of the zones of occupation after the war.

He consequently ordered General de Lattre on March 29 to cross the Rhine and rush to Karlsruhe and Stuttgart, ahead of General Patch and his army, "even if the Americans do not agree and if you [have to] cross [the Rhine] in row boats. It is a question of major national interest."[3]

De Lattre and the First French Army immediately left the Black Forest region, leaving a German army behind, in disregard of General Devers' orders. De Lattre made a swift advance, captured Karlsruhe on April 4, and entered Stuttgart on April 20. Devers, irritated by the independence of the French, ordered General de Lattre to evacuate that city immediately. The former scenario was repeated: De Lattre cabled de Gaulle, who answered: "I order you to maintain the French garrison at Stuttgart and to institute [a French] military government. . . . In the event of American comments you will reply that the orders of your government are to hold and administer the territories conquered by our troops until such a time as the French occupation zone has been fixed in agreement between the interested governments."[4]

General Devers of course referred the whole matter to General Eisenhower. For the second time the Supreme Allied Commander had to solve a serious problem arising from the independence of the French army, which considered itself responsible to its government in Paris and not to him. In his usual conciliatory manner he wrote to de

Gaulle on April 28, informing him that he had to report the matter to Washington, but that he wanted to avoid any problem that could impair the exemplary spirit of cooperation between French and American forces in the battle. He added, however, that giving direct orders to the First French Army for political reasons, in contradiction to instructions given by the military command, was in violation of an agreement between the French government and the government of the United States, prescribing that French divisions armed and equipped by the United States were under the orders of the Combined Chiefs of Staff. De Gaulle replied that the situation was in no way the responsibility of Eisenhower, but resulted from the lack of agreement between the American and the British governments and between those governments and the French government concerning the occupation of German territories.

The French consequently did not evacuate Stuttgart and refused to permit its use by General Patch. "So unyielding were the French in their assertion that national prestige was involved," stated Eisenhower, "that the argument was referred to me. I instructed U.S. General Devers to stand firm and to require compliance with his plan. The French General still proved obstinate and referred the matter to Paris. General de Gaulle continued to maintain an unyielding attitude on the governmental level in his reply to a firmly worded message from the President of the United States on the subject. General Eisenhower then warned the French commander that under the circumstances, "it was necessary for me to inform the combined chiefs of staff that I could no longer count with certainty on the operational use of any French Forces they might be equipping in the future."[5] This threat of a possible curtailment of equipment for the French Forces proved effective. In fact, the Americans gained the facilities.

A third conflict arose on another front, after the war was over. The French armies under the command of General Juin had proved effective in Italy, and won praise from the American and British commands. After the capitulation of Rome, they had moved swiftly in June to northwest Italy. De Gaulle considered that the time had come to annex to France a small area on the western slope of the Italian Alps, where the population was ethnically French and spoke French. This small territory had been the object of many disputes between France and Italy since 1860. However, the Supreme Allied Command had decided to extend the jurisdiction of its own military government over this small portion of land, which the French Forces now occupied under the orders of General Paul Doyen.

De Gaulle refused to let the Allies interfere with his occupation of the land and claimed that he was not bound by the Allied Command in Italy because the armistice with Italy had been signed by the Americans and the British without France. He concluded that "the question of the future delineation of the French-Italian frontier is an affair which concerned France and Italy" and no one else. The French military commander Gen. Paul Doyen received stiff orders from de Gaulle to oppose any move from the Americans or the British. He accordingly told General Grittenbeyer of the U.S. Fourth Army Corps, who was acting for the Allied Military Command, that his instructions, direct from General de Gaulle, were to make as clear as possible to the Allied Command that "I have received the order to prevent the setting up of the Allied Military Government in the territories occupied by our troops and administered by us, with all necessary means without exception."[6]

General Alexander, Commander of the Allied armies in Italy, was indignant. On June 5 he asked the Combined Chiefs of Staff for the authority to complete the occupation of northwest Italy "using force if necessary."

The next day the Department of State protested vigorously to the French Foreign Minister concerning the violation of the Franco-American agreement regarding the cooperation of the French Forces with the Allies, stating that the position adopted by General Doyen would create a "highly" inflammable situation. It would "confirm the fears that the French government intends to use force to obtain its political aims."

President Harry Truman, who had not shared Roosevelt's personal dislike of de Gaulle, this time felt outraged by his attitude. On June 7 he sent a long telegram through his embassy in Paris[7] stating that he was indignant to learn that the First French Army, under the command of General Eisenhower, Supreme Allied Commander for the Western front, had ignored the orders that it had received to withdraw to the frontier in execution of agreements for the occupation and the organization of the Allied military government. The President stated that the notices sent by General Doyen "made the unbelievable threat that French soldiers bearing American arms will combat American and Allied soldiers whose efforts and sacrifices had, so recently and so efficiently, contributed to the liberation of France itself."

Truman insisted that de Gaulle reconsider the whole question. If not, he would inform the people of the United States, "who would be profoundly shocked if they were aware of the nature of the action which your military officers, presumably with your approval, had threatened to take." He concluded that as long as a threat existed by the French government against American soldiers, he "considered it imperative to suspend the delivery of arms and ammunition to the French troops. Rations will continue to be supplied."[8]

De Gaulle replied the same day that it had "obviously never been the intention of the French government, nor of General Doyen, commander of the Alpine Detachment, to oppose by force the presence of American troops in the little zone occupied by us."[9] In fact, President Truman never lifted the embargo against military deliveries to the French Army, but gasoline and rations continued to be supplied to the French Forces occupying Germany.

This third incident was not communicated to the press at that time to avoid arousing public opinion and creating further dissensions among the Allies.

The French soon after evacuated the small villages of Cuneo in the Valley of Aosta. However, following the Peace Treaty, the Italian government ceded these territories to France. A plebiscite was held and the population overwhelmingly chose to join France.

In all three instances, de Gaulle used the army as an instrument of national policy. He acted in the name of France, now an independent and sovereign country, for whom he could decide unilaterally its national interest, without consulting his allies, and without negotiation.

The detailed account of these three incidents, occurring during the tenure of Harry S. Truman, who bore neither prejudice nor distrust towards de Gaulle, clearly illustrates not only de Gaulle's extraordinary character but the persistence with which he pursued his principal objective, namely, demonstrating that the nation of France had not been erased from the map after the disaster of 1940. His pursuit of this objective is the reason he had continuously challenged, with tiny military forces, Roosevelt's policies. After France's liberation, and indeed throughout his presidency, de Gaulle continued to appreciate the political importance of military power.

It may be concluded that, in the case of the three incidents discussed here, de Gaulle might have obtained the same results through negotiations with the Allies. Had he attempted to negotiate, however, he would have been doing so from a position of relative weakness, as supplicant, instead of acting from a position of strength and defiance. His actions, therefore, were an attempt to place France on an equal footing with the Great Powers, the victors of the war—the United States, Great Britain, and the USSR.

CHAPTER XXV

Allies in Conflict

This account of events which transpired during the years 1940 through 1945 may seem to relate nothing but a series of quarrels among Frenchmen, between Frenchmen and Americans, or between Roosevelt and de Gaulle. But these disputes—as acerbic and ubiquitous as they were—only served to mask underlying differences of principle that existed between de Gaulle and Roosevelt. When these differences manifested themselves over the course of the war, the incessant rivalry and hostility each leader bore the other only magnified problems that otherwise might have been mitigated by the conduct of skillful and tactful diplomacy.

From the outset, Roosevelt and de Gaulle had very different opinions as to the conduct of the war. De Gaulle was resolved to fight with all his resources alongside England and the United States, but only under the condition that the latter acknowledge and accept the objectives of the war for which France was fighting. He declared more than once that "Free France intends to march alongside her allies with the express understanding that they in turn will march alongside of her."[1] Roosevelt felt otherwise. Winning the war as quickly as possible, with the minimum loss of human life, was his first priority; both foreign and domestic policies were given secondary importance.[2] These two opposing outlooks exacerbated the fierce conflict between the two statesmen.

Roosevelt and de Gaulle's strategic objectives were also diametrically opposed. After France's defeat, the United States favored a policy of "expediency." Its aim was the total neutralization of French territories and colonies, its army, and especially its navy. To this end, the United States continued to maintain an embassy in Vichy. Considerable efforts had to be expended to prevent Vichy France from declaring war on England and to prevent the use of French colonies as German bases. There was also, of course, the danger that the French fleet would join the Nazis.

Free France's basic doctrine was the complete opposite. It wished to bring all French territories in the Empire, as well as all Frenchmen everywhere, into active combat under de Gaulle's authority. French neutrality had to be done away with no matter what the cost. The United States, on the other hand, was adopting an opportunistic policy. It favored French neutrality and its corollary, support of Pétain, as long as he did not lean too far to the Nazis' side.

It is true that, as the danger posed by the Japanese and the Germans diminished, the United States' opportunistic policy shifted, especially after the U.S. landing in North Africa. It was then that an effort was made to enlist the support of Vichy "neutrals," and even of the collaborationists. The United States attempted to enlist the support of Marshal Pétain, General Weygand, and, finally, Darlan in order once again to involve all of France in combat on the Allied side. To American strategists, North Africa suddenly appeared to be a base from which they could liberate Europe; therefore, the policy of fostering French neutrality was eventually abandoned.

The second conflict of principle between de Gaulle and Roosevelt stemmed from the American policy of directly contacting local authorities. Some of the colonies were loyal to de Gaulle, but the Americans were unwilling to initiate contact with him for the purpose of establishing bases or coordinating military policies in those territories. Roosevelt instead had questioned French sovereignty over these lands ever since the Armistice of 1940. This attitude had longstanding roots in U.S. policy and was established after years of dealing with Latin American republics, where revolutions were frequent and the authority of the State was, therefore, uncertain. But this posture, which ran counter to the principle of French sovereignty and of national unity, was also contrary to de Gaulle's way of thinking. It was only later, when the provisional government of the French Republic had gained official recognition, that these conflicts were resolved.

Finally, the United States was also categorically anticolonialist, which led inevitably to clashes with de Gaulle. The United States wanted to ensure that all countries under French "control" be liberated as quickly as possible—at the very latest immediately after the end of the war. "How can you protest against foreign occupation of your country while France herself continues to maintain colonies?"

was more or less the American sentiment. All Americans, whether liberal or conservative, Republican or Democrat, were in agreement on this issue.

Free France, however, insisted on her integrity concerning the maintenance of her colonial empire. Under no circumstances whatsoever would de Gaulle and his followers permit a foreign power to interfere in France's overseas sovereignty. Consequently, conflicts arose regarding the landing of American troops in New Caledonia and in North Africa, and the winning over of Dakar. In the years following the war, France finally divested itself of its colonies on its own, and the colonial issue was consequently no longer a cause of conflicts.

Thus, with respect to three issues—French neutrality, independent American contacts with local authorities, and anti-colonialism—Free France and the United States held widely diverging points of view. These differences persisted until France was liberated, and for even a short time beyond. During the war they appeared serious, but discreet and subtle diplomacy could have smoothed over differences. It is very unfortunate that Free France did not have someone in Washington who was respected by the Americans and who knew how to set their minds at rest as to Free France's real objectives in the war. This person could have played down, rather than exacerbated, de Gaulle's violent outbursts. De Gaulle had a difficult character, but he can scarcely be faulted for the fact that not a single high-ranking diplomat rallied to his cause during the first years of his movement, and that many influential Frenchmen undermined his actions continuously.

For his part, de Gaulle never stopped contending with the Americans. In them he saw "a taste for hegemony,"[3] and it must be remembered that he was extremely sensitive when it came to matters concerning France's welfare, the integrity of her empire, or his own personal prestige.

While Churchill and other Allied heads of state—Belgian, Norwegian, Danish, Dutch, Greek, Chinese—sided with Roosevelt or at least negotiated with him, de Gaulle did not. This self-proclaimed leader, who was opposed by his own people abroad and sometimes at home, and who headed only a small group of volunteers, persisted in crossing swords with Roosevelt. To the President of the United States of America, this was unpardonable.

The policy of the American administration during the whole period from 1940 to 1945 was also somewhat strange: it officially recognized the government of Vichy, a vassal of the Nazis, which had its embassy in Washington. But during the same period it accepted a Free French Delegation, the arch-enemy of Vichy. The United States was dealing at the same time with both an "official" government and its determined opposition. There were seemingly endless paradoxes. The United States was granting lend-lease equipment and war material to Free France, first through the British, and then directly—an unusual way to support a non-recognized entity against a recognized government. Harold L. Ickes, Secretary of the Interior, attended the July 14 Free French celebration of Bastille Day in 1941, and made a fiery speech praising the Resistance. And when the Free French had an efficient military recruiting bureau in New York, the administration enticed General Giraud to open a competing office in the same city.

There was also another paradoxical situation: as the war was developing and the United States was increasing its involvement, the relations between the President and de Gaulle became worse instead of better. To add to the confusion, the worsening relations between Roosevelt and de Gaulle did not preclude an ever-increasing supply of war materials from the United States to Free France, whose president was de Gaulle!

After the U.S. Army landed in North Africa, the elimination of de Gaulle became one of the principal objectives of Roosevelt's policy toward France. Indeed, the President never ceased to oppose the General, and carried out anti-Gaullist plans singlehandedly. More than once the President instructed his envoys to bypass the State Department and communicate directly with him, while at the same time the War Department was maintaining good relations with the General. The Office of Strategic Services (OSS) and the Secret Service also favored de Gaulle, and the American press, always independent, gave him full support.

To the chaos of the decision-making process in Washington one must add the incessant intrigues of the French exiles. The White House and the Free French headquarters spent a great deal of time fighting each other, to the point of losing sight of the principal objective of the war. Despite the squabbles and the endless confusion, the wartime record was a mixed one. On the field of battle, American and French soldiers fought bravely side by side, despite the attitudes of their leaders. On the diplomatic front, however, things were not always simple, and fighting the same enemy did not make for true allies.

Epilogue

*War is against our enemies; peace is against
our friends.*

—Charles de Gaulle

Nearly half a century has passed since the end of the Second World
War and the confrontations between Roosevelt and de Gaulle.
Although he won the war, Roosevelt's dream of establishing permanent peace in the world was not realized. And while de Gaulle succeeded in recreating an independent France, he did not resuscitate it
as a major world power as he had hoped to do. France became a great
Western power between two superpowers. And although de Gaulle
did not rule his native country as a dictator, as Roosevelt feared he
might, he did remain a proud and difficult ally.

The wartime conflicts between de Gaulle and Roosevelt seem to be
far behind us, but are they? During the war, de Gaulle's policy toward
America consisted mainly of challenges to the President in order to
promote the principle of independence in international affairs. He
tried to establish a position with the other superpower, the Soviet
Union, to counterbalance any dependence on the United States. To
further this aim, he went to Moscow in December 1944 to obtain a
treaty of alliance and assistance with Stalin. According to the agreement, both countries pledged not to participate in any action directed
against the other. He was later to be disappointed by Stalin and Roosevelt when they both refused to invite him to the Yalta Conference
in February 1945, where plans for the postwar world were discussed
and agreed upon in his absence.

As president of the Fifth Republic, de Gaulle fought to restore

France to her prewar position as a leader in international affairs. He wanted to reestablish France to an exalted position of grandeur, and proposed to the United States and to Great Britain the creation of a triumvirate to direct all world affairs. This offer was rejected by President Eisenhower and later by John Kennedy. In their view, France had lost most of her prestige since the defeat of 1940 and was a difficult and unreliable ally. They also feared that by accepting de Gaulle's proposal they might antagonize other European governments. Finally, de Gaulle attempted in vain to organize all Western nations in a close alliance to form a third force to counterbalance the two superpowers.

De Gaulle, a realist, soon discovered that the power of the United States, and its power alone, could guarantee the independence and freedom of the Western democracies. Only the United States could prevent invasion by the Soviet superpower. He concluded, then, that in all major conflicts between the United States and the Soviet Union, he had no alternative but to side with the United States for the survival of his own country. Consequently, de Gaulle joined with the United States without hesitation in the two Berlin crises. In May 1960, when the U.S. spy plane U-2 was shot down by the Soviets, he declared to President Eisenhower, "Whatever happens, I will be with you."[1] And his attitude was just as clear during the Cuban Missile Crisis—he did not hesitate to declare to Dean Acheson, President Kennedy's former envoy, "If there is a war, I will be with you, but there will be no war."

On other occasions, when the Western democracies were not threatened by the Soviets, he showed his independence by opposing the United States at every turn. This attitude was particularly clear when problems arose in the Third World. He criticized and opposed United States involvement in Vietnam, and denounced the participation of the U.S. marines in the Dominican insurrection by stating that France "disapproves of the action of the United States and requests the withdrawal of American forces." He also opposed, constantly and with vigor, all American policies in the Middle East.

And in 1964 de Gaulle refused to attend the official ceremony to commemorate the twentieth anniversary of the landing of American Forces in Normandy on June 6, 1944.

The policy of relying upon ultimate American protection for his country and Western Europe, while resisting its influence in all other respects, led de Gaulle to take a further paradoxical position that has not always been understood: between 1960 and 1966 he gradually withdrew France from NATO, the North Atlantic Treaty Organization.[2] But to further French interests, he nevertheless remained an active member of the Atlantic Alliance. The United States, for its part, acted without consulting France and sometimes took positions against her. This was the case when the United States joined the USSR in forcing, during the Suez crisis in 1956, the Anglo-French expeditionary forces to evacuate Egypt. America's anticolonialist tradition was also apparent during the Tunisian revolt and the Algerian war, when the United States did not support the French position.

The underlying policies of postwar America and France have not greatly changed. Each nation follows an independent and sometimes conflicting course, but despite the problems each creates for the other and over which so much political energy is spent they are nonetheless united in times of major crisis.

Despite the fluctuating character of Franco-American relations over the decades, there remains a deep feeling of solidarity and friendship between the two peoples, who share a common faith in human rights and have been allies in three great wars: the War of Independence and two World Wars. As President Roosevelt said in a broadcast to the French on November 7, 1942, *"Il n'y a pas deux nations plus unies par les liens de l'histoire et de l'amitié mutuelle, que le peuple de France et les États-Unis d'Amérique."* ("There are no two nations more united by the bonds of history and of mutual friendship than the people of France and the people of the United States of America.")

I have myself, more than once, witnessed this feeling of friendship in the streets of Paris as well as in the small villages of France. It is perhaps best expressed by the women of a small village in Normandy, Sainte Mère Eglise, whom I have seen make their yearly pilgrimage to place flowers on the graves of the young soldiers who came from so far to fight and die, to make them free.

Notes

CHAPTER I

1. Edgar de Larminat, *Chroniques Irrévérentieuses* (Paris: Plon, 1967), p. 37.
2. Charles de Gaulle, *Mémoires de Guerre* (Paris: Plon, 1954), 1:267.
3. de Larminat, *Chroniques,* p. 57. Col. (later Gen.) Edgar de Larminat was a brilliant officer. He had insisted in vain that his superior, General Mittelhauser, join the British; and he wanted entire battalions of French soldiers to leave Lebanon and join the British in Palestine. But General Wavell, in command of British forces in the Middle East, feared that de Larminat's actions would lead to much trouble, and refused to let him speak on the radio from Jerusalem or Cairo to make an appeal to the French army.

CHAPTER II

1. John Gunther, *Roosevelt in Retrospect* (New York: Harper, 1950), 314.
2. Warren F. Kimball, *Churchill and Roosevelt. The Complete Correspondence* (Princeton: Princeton University Press, 1984), 1:47.
3. Kimball, *Churchill and Roosevelt,* 1:52.
4. Winston Churchill, *The Second World War* (Boston: Houghton Mifflin), 2:197.
5. See Kimball, *Churchill and Roosevelt,* 1:43–71.
6. deGaulle, *Mémoires,* 1:503.
7. United States *Statutes at Large,* 54:63.
8. Robert Sherwood, *Roosevelt and Hopkins* (New York: Harper, 1948), pp. 187–91.
9. James MacGregor Burns, *Roosevelt 1940–1945* (New York: Harcourt, Brace, Jovanovich, 1970), p. 28.

CHAPTER IV

1. Letters quoted in extenso in Raoul Aglion, *De Gaulle et Roosevelt* (Paris: Plon, 1984), 241–47.

CHAPTER V

1. de Gaulle, *Mémoires,* 1:267.
2. Ibid., p. 471.

3. Jacques Maritain, À *Travers le Désastre* (New York: Éditions de la Maison Française, 1944), p. 115.

4. Roussy de Sales, *L'Amérique Entre en Guerre* (Paris: La Jeune Parque, 1948), p. 216.

5. de Gaulle, *Mémoires,* 1:482.

CHAPTER VI

1. de Sales, *L'Amerique,* p. 240.

2. Ibid., p. 267.

3. Ibid., p.269.

4. St.-John Perse, *Oevres complètes* (Paris: Galimard, 1972), p. 632.

CHAPTER VII

1. de Gaulle, *Mémoires,* 1:269.

2. François Kersaudy, *Churchill and de Gaulle* (New York: Atheneum, 1983), p. 83.

3. Cordell Hull, *Memoirs* (London: Hodder & Stoughton, 1948), pp. 1160–64.

4. de Gaulle, *Mémoires,* 1:83.

5. Raoul Aglion, *L'Épopée de la France Combattante* (New York: Édition de la Maison Française, 1943), p. 164.

CHAPTER VIII

1. "Foreign Relations of the United States," (hereafter USFR) (Archives of the United States, 1940), 2:504–5.

2. An early controversial hero of the Free French Navy, Muselier was retired and lived in the South of France when the war broke out. When he learned that the Germans were in Paris, fearing they would find the secret strategic papers of the navy, he rushed to the capital. He reached the archives before the enemy did and succeeded in burning them. He then attempted to return to the south of France. It was not easy. The train he took had to stop after two hundred miles for lack of coal. He then found a bicycle, then used a peasant's horse cart, and finally commandeered a fire engine that took him to a small French port where he took a transfer to Gibraltar. The British Coast Guard who received him there in rags and black with smoke could not believe he was an admiral. He soon went to London. As he outranked de Gaulle he wanted to take his place. Of course General de Gaulle refused, but appointed him head of the Free French navy and sent him with a flotilla on an expedition in the North Atlantic.

3. Hull, *Memoirs,* 1130; also Churchill, *Second World War,* 3:6.6.6–6.6.7.

4. Émile Muselier, *De Gaulle contre le Gaullisme* (Paris: Chêne, 1946), p. 305.

5. USFR, 2:115.

6. Churchill, *Second World War,* 3:667.

7. USFR, 1942, 2:508.

8. Hull, *Memoirs,* p. 1131; also *New York Times,* Dec. 31, 1941, p. 1 (for text in English and French).

9. Churchill, *Complete Speeches,* 6:6543.

10. USFR, 1942, 2:666.

11. Muselier, *De Gaulle contre le Gaullisme,* p. 304.

12. Sherwood, *Roosevelt and Hopkins,* p. 489.

13. *Complete War Memoirs of Charles de Gaulle* (New York: Simon & Schuster, 1978), pp. 216–17; and also de Gaulle, *Mémoires de Guerre—Le Salut* (Paris: Plon, 1954), p. 505.

CHAPTER IX

1. USFR, 1942, 2:509.

2. William Langer, *Our Vichy Gamble* (New York: 1947).

3. USFR, 1942, 2:510.

4. Ibid., 2:508.

5. Ibid., 2:504.

6. Ibid., p. 509 (also conversation of author with François Charles Roux, later Ambassador of France).

7. Ibid.

CHAPTER X

1. Joseph P. Lash, *Eleanor Roosevelt* (New York: Doubleday, 1964).

2. Henri de Kérillis, *Français, Voici la Vérité.* (New York: Éditions de la Maison Française, 1942), p. 312.

3. Ibid., p. 312.

4. de Kérillis, *De Gaulle Dictateur* (Montreal: Beauchemin, 1945), p. 9.

5. Eve Curie, *Journey Among Warriors* (New York: Doubleday, 1943).

CHAPTER XI

1. Fritsch-Estrangin, *New York entre de Gaulle et Pétain* (Paris: La Table Ronde, 1969), p. 172.

CHAPTER XII

1. USFR 1941, 2:579. Telegram from Mallon, U.S. Consul.

2. Ibid., p. 582.

3. Ibid., p. 583.

4. Ibid., p. 584.

5. Ibid., p. 579.

6. Ibid.

7. Ibid., pp. 579–82.

8. Ibid.

9. Ibid., p. 582.

CHAPTER XIII

1. USFR, 1942, 2:550.

2. Ibid., p. 522.

CHAPTER XIV

1. Pierre Tissier, *Le Gouvernement de Vichy* (London: Harrap, 1942). Also Robert Aron, *Histoire de Vichy* (Paris: Arthème Fayard, 1956); Robert O. Paxton, Vichy-France 1940–1944 (New York: Random House, 1982).

2. Tissier, *Le Gouvernment de Vichy,* p. 120.

3. J. R. Tournoux, *Pétain et de Gaulle* (Paris: Plon, 1964), p. 258. (Pro-German instructions of collaboration to General Dentz in Syria). See also Paxto, *Vichy-France.*

4. Fritsch-Estrangin, *New York,* p. 45.

5. *Herald Tribune,* August 31, 1941.

6. H. Montgomery, *Room 3603* (New York: Farrar, Straus, 1963), p. 97.

7. Ibid., p. 101.

8. A copy of this letter was given by Hervé Alphand to the author at that time. Extracts were published in R. Aglim *De Gaulle et Roosevelt* (Paris: Plon, 1984), p. 161.

CHAPTER XV

1. André Weil-Curie, "Du Côté de Carlton Gardens," *Revue des Deux Mondes,* Paris, March 15, 1987.

2. *Life,* August 24, 1942, p. 87.

3. Ibid.

4. Author's notes on meeting.

5. de Gaulle *Mémoires* 2:381. Also USFR, 1942, 541–42.

6. USFR, Ibid., 544.

7. Ibid., p. 546.

8. Ibid. Also de Gaulle, *L'Unité,* 411.

9. USFR, ibid.

10. Ibid., pp. 546–47. See also Roussy de Sales, *L'Amérique,* p. 368.

11. Private conversation between François Charles-Roux and the author, 1984.

12. de Gaulle, *Mémoires,* 2:408.

13. USFR, ibid., p. 548.

14. Ibid., p. 549.

15. *La Lettre de la France Combattante,* Vol II. London 1942–1943 (issued by the Press Service, Free French Headquarters).

16. USFR, ibid., p. 556.

CHAPTER XVI

1. Kimball, *Churchill & Roosevelt,* 1:583.

2. Burns, *Roosevelt,* p. 297. Also Churchill, *Second World War,* 4:635.

3. Churchill, *Second World War,* 4:636.

4. *Free France,* Vol. II, No. 11, p. 306. Free French Information Service, NY, 1942.

CHAPTER XVII

1. These events that took place in Algiers were reported to me in conversations I had with Gaston Palewski, Chef de Cabinet (chief of the civilian staff) of General de Gaulle, and Louis Vallon of the underground resistance. They are confirmed by Harriman, Sherwood, Pendar and other Americans.
2. Kimball, *Roosevelt and Churchill*, 2:209, May 8, 1943, Roosevelt to Churchill.
3. Averell Harriman, *Special Envoy* (New York: Random House, 1975), p. 187.
4. de Gaulle, *Mémoires*, 2:79.
5. Kenneth Pendar, *Adventures in Diplomacy*, (London: Cassel, 1966), p. 148.
6. de Gaulle, *Mémoires*, 2:79.
7. Sherwood, *Roosevelt and Hopkins*, p. 685.
8. W. Churchill, *Second World War*, 4:682.
9. de Gaulle, *Mémoires*, 2:80.
10. Kimball, *Churchill and Roosevelt*, 2:209.
11. Harriman, *Special Envoy*, p. 185.
12. de Gaulle, *Lettres, notes et carnets*, 47-1941-51943:518.
13. Institut Charles de Gaulle, *Espoir*, no. 43, 29.
14. Eleanor Roosevelt. *Autobiography*, 248.
15. de Gaulle, *Mémoires* 2:86.
16. Kimball, 2:255.

CHAPTER XVIII

1. de Kérillis, *De Gaulle Dictateur*, p. 222.
2. Alphand, *L'étonnement d'être* (Paris: Fayard, 1977), p. 147.

CHAPTER XIX

1. Kimball, *Churchill and Roosevelt*, p. 181.
2. de Gaulle, *Mémoires*, 2:223.
3. Béthouard: *Cinq Années*, d'espoir (Paris: Plon), 243.
4. de Gaulle, *Mémoires* 2:223–224.
5. Ibid.
6. Ibid.
7. Ibid.
8. W. Donovan's memorandum to President Roosevelt, June 15, 1944.
9. Anthony Cave Brown, *Wild Bill Donovan, the Last Hero* (New York: Times Books, 1982), p. 561.
10. Ibid.

CHAPTER XX

1. de Gaulle, *Mémoires*, 2:237–240.
2. Samuel I. Rosenman, "Roosevelt's toast to de Gaulle," *Public Papers and Addresses of F. D. Roosevelt* (New York: Random House), 13:1914–16.

3. Eleanor Roosevelt, *Autobiography,* p. 269.

4. Rosenman, "Roosevelt's toast," pp. 1914–16.

5. de Gaulle, *Mémoires,* 2: 239.

6. Ibid.

7. *FDR Library,* July 11, 1944, Press Conference 24, 12, 13.

8. de Gaulle, in *Mémoires,* "Letter from Roosevelt to Joseph Clark, Congressman," 2:240.

9. Ibid., p. 210.

10. Records of the French embassy in Washington, D.C., and *New York Herald Tribune,* July 12, l944.

11. *New York Herald Tribune,* July 11, 1944.

12. Ibid., July 16.

13. Ibid., August 4.

CHAPTER XXI

1. Alphand, *L'Étonnement d'Être,* p. 142.

2. *New York Post,* June 20, 1944.

3. Prime Minister to Foreign Secretary, May 21, l943, p. 181.

4. Léger to President, January 31 (folder 1–44), 1944, F.D.R. Library.

5. Letter from Alexis Léger to President, November 8, 1943, F.D.R. Library.

6. F.D.R. Library, Secretary's file, Box 5.

7. USFR, Diplomatic papers, Vol. II, Europe, pp.185-1943.

CHAPTER XXII

1. USFR, Diplomatic papers, Vol. II, Europe, pp. 185–1963.

2. *New York Times,* September 10, 1944.

3. Curiously enough, in April 1944, while Roosevelt was procrastinating, Himmler, Hitler's heir to the Nazi empire, recognized de Gaulle as head of the French government. He had Goering's backing to send him a message offering a separate peace and an alliance: "You have won.... But what are you going to do? Hand yourself over to the Anglo-Saxons? They will treat you like a satellite and you will lose your honor. Associate yourself with the Soviets? They will impose their law and will liquidate you personally.... In reality the only path that will lead your people to greatness and independence is an understanding with defeated Germany. Proclaim it right away! Make contact without delay while the men who run the Reich still enjoy the de facto power and want to lead their country in a new direction ..." deGaulle received this message with contempt. He did not answer. (de Gaulle, *Mémoires,* 3:176).

4. de Gaulle, *Mémoires,* 3:44.

CHAPTER XXIII

1. de Gaulle, *Mémoires,* 3:391.

2. Ibid., p. 401.

3. Ibid., p. 88.

4. Ibid.

5. Ibid., p. 89.

6. Ibid., pp. 88–89.

7. Ibid., 402.

8. Ibid., p. 89.

CHAPTER XXIV

1. G. R. Tournoux, *La Tragedie du Général* (Paris: Plon, 1967), p. 326.

2. See de Gaulle *Le Fil de l'Épée* (Edit. Paris: Berger, 1944).

3. de Gaulle, *Mémoires,* 3:153.

4. Ibid.

5. Eisenhower, *Crusade in Europe,* p. 450.

6. de Gaulle, *Mémoires,* 3:538.

7. Ibid.

8. Harry Truman, *Memoirs,* (New York: Doubleday 1955), pp. 239–42.

9. de Gaulle, *Mémoires,* 3:539.

CHAPTER XXV

1. de Gaulle, *Mémoires,* 3: 529–33.

2. USFR Department of State to the British Embassy, 1942, p. 523.

3. de Gaulle, *Mémoires,* 1:531.

EPILOGUE

1. Alfred Grosser, *Les Occidentaux,* p. 239.

2. The NATO Treaty was signed in Washington on April 4, 1949.

Bibliography

Aglion, Raoul. *War in the Desert*. New York: Henry Holt, 1942.

————. *The Fighting French*. New York: Henry Holt, 1943.

————. *L'Épopée de la France Combattante*. New York: Editions de la Maison Française, 1944.

————. *De Gaulle et Roosevelt*. Paris: Plon, 1984.

Alphand, Hervé. *L'Étonnement d'Être*. Paris: Fayard, 1977.

Amouroux, Henri. *Le 18 Juin 1940*. Paris: Fayard, 1964.

Aron, Robert. *Histoire de Vichy*. Paris: Arthème Fayard, 1954.

Aron, Raymond. *The Century of Total War*. Boston: 1955.

Bethouard, A. *Cinq Années d'Espérance*. Paris: Plon, 1968.

Billotte, Pierre. *Le Temps des Armes*. Paris: Plon, 1972.

Brantz, A. *Turn of the Tide*. London: Collins, 1957.

————. *Triumph of the West*. London: Collins, 1959.

Blum, Suzanne. *Vivre sans la Patrie*. Paris: Plon, 1975.

de Boisdeffre, P. *Le Revue des Deux Mondes*. Paris, December 1984.

Brown, Anthony Cove. *Wild Bill Donovan: The Last Hero*. New York: Times Books, 1962.

Bullitt, William. "How We Won the War and Lost the Peace." Life, 25 (August 30, 1948).

Burns, James MacGregor. *Roosevelt, the Soldier of Freedom*. New York: Harcourt, 1970.

Catroux, Général Georges. *Dans la Bataille de la Méditerranée*. Paris: Julliard, 1949.

Chaban-Delmas, Jacques. "Charles de Gaulle." *Paris Match*, Edition No. 1, 1980.

Churchill, Winston. *The Second World War*. 6 vols. London: Cassel, 1948–53.

Coleville, John. *The Fringes of Power.* London/New York: Norton, 1978.

Conte, Arthur. *Yalta ou le Partage du Monde.* Paris: Lafont, 1956.

Cook, Don. *Charles de Gaulle.* New York: Putnam & Sons, 1984.

Cot, Pierre. *Le Procès de la République.* New York: Editions de la Maison Française, 1944.

Cremille, *Histoire de la France Libre.* Geneva: Cremille, 1972.

Crosier, Brian. *Charles de Gaulle.* New York: Scribner, 1973.

Curie, Eve. *Voyage parmi les guerriers.* New York: Editions de la Maison Française, 1945.

de Gaulle, Charles. *Mémoires de Guerre.* 3 vols. Paris: Plon, 1954–59.

———. *Lettres, notes et carnets.* Paris: Plon, 1981, 1982, 1983.

Divine, R. A. *Roosevelt and World War II.* New York: Penguin Books, 1969.

Duroselle, Jean Baptiste. *Tout Empire Périra.* Paris: Publication Sorbonne, 1982.

———. *L'Abîme. T. N.,* Paris, 1982.

Eisenhower, David. *Eisenhower at War.* New York: Random House, 1986.

Eisenhower, Dwight. *Crusade in Europe.* New York: Doubleday, 1948.

Espoir, Revue de L'Institut Charles de Gaulle, Paris.

Feis, Herbert. *Churchill, Roosevelt, Stalin.* Princeton: Princeton University Press, 1957.

Ferro, Maurice. *De Gaulle et l'Amérique.* Paris: Plon, 1973.

Freitsch-Estrangein, Guy. *New York entre de Gaulle et Pétain.* Paris: La Table Ronde, 1969.

Funk, Arthur. *Charles de Gaulle: The Crucial Years 1943–1944.* Norton/University of Oklahoma, 1959.

Gilbert, Martin. *Winston Churchill.* New York: Houghton Mifflin, 1987.

Gillois, A. *Histoire secrete des Français Libres.* Paris/London: Hachette, 1973.

Grosser, Alfred. *Les Occidentaux.* Paris: Fayard, 1981.

Gunther, John. *Roosevelt in Retrospect.* New York: Harper, 1950.

Harriman, Averell. *Special Envoy.* New York: Random House, 1975.

Hoffman, Stanley. *Decline or Renewal of France Since 1930.* New York: Viking Press, 1974.

Hull, Cordell. *Memoirs.* London: Hodder & Stoughton, 1948.

Johnson, Paul. *Modern Times.* New York: Harper & Row, 1983.

de Kérillis, Henri. *De Gaulle Dictateur.* Montreal: Beauchemin, 1945.

———. *Français, Voiçi la Vérité,* New York: Editions de la Maison Française, 1942.

Kersaudy, François. *De Gaulle et Churchill.* Paris: Plon, 1981.

Kimball, Warren F. *Churchill and Roosevelt; Complete Correspondence.* Princeton: Princeton University Press, 1984.

Lacouture, Jean. *de Gaulle.* Paris: Le Seuil, 1965.

———. *Le Rebel.* Paris: Le Seuil, 1984.

Langer, William. *Our Vichy Gamble.* New York, 1947.

Lash, Joseph. *Eleanor and Franklin.* New York: New American Library, 1973.

de Larminat, Edgar. *Chroniques Irrévérencieuses*. Paris: Plon, 1967.

Laurent, Anne. *Les Rivaux de Charles de Gaulle*. Paris: Laffont, 1977.

Lottman, Herbert R. *Pétain, Hero or Traitor*. New York: William Morrow Co.

Macmillan, Harold. *War Diaries*. New York: Saint Martin Press, 1984.

Macridis, Roy. *De Gaulle—Implacable Ally*. New York: Harper & Row, 1966.

Maritain, Jacques. *À Travers le Désastre*. New York: Editions de la Maison Française, 1944.

Michel, Henri. *Histoire de la France Libre*. Paris: Presses Universitaires de France, 1972.

Montgomery, H. *Room 3603*. New York: Farrar, Straus, 1963.

Murphy, Robert. *Diplomat Among Warriors*. New York: Doubleday, 1964.

Muselier, Emile: *De Gaulle contre le Gaullisme*. Paris: Editions du Chêne, 1946.

Paxton, Robert, O. *Vichy-France*. Old Guard-New Order 1940–1944, New York: Random House, 1982.

Pendar, Kenneth. *Adventures in Diplomacy*. London: Cassel, 1966.

Pertinax (André Géraud). *Les Fossoyeurs*. 2 vols. New York: Editions de la Maison Française, 1943.

Roosevelt, Eleanor. *The Autobiography of Eleanor Roosevelt*. New York: Harper & Row, 1937.

Roosevelt, Elliott. *F.D.R., His Personal Letters*. New York: Duell, 1950.

Rosenman, Samuel. *Public Papers and Addresses of F. D. Roosevelt*. New York: Random House, 1943.

Rougier, Louis. *Les Accords Pétain-Churchill*. Montreal: Beauchemin, 1945.

de Roussy de Sales, Raoul. *L'Amérique entre en Guerre*. Paris: La Jeune Parque, 1948.

Saint-John Perse. *Oeuvres Complètes*. Paris: Editions Galimard, 1972.

Sherwood, Robert E. *Roosevelt and Hopkins: An Intimate History*. New York: Harper, 1948.

Shoenbrun, D. *The Three Lives of Général de Gaulle*. New York: Atheneum, 1965.

Smith, Gaddis. *American Diplomacy During the Second World War*. New York: John Wiley, 1965.

Soustelle, J. *Envers et Contre Tout*. Paris: Laffont, 1947–50.

Spears, Sir Edward. *Two Men Who Saved France*. London: Eyre and Spottiswood, 1966.

Tissier, Pierre. *Le Gouvernement de Vichy*. London: Harrap, 1942.

Torrès, Henri. *La France Trahie, Pierre Laval*. New York: Brentano, 1941.

———. *La Machine Infernale*. New York: Brentano, 1943.

Tournoux, J. R. *Pétain et de Gaulle*. Paris: Plon, 1964.

Truman, Harry S. *Memoirs*. 2 vols. New York: Doubleday, 1955.

Viorst, Milton. *Hostile Allies: FDR and de Gaulle*. New York: Macmillan, 1965.

Weil-Curiel, André. *Le Temps de la Honte, le Jour se Lève a Londres*. Paris: Editions du Myrte, 1945.

Welles, Sumner. *The World of Four Freedoms*. New York: Morningside Heights, 1943.

———. *The Time for Decision.* New York: Harper, 1944.

White, Dorothy Shipley. *Seeds of Discord.* Syracuse: Syracuse University Press, 1964.

Archives of the United States, USFR, Vol. II.

Index